MW00576595

Asanga Abeyagoonasekera's new work i *Lankan strategic thinking and a useful te... ,... stand the emerging dynamics of the Indo-Pacific.*

Walter Russell Mead, Distinguished Fellow Hudson Institute, Columnist, *The Wall Street Journal*, Professor of Foreign Affairs and Humanities Bard College

This book is a treasure trove of discussions by one of Sri Lanka's leading experts on the many dilemmas that the country now faces. For anyone wanting to understand Sri Lanka's contemporary foreign policy and security challenges, it is a must read.

Dr. David Brewster, Senior Research Fellow, National Security College, Australian National University

As the maritime rivalries heat up in the Indo-Pacific and the world turns its attention to Sri Lanka at the heart of this strategic geography, Asanga Abeyagoonasekera offers rich insights into the strategic dynamics of the island nation. A good place to start for anyone interested in contemporary Sri Lanka.

C. Raja Mohan, Director, Institute of South Asian Studies, National University of Singapore

Replete with well sieved information and interspersed with nuanced commentary, Asanga has written, with extraordinary verve and energy, a must-read account of Sri Lanka's political dynamics and the interplay with the global power shift.

Uttam Kumar Sinha, Security Analyst and Author, Manohar Parrikar Institute for Defence Studies and Analyses, New Delhi

Beauty can be a curse. Sri Lanka is a jewel of an island perfectly positioned astride the sea lane connecting East and West. And it has been so from the beginning of time. Perhaps it is only to be expected that many would cast covetous eyes on its stunning landscape, its resources and its location. When the people of Sri Lanka are united, they harness its natural endowments and prosper from external relations. When they are not, external forces exacerbate internal divisions. In a series of thoughtful essays in Conundrum of an Island: Sri Lanka's Geopolitical Challenges, *Asanga analyses the internal and external challenges confronting Sri Lankan society and discusses ways of addressing them. Despite a clinical awareness of past tragedies and the pitfalls which lie ahead, Asanga never loses hope that good leadership can point a happier way forward for a people who deserve better.*

George Yeo, Former Foreign Minister of Singapore

Sri Lanka faces both longstanding domestic, political and cultural fissures as well as a turbulent Indo-Pacific strategic environment. There is no better guide to both than Asanga Abeyagoonasekera.

Dr. Parag Khanna, Author of *The Future is Asian* and *Connectography*

The world is rapidly changing. The escalating US–China competition, rising tension in the India–China border, COVID-19 pandemic and the US presidential election are examples. What should Sri Lanka do in this context? The book presents some answers. It is no doubt that this is an important book.

Dr. Satoru Nagao, Visiting Fellow at Hudson Institute, USA

Asanga Abeyagoonasekera explores various contemporary issues faced by Sri Lanka. He examines events such as the recent terror attack and the pandemic, as well as a multitude of political challenges confronting the island.

Dr. Karen S. Miller, Chair Political Science, Criminal Justice, and Organizational Leadership, Northern Kentucky University

Asanga so aptly brings out how Sri Lankan foreign policy today stands at the crossroads; exploring and crafting new incarnations of its non-alignment and neutrality while fine-tuning its responses in its novel and multifaceted engagements with the 21st century geopolitics. In his most forthright manner he underlines how, among others, the challenges lie in the fact that national leaders continue to "lack in articulating a clear foreign policy and oscillate between the two increasingly divided factions of Washington and Beijing" while India remains their most important neighbor to reckon with. At the same time, in spite of such tumultuous geopolitics, the fundamentals of foreign policy remain undergirded by Sri Lanka's principled efforts at ensuring a rule-based order while protecting democratic values in its deliberations and discourses, which make this volume a must read on Sri Lankan foreign policy.

Professor Swaran Singh, Diplomacy and Disarmament Division, Jawaharlal Nehru University

A book that goes to the heart of the challenges of our time — not only for Sri Lanka, but for nations and their people the world over.

Dr. James Ross, Managing Director, Ulysses Arts Oxford

Sri Lanka is a beautiful Indian Ocean island, but whose politics and institutions are often ignored. Conundrum of an Island: Sri Lanka's Geopolitical Challenges, *from Asanga Abeyagoonasakera intends to remedy that situation. It is a collection of essays about Sri Lanka's domestic and geopolitical challenges. Starting from the deadly terrorist attack of April 21, 2019, it does question the deeper reasons for the horrendous event and the numerous sources of instability of a country where a 30-year-long civil war ended only a decade ago. From corruption to the difficulties of reconciliation and the relations with regional and global powers, the author leaves no stone unturned. The book also examines the state's weak but evolving institutional mechanisms. In the process, the author takes us back and forth from his island to Beijing and Washington, and from Sri Lanka's domestic vulnerabilities and instability to regional and global rivalries.* Conundrum of an Island: Sri Lanka's Geopolitical Challenges *is indeed a valuable contribution to the understanding of the local and regional dynamics and a must read for whoever wants to understand Sri Lanka's predicament as well as the intricacies of its defense and security policies.*

Frédéric Grare, Senior Fellow, Carnegie Endowment for International Peace

Asanga has powerfully captured the multiple challenges that Sri Lanka is facing through exhaustive and lucid analyses that reflect his profound knowledge and understanding of security policy making in Sri Lanka that he was associated with in his capacity as Director General of INSSSL.

This book is an in-depth, incisive and insightful examination of Sri Lanka's multiple foreign policy and security challenges. The book is a must read for academics and policy makers and those interested in understanding the emerging power dynamics in the Indian Ocean and the role Sri Lanka is poised to play.

Smruti S. Pattanaik, PhD, Research Fellow, Manohar Parrikar Institute for Defence Studies & Analyses (MP-IDSA)

Conundrum of an Island: Sri Lanka's Geopolitical Challenges *by Asanga Abeyagoonasekera is a must read for national security scholars and practitioners. He has posed important questions about whether Sri Lanka has ever attempted developing a National Defense Policy for itself despite the fact that it has been scourged by terrorism for several decades. The question becomes even more pertinent in the context of the changing geopolitics and Sri Lanka's geostrategic location in the Indian Ocean. Abeyagoonasekera's chapters on the Indian Ocean geopolitics in the context of China's Belt and Road Initiative is packed with a lot of information and examines the implications for Sri Lanka of China's growing footprint in the Indian Ocean.*

Dr. Rajeswari Pillai Rajagopalan, Distinguished Fellow and Head, Nuclear and Space Policy Initiative, Observer Research Foundation

CONUNDRUM
OF AN ISLAND

Sri Lanka's Geopolitical Challenges

To AMB. Schaffer,
With best wishes!
08/27/2021

CONUNDRUM OF AN ISLAND

Sri Lanka's Geopolitical Challenges

Asanga Abeyagoonasekera

World Scientific

NEW JERSEY · LONDON · SINGAPORE · BEIJING · SHANGHAI · HONG KONG · TAIPEI · CHENNAI · TOKYO

Published by

World Scientific Publishing Co. Pte. Ltd.

5 Toh Tuck Link, Singapore 596224

USA office: 27 Warren Street, Suite 401-402, Hackensack, NJ 07601

UK office: 57 Shelton Street, Covent Garden, London WC2H 9HE

Library of Congress Cataloging-in-Publication Data

Names: Abeyagoonasekera, Asanga, author.

Title: Conundrum of an island : Sri Lanka's geopolitical challenges / Asanga Abeyagoonasekera,
 Institute of National Security Studies Sri Lanka (INSSSL), Sri Lanka.

Description: Hackensack, New Jersey : World Scientific, [2021] |
 Includes bibliographical references and index.

Identifiers: LCCN 2020041552 (print) | LCCN 2020041553 (ebook) |
 ISBN 9789811227844 (hardcover) | ISBN 9789811229336 (paperback) |
 ISBN 9789811227851 (ebook for institutions) | ISBN 9789811227868 (ebook for individuals)

Subjects: LCSH: Geopolitics--Sri Lanka. | National security--Sri Lanka. |
 Internal security--Sri Lanka. | Sri Lanka--Politics and government--1978- |
 Sri Lanka--Foreign relations--21st century.

Classification: LCC JQ655 .A73 2021 (print) | LCC JQ655 (ebook) | DDC 320.95493--dc23

LC record available at https://lccn.loc.gov/2020041552

British Library Cataloguing-in-Publication Data

A catalogue record for this book is available from the British Library.

Copyright © 2021 by World Scientific Publishing Co. Pte. Ltd.

All rights reserved. This book, or parts thereof, may not be reproduced in any form or by any means, electronic or mechanical, including photocopying, recording or any information storage and retrieval system now known or to be invented, without written permission from the publisher.

For photocopying of material in this volume, please pay a copying fee through the Copyright Clearance Center, Inc., 222 Rosewood Drive, Danvers, MA 01923, USA. In this case permission to photocopy is not required from the publisher.

For any available supplementary material, please visit
https://www.worldscientific.com/worldscibooks/10.1142/12028#t=suppl

Desk Editors: Balasubramanian Shanmugam/Lai Ann

Typeset by Stallion Press
Email: enquiries@stallionpress.com

Printed in Singapore

*This book is dedicated to the victims of the
4/21 Easter Sunday Terror Attack in Sri Lanka*

&

*Late Emeritus Prof. Vini Vitharana,
who was an inspiration for my work.*

Scaffolding

Masons, when they start upon a building,
Are careful to test out the scaffolding;

Make sure that planks won't slip at busy points,
Secure all ladders, tighten bolted joints.

And yet all this comes down when the job's done
Showing off walls of sure and solid stone.

So if, my dear, there sometimes seem to be
Old bridges breaking between you and me

Never fear. We may let the scaffolds fall
Confident that we have built our wall.

Seamus Heaney*

* Seamus Heaney (1988). "Scaffolding," Opened Ground: Selected Poems 1966–1996.

Contents

List of Abbreviations

ACSA	—	Acquisition and Cross-Servicing Agreement
AFAS	—	ASEAN Framework on Services
AIIB	—	Asian Infrastructure Investment Bank
AML	—	Anti-Money Laundering
ARF	—	ASEAN Regional Forum
ASEAN	—	Association of South East Asian Nations
ATC	—	Australian Tamil Congress
BDN	—	Blue Dot Net
BESA	—	Basic Exchange and Cooperation Agreement
BIMSTEC	—	Bay of Bengal Initiative for Multi-Sectoral, Technical, and Economic Cooperation
BJP	—	Bharatiya Janata Party
BRI	—	Belt and Road Initiative
BTF	—	British Tamil Forum
CBMs	—	Confidence Building Measures
CEPT-AFTA	—	Common Effective Preferential Tariff Scheme for the ASEAN Free Trade Area
CFT	—	Countering the Financing of Terrorism
CIA	—	Central Intelligence Agency
CIABOC	—	Commission to Investigate Allegations of Bribery or Corruption
CICA	—	Conferences on Interaction and Confidence Building Measures in Asia
CID	—	Criminal Investigation Department

CKDu   — Chronic Kidney Disease of Unknown Etiology
COMCASA   — Communications Compatibility and Security Agreement
CPEC   — China Pakistan Economic Corridor
CPIB   — Corrupt Practices Investigation Bureau
CTC   — Canadian Tamil Congress

DNA   — Deoxyribonucleic acid

ERM   — Ethnic Rebellion Model

FATF   — Financial Action Task Force
FDI   — Foreign Direct Investment
FIU   — Financial Intelligence Unit
FOIP   — Free and Open Indo-Pacific

G20   — Group of Twenty
G7   — Group of Seven
GTF   — Global Tamil Forum

ICSR   — International Center for the Study of Radicalisation
ICWA   — Indian Council of World Affairs
IMAC   — Information Management and Analysis Center
IMF   — International Monetary Fund
IONS   — Indian Ocean Naval Symposium
IORA   — Indian Ocean Rim Association
IPSR   — Indo-Pacific Strategic Report
IS   — Islamic State
ISIL   — Islamic State of Iraq and the Levant
ISIS   — Islamic State of Iraq and Syria
ITAC   — Integrated Threat Assessment Centre

JVP   — Janatha Vimukthi Peramuna

KGB   — Komitet Gosudarstvennoy Bezopasnosti translated as Committee for State Security

LEMOA   — Logistics Exchange Memorandum of Agreement
LNG   — Liquefied Natural Gas
LTTE   — Liberation of Tamil Tigers Eelam

MCC   — Millennium Challenge Corporation
MIND   — Munasinghe Institute of Development

MoU	— Memorandum of Understanding
MRCC	— Maritime Rescue Coordination Center
NAFTA	— North American Free Trade Agreement
NATO	— North Atlantic Treaty Organization
NCCC	— National Cyber Coordination Center
NCCT	— National Council of Canadian Tamils
NCSC	— National Cyber security Coordinator
NDAA	— National Defense Authorization Act
NDP	— National Defence Policy
NMDA	— National Maritime Domain Awareness
NSA	— National Security Advisor
NSC	— National Security Council
NTJ	— National Thowheed Jama'ath
NTS	— Non-Traditional Security
OAS	— Organization of American States
OBOR	— One Belt One Road
OCDS	— Office of the Chief of Defence Staff
ODA	— Official Development Aid
OPV	— Offshore Patrol Vessels
PCA	— Prevention of Corruption Act
PCoI	— Presidential Commission of Inquiry
PLA	— People's Liberation Army
PRP	— Pivotal Regional Partnerships
PSC	— Parliament Select Committee
PSFTA	— Pakistan–Sri Lanka Free Trade Agreement
RAM	— Risk assessment model
RCEP	— Regional Comprehensive Economic Partnership
RTI	— Right to Information
SARS	— Severe Acute Respiratory Syndrome
SAARC	— South Asian Association for Regional Cooperation
SALW	— Small Arms and Light Weapons
SIPG	— Shanghai International Port Group
SLOC	— Sea Lines of Communication
SOFA	— Status of Forces Agreement
SQM	— Square Meter

TEU	—	Twenty-foot Equivalent Unit
TNA	—	Tamil National Alliance
TNC	—	Tamil National Council
TNS	—	Transnational Security
TPP	—	Trans-Pacific Partnership
TRC	—	Truth and Reconciliation Commission
TTF	—	Technology Transfer Facility
TYO	—	Tamil Youth Organisation
UK	—	United Kingdom
UN	—	United Nations
UNCLOS	—	United Nations Convention on the Law of the Seas
UNESCO	—	United Nations Educational Scientific and Cultural Organization
UNHRC	—	United Nation Human Rights Council
US	—	United States
UWO	—	Unexplained Wealth Order
WEF	—	World Economic Forum
WMD	—	Weapons of Mass Destruction
WTCC	—	World Tamil Coordinating Committee

Acknowledgments

I have written this book by gathering information from academics, government officers, researchers, and practitioners of foreign policy and security studies. I thank all of them for providing me with useful and timely insights and material. The wise counsel and critique of numerous senior academics from across the world have shaped my writing, and for that I am grateful. I thank senior scholars and government officers from many corners of the world who have recommended and appreciated my writing and invited me to present my work. I am grateful for their continuous support.

A special word of thanks to Ramla Wahab Salman and several editors from think tanks from around the world for their support through the years of research and publication. I recognize the dedication and inexhaustible patience of two of my researchers, Ruwanthi Jayasekara and K. D. Vimanga, along with Gayathri de Zoysa, who worked on initial copyedits. I am grateful for their time and dedication.

I thank Chua Hong Koon and the editor Lai Ann at World Scientific Publishing Company for all the kind assistance given to make this project a success.

Finally, I thank my wife Kumudu, and my two children Avish and Arya, to whom I owe so much.

Introduction

I was three minutes away from the attack. My family and I witnessed the carnage of the extremist Easter Sunday terrorist attack at the Shangri La Hotel on April 21, 2019. The multiple-location suicide bombings were the largest terror attack carried out in the island nation's history. However, like most Sri Lankans, it was not my first experience of a terror attack. The island was engulfed in an almost three-decade civil war with Tamil Tigers (LTTE) and two youth insurrections, killing tens of thousands of many innocent lives.

At the time of the Easter Sunday attack, I was serving as the Director-General of the Institute of National Security Studies Sri Lanka (INSSSL). INSSSL is a national security think tank under Ministry of Defence which was established by President of Sri Lanka in 2016 for the purpose of research. In a President's Monthly Threat Forecast (MTF) submitted from 2017 January, we continuously predicted a security threat from the Islamic extremist terror circle, particularly in the January 2019 MTF to the President. Why did such vital information go unheard? How did Sri Lankan intelligence miss out the vital intelligence information provided by Indian intelligence multiple times? Was Sri Lanka chosen for the attack to be staged? What are the underlying factors? What security threats and geopolitical effects do the nation and the region have to face in the near future? These are some vital questions discussed in this book.

This book is a compilation of essays on several themes intended to provoke thought and understanding of everyday political and social life on an island facing constant geopolitical and domestic political challenges. The themes of this books are *4/21 Terror Attack and National Security*;

China, BRI, and Sri Lankan Foreign Policy; *Geopolitics*; *China, BRI, and Sri Lankan Foreign Policy*; *Geopolitics*; *Sustaining Democracy and Facing a Pandemic*; and *Domestic Political Stability, Leadership, and Economic Crime.*

Most essays have tried to capture the domestic viewpoint, drawing a wider picture of the global geopolitical tapestry. It is as if a catapult is pulled from the local end, touching the regional dynamics and reaching out toward the global arena and returning to address the domestic landscape. The chapters enframe a variety of domestic political incidents, conflicts of various actors, and the *Conundrum of an Island* in the Indian Ocean stuck in a triangular maritime power dynamics of US, China, and India. I look at influences from foreign nations on Sri Lanka's foreign policy and the dynamics of security challenges in the larger geosphere and marine sphere of South Asia and the Indian Ocean, respectively. I have always attempted to offer an Olympian viewpoint of the challenges the nation faces, attempting to find connections and patterns toward a greater outside geopolitical influence impacting domestic politics.

The rising China factor in the global arena and in the island nation from its infrastructure diplomacy connecting to the Belt and Road Initiative (BRI) initiative to the Indo-Pacific strategy by the US and Sri Lanka's strong relationship with its neighbor India is reflected in its balanced foreign policy. Has China made inroads to the nation from its "debt trap diplomacy" and "predatory loans"? Why was Millennium Challenge Corporation's (MCC) Compact loan (a US initiative) rejected? Why did Sri Lanka withdraw from its own co-sponsored UNHRC Resolution in 2020? These are some questions the book will discuss.

The book follows *Sri Lanka at Crossroads* (2019, World Scientific), which examines Sri Lanka's strategic position and potential within a new world order. The book consists of a collection of my essays written for Hudson Institute (US), Observer Research Foundation (India), Cambridge University (UK), *South Asia Journal*, and ISAS (Singapore), among several others.

I have served 15 years in Sri Lankan government, working mostly along with researchers, academics, and practitioners of foreign policy and security policy. In this time, I have been fortunate to interact with remarkable individuals at various regional and global think tanks. The basis of the analysis of these essays is garnered from the knowledge I have gathered from the continuous interactions with a vast and diverse intellectual and research community. I am thankful to all of them for their continuous support in my work.

I have reproduced Seamus Heaney's poem "Scaffolding" as a reminder to build strong structures so that *we may let the scaffolds fall*. We have failed to invest and build strong structures to protect human lives. I hope this work would bring some insight for better policymaking in the region and in the global arena.

The book is dedicated to the victims of the 4/21 Easter Sunday Terror attack and late Prof. Vini Vitharana who has inspired my work.

Asanga Abeyagoonasekera
Colombo, July 2020

Chapter 1

4/21 Terror Attack and National Security

All along the history of this country, when such events happen, very often no proper inquiries were conducted, and after some time everybody forgot about these things,...Therefore, no proper justice was done or given to the people affected by these bomb blasts and other things in the past.

Malcolm Cardinal Ranjith, Archbishop of Colombo*

---

*Archbishop Malcolm Cardinal Ranjith, "A year after Easter bombings in Sri Lanka, recovery still a work in progress." Available at: https://cruxnow.com/church-in-asia/2020/04/a-year-after-easter-bombings-in-sri-lanka-recovery-still-a-work-in-progress/.

Easter Sunday in Sri Lanka: Crisis, Correction, and Hope[1]

What happened on September 11th is at least, theoretically, small stuff compared to what can happen.

Robert D. Kaplan

I was 16 when I witnessed the horror of terrorism first hand: an LTTE blast took my father's life.

When the long battle with the Tamil Tigers ended in 2009, I was relieved that my children would not have to go through what I did.

I was wrong.

On April 21, 2019, I covered my seven-year-old child's eyes while my family was evacuated from the emergency exit of Shangri La Hotel, Colombo, soon after the two suicide attacks which shook the entire building. The steps were soaked in blood. Lifeless bodies were carried out, and many body parts blown off. Unfortunately, not all families were lucky enough to escape through the fire exit like us. My family is still in shock and living in fear, like many others today. I sympathize with the victims and their families who have lost their loved ones and friends.

Had I been 3 minutes earlier to the lift, I would not be writing this piece.

Since that day, the questions asked by my six- and seven-year-old children are hard for me to answer. Why do people kill each other? How many bad people are there in the world? Why do people make bombs? It goes on. For my young son's peace of mind and happiness, I painted a heroic story that life will all be better soon after a superhero saves us.

In my capacity as the Director General of the National Security think tank, I see this event as gross national security negligence.

The 2019 Easter Sunday attacks stand apart from the previous faces of terror. Nine extremists turned the entire nation to a state of fear by killing the innocent. The targets were Christians and foreign nationals to get maximum global attention.

Sri Lanka is a geostrategically blessed paradise island that lives with an "existential threat," (as outlined further in my book). This is due to its internal politics, which is in a state of disarray, and external geopolitics. Countries facing an existential threat for a long period of time tend to become a "national security state," according to John J. Mearsheimer. In its 71 years of independence, Sri Lanka has fought a brutal war against terror for almost 30 years. Today, there is another phase of terrorism: violent extremism.

Certain liberal values introduced by the former government made our nation vulnerable and a soft target for terrorists to breed and function. What was seen by the West as an autocratic state under the former Sri Lankan president, Mahinda Rajapaksa, was reset overnight, tagging Sri Lanka to a global liberal order. This was done at the expense of an ensured demilitarization and the complete dismantling and weakening of the country's military apparatus.

Under the tenets of liberalism, the Sirisena government ushered in measures, which brought prosperity to individuals, without fully understanding its setbacks. The principle of liberalism was confused with nationalism. Some policymakers pitted one against the other to push agendas forward.

Many extra-regional nations came forward with certain agreements which had direct and indirect influences on our national security. Noncooperation with some powerful nations may lead to the assumption that certain powerful nations may have used a backdoor to enter the island using terror.

Cardinal Malcolm Ranjith, at a press conference, warned that "powerful nations could be behind these attacks." The Sri Lankan national security apparatus should invest in serious research and investigation in this critical area. This lacuna is due to the lack of support by certain policymakers. A glance at the support extended to Sri Lanka's national security think tank will reveal its rank on the State's list of priorities. The National Defence Policy is the leading government document that provides an exhaustive list of all threats faced by the island nation. However, it remains a classified document, locked inside a cupboard for three years, and none of the policymakers bothered to take this forward.

The Institute of National Security Studies Sri Lanka (INSSSL), at its internal Ministry of Defence discussion held in 2017 March, identified the threat of extremism that could trigger in Sri Lanka and documented in its monthly threat forecast written in March and October of 2017 and subsequently in January of 2019 after the discovery of 100 detonators and explosives in the west coast of the island nation. How did such warnings go unheard?

This gross negligence was clearly due to the malfunction of processes within the government, perhaps due to political meddling within intelligence agencies and political division. The consequence is devastating and has dragged the entire nation to a "state of fear," claiming more than 269 innocent lives.

Extremism presents a clear threat to a state's national security when the consequences of an extremist act cannot be managed. Extremist groups can operate in emerging democracies, while also finding operational space in failed or failing states. Post-war Sri Lanka was a soft target for extremism to creep in due to political instability, heightened by two sets of instructions flowing in from the former bipartisan government. I have indicated multiple times the grave danger to national security from the existing political instability of the country.

It had not even been a month since President Trump announced, "we just took over 100% of the [IS] caliphate,"[2] in a victorious speech proclaiming the end of Islamic State's (IS) control of territory as the last bullet was fired in the IS-held Syrian town of Baghouz, on the banks of the Euphrates river. Lina Khatib, an expert from Chatham House, UK, who analyzed the victory of the US-, British-, and French-backed Kurdish and Arab coalition, said: "The group itself has not been eradicated, the ideology of IS is still very much at large."[3] She states that IS will revert to its insurgent roots as it moves underground, using the territorial loss as a call to arms among its network of supporters.

Joseph Votel, the former top American general in the Middle East, warned: "(The caliphate) still has leaders, still has fighters, it still has facilitators, it still has resources, so our continued military pressure is necessary to continue to go after that network."[4]

Similarly, Prof. Rohan Gunaratna, an international terrorism expert, analyzed how this spilled over to the Sri Lankan attack. He stated, "With a vengeance, the returnees from Iraq and Syria and diehard supporters and sympathizers in their homelands responded to the call by the IS leadership to avenge Baghouz, the last IS stronghold. The indoctrinated personalities and cells attacked Buddhist shrines and broke Buddha images."[5]

At least 41,490 international citizens traveled to Syria and Iraq to join ISIS, according to ICSR, i.e. approximately 50 each month. A total of 41 Sri Lankan Muslims from two extended families travelled to Iraq and

Syria. In the last several years, many individuals migrated as refugees to Sri Lanka from Muslim nations.

The members of the IS branch that carried out the attacks in Sri Lanka believed in martyrdom. They were educated and mostly from upper middle-class families. The scale and complexity of the attacks is different when compared to that carried out by the LTTE. The extremist bombers were calm, and one bomber even gently touched a child's head outside the church moments before he carried out his suicide attack. This shows they were well trained for months and, perhaps, years.

Some commentators view the Easter Sunday attacks as retaliation to the 2019 Christchurch mosque attack, which occurred in March. The Christchurch footage was used for election campaigns in Turkey weeks after the attack. It was also used by a Sri Lankan political leader to win popular support, which would further create divides in the Christian and Muslim communities, in the same way President Trump imposed the ban on entry of Muslims into the US soon after his victory. The dangerous nature of such populist acts by politicians will further polarize and lead toward a clash among two great civilizations.

ISIS tentacles reached the National Thowheeth Jama'ath (NTJ) in Sri Lanka in 2017, among other groups globally. The spillover from the Baghouz defeat affected the island nation of Sri Lanka, a top tourist destination that was gearing up to participate in The Second Belt and Road Forum and celebrate its 10 years of success in eradicating terrorism, come May 2019.

The Sri Lankan Easter Day bombings caused the single largest loss of lives in a day due to terrorism in the island nation's history. Despite sophisticated security services the nation possessed during the three-decade — long battle against the LTTE, there were intelligence and security limitations. Multiple warnings were issued by Indian intelligence agencies before the attacks, and Islamic community leaders identified NTJ, the extremist cell which carried out the attacks, months and years earlier as posing a security threat. In the end, the entire nation fell victim to "a gross national security negligence." The reason for this intelligence failure could be explained as: intelligence information was withheld and did not reach the political decision makers. Such endemic security failures were in plain sight even in the US with regard to the 9/11 attacks. The CIA found that the available intelligence did not flow to the political decision makers.

Steps to strengthen military intelligence

First, the Sri Lankan government should take several immediate steps to strengthen military intelligence and the handling of cross-border intelligence sharing among other nations as this type of terrorism require a multi-pronged, multi-jurisdictional approach.

Second, it is necessary to protect our vulnerable communities, who could be targeted through the spread of misinformation and disinformation in social media, which could lead to communal riots. Religious leaders need to play a very important role to promote religious harmony in this environment.

Third, while operational intelligence to arrest the perpetrators of the attacks will continue, the analysis of intelligence data will be an important step to understand the root cause behind the attack.

Fourth, a complete post-audit of the security negligence should be performed by the government to identify where the limitations originated, which should then be rectified immediately. The accountability of negligence has to be pointed out, and those responsible should be charged or fired.

Finally, external support from other nations should be taken only for intelligence sharing and building capacity to combat extremism, and not to sign any other security agreements that could have security implications in the long run.

In the coming months, the deradicalization of the radicalized youth will be another essential measure that would require substantial investment of time and resources. The government and the civil society will have to share the enormous duty of managing the spread of hatred and division among different ethnic and religious groups. A collective effort from the Sri Lankan society is necessary to defeat extremism in the island nation.

Similar to the manner in which the Sri Lankan Muslim society assisted in defeating the LTTE, they will assist in eradicating extremism within the island. The simplest act of kindness and service from each one of us to reclaim unity will be an honor to respect the lives we lost in 4/21.

Sri Lanka will respond to terror with strength and hope — more unified than ever before.

Bombings and Ballots: Uncomfortable Truths from South Asia[6]

Terrorism has become a festering wound. It is an enemy of humanity.

Atal Bihari Vajpayee

Do terrorist bomb explosions and elections have a relationship? In South Asia, a region engulfed with a high level of terrorist activity, the record clearly shows that terrorists see the run-up to an election as an opportune time to act. India and other South Asian nations have faced terrorism during their election times. Erica Chenoweth, an eminent political scientist, explains that high levels of political competition in democracies relative to non-democracies help explain why democracies experience more terrorism than non-democracies.

On May 21, 1991, in Sriperumbudur, Tamil Nadu, India, the then Indian Prime Minister Rajiv Gandhi was campaigning for the forthcoming national elections, when a 17-year-old suicide bomber, Thenmozhi Rajaratnam, also known as Danu and a member of LTTE leader Prabhakaran's Black Tiger suicide squad,[a] successfully carried out a suicide attack. Rajiv Gandhi's assassination had a significant impact on the Indian elections. The pre- and post-bombing election results varied greatly between phases since the assassination took place after the first round of polling. The Congress Party did poorly in the pre-assassination phase but did well in the post-assassination phase, securing a victory for the Congress coalition with the Prime-ministership of P. V. Narasimha Rao. Before the 2019 Indian general election, in which Rahul Gandhi, the son of Rajiv Gandhi, was leading the Congress Party, a suicide attack killed more than 40 Indian soldiers on Valentine's Day in Pulwama, Jammu and Kashmir.

The Indian election was directly impacted by the bombing and the subsequent India–Pakistan dispute, giving Modi a springboard to emerge from criticisms over unaccomplished economic targets and the higher unemployment rate and carve out a different election narrative. Milan Vaishnav, the Director of the South Asia Program at the Carnegie

---

[a]Black Tigers were a wing of Liberation Tigers of Tamil Eelam (LTTE). They were specially selected and trained by LTTE to carry out suicide attacks.

Endowment for International Peace, explains that the Pakistan crisis provided Modi with a golden narrative. "The thing about a national security crisis is that it plays up decisiveness, leadership, and nationalism. These are three characteristics he often touts."[7] The retaliation to hunt down terrorists played out well in favor of PM Modi's election campaign, framing him as a defender of the nation. PM Modi's comments, such as: "Even if they go below the seven seas, I will find them," worked well to secure a clear majority from voters who saw his leadership as an integral part of India's national security.

In Pakistan, Prime Minister Benazir Bhutto was shot and bombed at her election rally in Rawalpindi on December 27, 2007, a few weeks before the Pakistani general election. The suicide attack was carried out by a 15-year-old man, Bilal, a horrific moment impacting the Pakistani elections. The election resulted in PM Bhutto's Pakistan People's Party (PPP) coming back to power.

Similarly, in Sri Lanka, bombs and elections are not uncommon to the general public. On October 24, 1994, Gamini Dissanayake, the 52-year-old UNP presidential candidate, was completing his election campaign when a female LTTE suicide bomber carried out an attack two weeks before the presidential election. The bombing had a significant impact on the UNP's party leadership, and many experienced politicians lost their lives, which had a significant impact on the election. Post-assassination, his wife, Srima Dissanayake, was defeated by Chandrika Bandaranaike Kumaratunga (CBK) of SLFP. Another attack was carried out by LTTE during CBK's second term election on December 18, 1999, in which she was targeted at her Town Hall election rally in Colombo, where she injured her right eye. This attack had a direct impact on the voters in the Presidential elections, where she managed to secure the sympathy vote by appearing before television after the attack, resulting in an election victory against Ranil Wickremesinghe.

If all five scenarios are analyzed (Table 1), the directly targeted assassination attempts have worked in favor of the candidate or his predecessor who was the targeted victim, resulting in victory over the opposition. There is only one scenario in which the opponent won.

The 4/21 Sri Lanka extremist attack, which killed 250 innocent civilians, forced the then Sri Lankan government to change its narrative from tackling corruption/war on drugs toward fighting terrorism and national security. As the impact settles down over time, it is important to analyze the impact on the upcoming election.

Table 1. Terrorist attacks and election outcomes.

	Candidate	Opponent
Rajiv Gandhi (1991)	Won by Congress coalition P.V. Narasimha Rao	
Gamini Dissanayake (1994)		Won by CBK
CBK (1999)	Won by Peoples Alliance	
Bhutto (2007)	Won by Pakistan Peoples Party	
Modi (not direct target) 2019	Won by BJP	

In the 2019 Sri Lankan election, anything that turns the discussion to terrorism or national security will help the presidential candidate who has a background on the subject.

According to Daniel Benjamin, a Senior Fellow at The Brookings Institution Think Tank in Washington, D.C., terrorists want to demonstrate that they are central players in determining outcomes, and they especially want to portray to their audience that they make a powerful impact on the world stage.

Do the terrorists try to tilt events to help preferred candidates or political parties during elections? There is not sufficient precision to ensure the terrorist act can get a candidate elected. However, there is clear evidence in South Asia that bombs during elections have a significant impact on electoral outcomes. Terrorist attacks do not necessarily affect voting patterns, but they leave a significant fingerprint on pre- and post-election outcomes.

Democracies provide their citizens with many peaceful channels to express their grievances, and discontented individuals could easily organize and conduct violent attacks on the state using civil freedom in democracies. According to Princeton scholar Deniz Aksoy's paper titled "Elections and Timing of Terrorist Attacks," "democratic election times are periods of heated political competition and this competition has implications for terrorist group activity."[8] Further, she found that only in democracies with least the permissive electoral institutions is there an increase in the volume of terrorist attacks.

Analyzing the volatile and torn democratic fabric of South Asian nations, it is important to understand and foresee probable underlying factors that could trigger terrorist attacks before elections which will assist to swing votes from pre-attack to post-attack. The highly emotional voter percentage will be sufficient to swing the votes toward the victim and influence the result. In South Asia, elections and terrorist attacks do have a strong correlation. Given the frequency of attacks during election campaigns, as most of us have experienced in the past, they will likely have a direct impact on the outcomes of future democratic elections.

Toward Post-Terror Stability in Sri Lanka[9]

A security expert who has studied the so-called Islamic State (IS) rightly said to this author that: "Your country was 'staged'." While the IS attempted to take credit for the attacks, they do not appear to have been directed by the group. Those who perpetrated the attacks seem to have been influenced by the IS, but the precise manner and extent is unclear. Nonetheless, the claims of responsibility by the IS have had a significant impact on national morale in Sri Lanka due to their concurrence with geopolitical concerns faced by the country. The Easter Sunday attacks worsened the prevailing crisis of national morale, which is connected in significant ways to Sri Lanka's position in relation to great power rivalry between the US and China.

Geopolitical context

With the expansion of the geopolitical reach of global liberal hegemony, the Indian Ocean has been a vital highway of the global energy market. The US naval presence in the island of Diego Garcia, located equidistant from several littoral states of the Indian Ocean, has aided US liberal hegemonic foreign policy by serving as a base for small and large missions carried out over the past few decades in the region. Many more future military expeditions may be carried out from this flexible strategic hub, projecting US military power in and beyond the Indian Ocean. However, in February 2019, the International Court of Justice ruled that Diego Garcia, which has insofar been administered by the UK, be transferred to Mauritius, signaling the need for the US to consider exploring alternative locations in the Indian Ocean.

Meanwhile, located less than 2,000 kilometers from Diego Garcia and at the center of Indian Ocean sea lines of communications is Sri Lanka. While Sri Lanka maintained a non-aligned stance in its foreign policy during the Cold War period, today its foreign policy is multi-aligned, as it struggles to strike a balance in the context of great power rivalries and internal political disunity. Akin to a tight-rope walker without a pole, any significant measure of stability remains elusive.

Small nations have always owed their independence either to the international balance of power or rejection of imperial aspirations. For Sri Lanka, crucial is its position in the global balance of power between the US and a rising China, increasingly viewed by the US as a national security threat (as evidenced by recent US trade sanctions). Former US Ambassador to Sri Lanka, Robert Blake, highlighted this in his interview in Colombo, where he said, "First, my advice to America is that it should not ask the countries to choose between China and the U.S. They do not want to choose. They want to have good relations with the U.S., China, India and others." Yet this cannot be achieved with US liberal hegemonic aspirations in the Indian Ocean region. In this context, any Sri Lankan foreign security agreement with global powers should be vetted by Sri Lanka's parliamentary body, with inputs from national security researchers, for otherwise Sri Lanka might be unprepared for unanticipated national security implications in the future.

A rigorous process must avoid conjecture and unsubstantiated allegations, instead feeding careful observations and research inputs into the security establishment. The independence of Sri Lanka will be in jeopardy if the US or China take a decisive turn to pull Sri Lanka closer toward their respective orbits, such as in the past when China has sought to gain a decisive and permanent advantage. The recalibration toward achieving a balance by former Prime Minister Ranil Wickremesinghe was viewed as a threat by China, as certain policies made the island country vulnerable to US-led liberal hegemony. It is essential, then, for Sri Lanka to stabilize itself on the metaphorical tight-rope, especially given that the US has stated in its most recent National Security Strategy that its number one threat is China and Russia, and number two is the IS.

The need to uplift national morale

National morale is the degree of determination with which a country supports the foreign policies of its government in times of peace or war. According to International Relations theorist Hans Morgenthau, it permeates all activities of a country, including its military establishment and diplomatic service.

In 2015, the Sri Lankan government divided its portfolios, leaving the President with national security, and the Prime Minister with external affairs. After the 30/1 UNHRC resolution on promoting reconciliation, accountability, and human rights in post-war Sri Lanka and subsequent constitutional crisis, there was deep polarization within the political establishment, which triggered a national security threat that perhaps went unnoticed for some time, but whose instability was felt by the entire country from time to time. More recently, after the Easter Sunday attacks, the Sri Lankan President flew to China to meet his Chinese counterpart, President Xi Jinping, while his Foreign Minister travelled to the US to meet US Secretary of State Mike Pompeo. Both left, perhaps, to seek assistance from the two polarized camps.

This polarization in the establishment harms the national morale of Sri Lanka. It threatens and limits the country's power to carry its agenda forward or stabilize internal politics. In this vulnerable environment, the risk of external threats creeping in to take advantage is extremely real.

Implementation of a National Defence Policy for Sri Lanka[10]

There are none so blind as those who do not see.

Matthew 9:26-27

The most deluded people are those who choose to ignore what they already know.

Abu Bakr al-Baghdadi, leader of The Islamic State of Iraq and the Levant (ISIL) and most wanted terrorist leader after Osama Bin Laden, was killed on October 26, 2019, in a US military raid by its Delta Force in the village of Barisha located to the northwest of Syria. The killing occurred in the de-escalation zone of Idlib. Baghdadi's rule extended over 88,000 sq. km, stretching across the Iraq–Syria border. He was cornered by US Special Forces in the dead-end of a tunnel, where he detonated an explosive suicide vest, killing himself and three of his children.

Six months earlier, the final known footage of al-Baghdadi was aired on the militant group's Al-Furqan media network, after the Easter Sunday attacks in Sri Lanka. The local extremist cluster that carried out the attack was influenced by Baghdadi and his terror network across South Asia.

Despite the threat of violent extremism spreading in the Island nation, which was being discussed and documented before the attack, it was not a priority due to shortcomings within the security establishment. This was highlighted by the recently released Parliamentary Select Committee (PSC) report, a post-audit of the 4/21 attack.[11] Identifying deficiencies within the establishment and lapses in its decision-making process on national security, the committee's report reveals the importance and urgency of security sector reforms to ensure the public safety of Sri Lankan citizens.

The report holds eight recommendations. The first is for Sri Lanka's defence establishment to implement "essential reforms in the security and intelligence sector" by undertaking a comprehensive review of national security priorities to identify gaps and weaknesses and areas that require reform and strengthening. The recommendations suggest coupling an immediate review of the present structures in place for security and intelligence and mapping out tasks, responsibilities, and possible areas of overlap. The PSC is of the view that the nation has not identified its national security priorities. It leaves the task of strengthening coordination among the security establishment and key stakeholders. The nation requires a National Defence Policy (NDP).

The Geneva Center for Security Sector Governance sees defence policy as part of a broader concept of a country's National Security Policy or National Security Strategy. "Defence policy encompasses defence planning and management, which are consecutive steps towards practical implementation of that policy, down to actual command and control. The lines that divide all these concepts or phases are often blurred in practice. In general, defence policy covers everything from ends to ways and means of achieving national defence objectives and is guided by codes and principles that are embedded in National Security Policy."[12] Several South Asian nations do not possess defense policies or are not shared with their public. Sri Lanka's closest neighbor India, for example, has been criticized for not having a defence policy, a requirement that has been discussed since the time of Prime Minister Narasimha Rao in the 1990s. According to Prime Minister Rao:

The first criticism has been a rather extraordinary kind of criticism to say that we have no National Defence Policy. I would like to submit respectfully that is not true. We do not have a document called India's National Defence Policy. But we have got several guidelines which are strictly followed and observed and those can be summed up as follows: First the Defence of national territory over land, sea and air encompassing among others the inviolability of our land borders, island territories, offshore assets and our maritime trade routes. Secondly, to secure an internal environment whereby our nation-state is insured against any threats to its unity or progress based on religion, language, ethnicity or socio-economic dissonance. Third, to be able to exercise a degree of influence over the nations in our immediate neighbourhood to promote harmonious relationships in tune with our national interests. Fourth, to be able to effectively contribute towards regional and international stability and to possess an effective out-of-the-country contingency capability to prevent destabilization of the small nations in our immediate neighbourhood that could have adverse security implications for us.[13]

S. Kalyanaraman, Research Fellow at the Manohar Parrikar Institute for Defence Studies and Analyses, India, explains: "one of the staples of the popular and even academic discourse on India's national security during the last few decades has been the assertion that India does not have a defence policy. Such a view is widely shared not only by Indian and foreign scholars and analysts but also by retired high-ranking civilian and military officials."[14] A National Defence Policy is a step toward moving away from reacting in an *ad hoc* manner, while promoting strategic thinking and action in the realm of national security.

Has Sri Lanka ever attempted to develop a National Defence Policy?

The first draft of the National Defence Policy (NDP) was prepared in 2016 by a team of distinguished military officers along with INSSSL, a national security think tank, under the leadership of Air Chief Marshal Kolitha Gunathilake, Gen. Udaya Perera, Gen. Shavendra Silva and several others. The policy was submitted to the then Secretary of Defence Karunasena Hettiarachchi, who was instrumental in initiating the process, but failed to take it forward due to his sudden transfer. The same policy was handed over to the subsequent Defence Secretaries, Kapila Waidyaratne and Hemasiri Fernando. A second attempt was made after the Easter Sunday bombings, under the leadership of General Shantha Kottegoda and 18 distinguished military officers along with the INSSSL. After much deliberations, a revised policy was handed over to President Maithripala Sirisena. Had this policy guideline been taken up seriously before the Easter Sunday attacks, Sri Lanka would have had progressive reforms in the security sector and perhaps saved many innocent lives. The

PSC report contains several key recommendations and findings high-lighted by the committee, mirrored in the NDP as policy guidelines.

Sri Lanka's first-ever NDP is an extensive document outlining 6 national defence interests and 13 objectives, while identifying Sri Lanka's defence capabilities and discussing the country's force structure modern-ization efforts. The document identifies the need and the extent to which force modernization ought to be facilitated for the future well-being of the defence forces. The purpose of the NDF is to ensure things are done in an organized manner and objectives are attained while respecting rules. The reforms discussed at the PSC, for example, of creating a National Security Advisor (NSA) and National Security Council (NSC), are clearly identi-fied and discussed in the NDP. The NSC will be established under a new secretary-general as a secretariat headed by the President, and it will have 15 permanent members, including the Prime Minister, NSA, State Minister of Defence, Minister of Law and Order, Secretary to President, Secretary of Defence, Secretary of Foreign Affairs, Secretary of Finance, Attorney General, Chief of Defence Staff, Tri Force Commanders, IGP, and Chief of National Intelligence.

The NDP should be available to the public and, like any other policy, go through a periodic review every three years. Such a policy gives strength to the entire system and improves decision-making abilities while prioritizing defence requirements. The strategies will be formulated by the respective forces and Office of the Chief of Defence Staff (OCDS) to achieve the security requirements from regime to regime.

In a rapidly changing, complex, global threat environment in the international geopolitical arena, Sri Lanka faces numerous security threats such as extremism, cyberattacks, financial and economic crimes, maritime intrusions, environmental degradation, and natural disasters. Sri Lanka has lost lives and property every year as a direct result of these threats. Examples of natural disasters include the mudslides in Aranayaka,[15] which killed more than 200 people and displaced 350,000, as well as the garbage dump collapse disaster.[16]

National security issues were at the forefront of the November 2019 presidential election. It is pivotal we stimulate and strengthen the process using an NDP. New threats require new strategies and new capabilities. They also create new responsibilities. One of the fundamental questions is how to optimally balance the resources the nation possesses and acquire new resources to address the rapidly changing security threats facing Sri Lanka.

A Reappraisal of Sri Lankan Maritime Defense[17]

The deep-sea contains earthly treasures that aren't remotely understood or developed. But if we want to obtain these treasures, then we must master key technologies for entering the deep sea, surveying the deep sea, and developing the deep sea.

President Xi Jinping[18]

Ruhuna, the southern kingdom of Sri Lanka, was established by King Mahanaga. The historic entrepôt to the Maritime Silk Road was located within this ancient kingdom, now situated in present-day Godawaya,[b] which, although rich in archaeological findings, is presently a small fishing hamlet at the mouth of the Walawe river.[c] A nearby temple possesses a stone inscription in Brahmi script dating back to the second century, stating that the customs duties collected at the port were dedicated to the Buddhist temple.[19] A few kilometers from Godawaya port lies the town of Hambantota, the much-discussed modern port that has been leased out to the Chinese.[20] It is an identified entrepôt for the 21st century Maritime Silk Road.

In 1804, Leonard Woolf, the British civil servant, husband of Virginia Woolf, and author of the popular novel *Village in the Jungle,* arrived in Hambantota to assume duties as the Assistant Government Agent. The British commenced the construction of its first coastal defence tower, "The Martello Tower" in the town.[21]

An Italian, Giovan Giacomo Paleari Fratino, designed the Tower of Mortella in the island of Corsica, Italy, in 1565, which was replicated by the British in Sri Lanka. Its construction highlighted the importance of coastal defence towers. Martello Towers are a feature across prominent imperial port cities across, including Hambantota.

The evolution of coastal maritime defence has evolved from towers looking for visible objects floating along the surface to invisible and submerged undersea stealth operations in the 21st century. Unfortunately, certain policymakers in the developing world are still living in the era of towers, expecting clear visibility of threats.

The inability of small nations to grasp the entirety of the contemporary geopolitical snapshot, and the lack of financial resources to build capabilities of their own, are among the numerous limitations that prevent

---

[b]Godawaya is a small fishing village that is situated in Hambantota, Southern Sri Lanka.
[c]Walawe is the fourth biggest river in Sri Lanka and this used to be the old river mouth; however, the river mouth has been blocked for many years due to sand deposits.

them from enhancing their modern maritime security capabilities. In such a vulnerable environment, most nations stretch their hand for assistance from global maritime powers.

The great maritime powers of this century have invested more in developing asymmetric advantages in the marine sphere than in the geosphere. Before the US House Armed Services Committee, Admiral Harry Harris, Head of the US Pacific Command, testified, saying that the United States "must maintain its asymmetric advantage in undersea warfare capability including our attack submarines, their munitions, and other anti-submarine warfare systems" to counter threats such as Chinese coercion.[22] It is not only Americans who are concerned about the growing maritime footprint of the Chinese in the Indian Ocean. According to Indian maritime expert Abhijit Singh, the "Indian navy also devotes considerable resource and effort in tracking PLAN [People's Liberation Army-Navy] subs."[23] He further explains, "China's submarine deployments in the Indian Ocean undercut the logic of India as a net security provider in South Asia. The attempt at eroding New Delhi's strategic primacy in its backyard makes the latter's need for a counterstrategy in the wider Indo-Pacific region urgent and imperative."

While China's scale of submarine buildup cannot be matched — not even by the US or India — another significant area of rapidly developing expertise is Beijing's oceanographic research investment, which now dwarfs that of any other country. In 2012, the Chinese national maritime research fleet comprised just 19 vessels. By the end of 2017, it had expanded to 50 ships, half of which were classed as distant-ocean vessels capable of conducting maritime research.[24]

According to Ryan D. Martinson and Peter A. Dutton's report titled "China's Distant-Ocean Survey Activities: Implications for U.S. National Security," published by the US War College, China's Qingdao National Lab conducts research to support China's naval development. "The Qingdao National Lab — in conjunction with the Ministry of Natural Resources (MNR) and the Chinese Academy of Sciences (CAS) — is leading an enormous project to build an integrated network of fixed and mobile sensors to monitor the undersea conditions in the Western Pacific, South China Sea, and the Indian Ocean." This project is intended to enable China to conduct large scale, real-time ocean observation. According to the report, "Project scientists are developing models for understanding — and ultimately predicting — the dynamic undersea environment. Project funders and participants openly acknowledge the security objectives driving their scientific work. Though the network is still being developed, existing infrastructure is already serving the oceanographic needs of the PLAN." Data collected from sea-based sensors is shared with the MNR's National Marine Environment Forecasting Center, which in turn supplies oceanographic and meteorological products to the PLAN. The same report notes that "[w]hen *Xiang Yang Hong 01, a* marine research vessel, was commissioned in 2016, authoritative sources stated that its various tasks would include 'comprehensive observation in the field of military oceanography." This is the same marine research vessel *Xiang Yang Hong 01* that berthed at the port of Colombo in Sri Lanka on April 9, 2019.[25] This was a few days before the brutal Easter Sunday bombings, where several Chinese oceanographers from the Chinese Academy of Sciences and the First Institute of Oceanography under the Ministry of Natural Resources of China were killed.

Some Western scholars point out the blurred civil–military nexus of the Chinese marine research model. On the other hand, the US marine research model clearly distinguishes between military and civil purposes, with US Navy ships used for military surveys and civilian ships engaged in marine scientific research. Regardless, China continues with its mission to be the lead player in exploring the ocean depths.

Under the United Nations Convention on the Law of the Sea (UNCLOS), the clearly defined purpose of marine scientific research is "to increase scientific knowledge of the marine environment for the benefit of all mankind."[26] It is unclear if all these powerful nations are actually engaged in this noble task, or whether they are simply trying to increase their military footprint in the oceans, using civilian oceanographers to develop models for understanding oceanic phenomena. These same models could be applied to the development of combat systems and tactics needed by the military fleet, thus the study of the ocean dynamics is especially important for undersea warfare.

The defence establishments of powerful nations will be fed with significant amounts of scientific oceanographic data collected from the oceans. The Indian Ocean will take the center stage in the present geopolitical context, where data from local waters will be a rich source of information for militaries to predict future trends and characteristics of the ocean.

The Indian Ocean has already become an undersea competitive arena for listening devices and passive sonar systems to track ships and submarines. The sophistication and the use of these data are different from the Cold War period, when the US installed a network of hydrophones on the seabed to detect Soviet submarines.

Today, unlike the Cold War, there will be multilateral maritime military collaborations among India, the US, and Japan to specifically monitor PLAN submarine activity in the South China Sea and the Indian Ocean Rim. Japan, "besides providing funds for the upgrading of naval

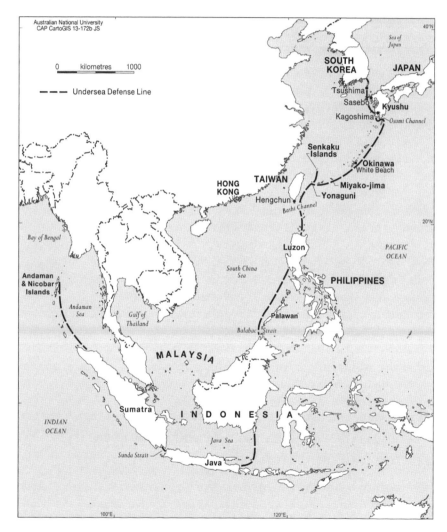

Figure 1. The US–Japan Fish Hook SOSUS Network.

Source: Desmond Ball and Richard Tanter, *The Tools of Owatatsumi: Japan's Ocean Surveillance and Coastal Defence Capabilities*, ANU Press, Australia, Map 4, p. 54.

air bases and construction of new electronic/signals intelligence stations along the Andaman and Nicobar chain of islands, plans to finance an undersea fiber-optic cable from Chennai to Port Blair." This network will likely be linked with the existing US–Japan "Fish Hook" sound surveillance (SOSUS) network, which monitors the activity of PLAN submarines (Figure 1).[27]

All these undersea activities will be transmitted to the shore to feed into the National Command Control Communication Intelligence (NC3I) Network of India's Information Management and Analysis Center (IMAC) and also linked with the National Maritime Domain Awareness (NMDA) project.[28] "In the NMDA project, the NC3I network will function as the communication backbone and the IMAC will continue to be the nodal centre, but will be rechristened as the NMDA Centre."[29]

Sri Lanka's role and policies in the marine sphere need to be understood by policy- and decision-makers of national security to fully account for the geopolitics above and beneath the Indian Ocean. Projects of vital national interest which we need to immediately contend with include the Maritime Rescue Coordination Center (MRCC),[30] which touches our surrounding ocean; the Jaffna (Palaly) International Airport[31] that covers our skies; and the Millennium Challenge Corporation (MCC) Compact grant from the US, assisting the management of our soil resources to make land policy decisions.[32] The compact programs under this grant cover strategic projects that should be carefully analyzed, discussed at a policy level in the parliament, and calibrated based on research inputs and longer-term thinking before inking any agreement.

As Sri Lanka heads to presidential polls in under a month, the incoming leader will require a wide geopolitical lens for decision making, well beyond traditional coastal defence.

Regional Approach to Non-Traditional Security: The Sri Lankan Perspective

Non-traditional security (NTS) threats such as transnational crime, terrorism, disaster relief, information security, and climate change, and health epidemics are now considered core national security issues. The rise of NTS threats presents new challenges for developing regional security architecture for South Asia. Sri Lanka faces enormous NTS threats relating to human, water, energy, and environmental security. Marking 70 years of independence in 2018, the country has faced nearly three decades of war with the LTTE Tamil Tigers and two youth insurrections in 1971 and 1989. Failing to arrive at a peaceful political negotiation, the Sri Lankan government followed a military approach in eradicating the LTTE,[33] completing one of the most successful military campaigns against a terrorist group in recent history. Since the victory over the LTTE in 2009,[d] Sri Lanka has faced external threats from LTTE lobby groups and internal attempts, including the recent assassination of two police officers.[34] The nation faced communal violence in Kandy in 2018,[35] which could recur in the future if ethnic and religious harmony is not promoted and fostered.

Sri Lanka also faces natural disasters, which claims the lives of around 300 people annually. The island nation is vulnerable to climate change and the effects of global warming. Despite having the highest human development index (HDI)[36] in the region and recently featuring in the efficiency driven category in the World Economic Forum (WEF) Global Competitiveness Report,[37] there is an imminent threat to human security. The Meethotamulla garbage dump disaster[38] was a clear indication of a failure to implement policy and provide secure living standards to citizens.

In this regard, it seems that Sri Lanka, being a small state in the South Asian region, has experienced number of NTS issues. Thus, this section would mainly attempt to analyze the economic and political security issues affecting Sri Lanka.

The following sub-sections would attempt to answer three main research questions. First, what are the social and political challenges faced by Sri Lanka due to NTS issues. Second, how can the post-conflict nation and its military adapt to NTS issues? Third, how to build a formal security architecture for South Asia?

NTS in South Asia

The South Asian region has about 23% of the world's population and 15% of the world's arable land, but receives less than 1% of global foreign investment and tourism revenues and accounts for only 2% of the global

---

[d]The civil war between the LTTE and the government of Sri Lanka protracted for over 25 years since 1983. The main objective of LTTE was to create an independent Tamil state. After failure of four rounds of peace talks, the final defeat of LTTE took place on May 18, 2009.

GDP. Of the 1.4 billion people in South Asia, 42% or 488 million live on less than a dollar a day. In terms of human development, all South Asian countries, with the exception of Sri Lanka, rank low.

Excessive spending on defense continues to have an adverse impact on the capacity of the countries in the region to provide adequate resources to spend on human security programs. South Asia's ratio of military expenditure as a percentage of GDP is one of the highest in the world.[39]

Environment degradation, infectious diseases, poverty, and extremism cannot be addressed only by military means and required a multi-stakeholder approach. The capacity of states to address these issues alone and independently is nearly impossible, and states are inadequately equipped to find solutions on their own. Approaches to NTS challenges require going beyond traditional security frameworks. A transformation from state-centrism to security of the individual is necessary when grappling with NTS challenges.

Political and economic security

One of the most important aspects of NTS is that people should be able to live in a society that honors their political security, including their basic human rights.

Political security comprises those rights by which citizens are given a share in the political life of the community, including that of the management of government. Further political security is the rights to political participation. Political participation can take many forms, and the most notable form is the right to vote. Political security also covers the right to join a political party, the right to stand as a candidate in an election, the right to participate in a demonstration, and freedom of association.

Sri Lanka is one of the oldest democracies in South Asia and rich in its democratic institutions. The nation has undergone many challenging political times, such as the recent constitutional crisis, and there have been amendments to strengthen the executive branch and also move power away toward the legislature. Despite all these attempts, democracy has survived due to the strength of an independent judiciary. Few months ago, economic security was at the helm of political discussions, which made Rajapaksa popular and Wickremesinghe unpopular. Today political security has gained prominence, making Wickremesinghe popular for preserving democracy and gaining his Premiership and Rajapaksa unpopular, thereby losing his position.

In the Sri Lankan Presidential election on January 8, 2015, voter participation rates reached more than 70% in several places in Sri Lanka.[40] Sri Lanka voter participation for the last 30 years has been more than 70%, which shows the nation is a rich democracy in terms of voter participation except for conflict-ridden years such as 1988–1989.

However, there are several cases of interference from political branches toward the judiciary. The Sri Lankan judiciary has played a pivotal role in restoring democracy and safeguarding government institutions to maintain stability. The recent Supreme Court decision, which brought back the former Prime Minister, was one such incident. Independence of the judiciary and respect toward judicial decisions are essential components of a democracy.[41]

The Sri Lankan government was reset by former President Sirisena inviting Mahinda Rajapaksa, the wartime President and the person who he contested against in the 2015 general election. Many observers have different perceptions and interpretations of this situation, one of which was an alleged breach of national security by his former Prime Minister Ranil Wickremesinghe. One could argue that the NTS threats faced by Sri Lanka, which provided legitimacy to delist branches of the terrorist outfit LTTE by the then foreign Minister Mangala Samaraweera,[42] and the mass-scale corruption in the Central Bank of Sri Lanka bond scam, were seen as national security threats. Sri Lanka and many other South Asian nations have become poor due to the high incidences of economic crimes and corruption scandals, which directly affect the nation's economy.

While the rubric of the NTS evolved first with 1994 UNDP report, which has a seven-part approach, another important element is human security: e.g. social safety nets that were championed by Japan, which became popular after 1997 Asian Financial Crisis, and the concept of human security focusing on reducing the human consequence of violent conflict, as advocated by Canada and Norway. Based on such conceptualizations, we now have a much broader understanding in this subject area.

There are eight characteristics identified by the UN to understand how an NTS policy was reached; this normative framework gives a comprehensive understanding of the decision-making process and could be seen as the conceptual underpinning of good governance. Participation, Rule of Law, Transparency, Responsiveness, Consensus Oriented, Equity and Inclusiveness, Effectiveness and Efficiency, and Accountability (Figure 2).

Sri Lanka and many other South Asian nations have limited capacity in these eight areas. For example, healthcare challenges include the

NTS Analysis

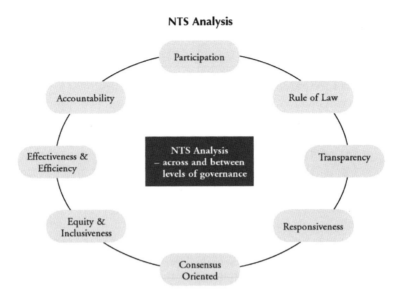

Figure 2.   NTS analysis.

Source: Caballero-Anthony M. and Cook Alistair D.B., Non-Traditional Security in Asia, ISEAS, Singapore, 2013, p. 11.

dengue epidemic,[43] which got out of control, and the chronic kidney disease of undetermined cause (CKDu),[44] which affected people in many parts of the Island. Natural disasters such as floods; landslides[45]; and man-made disasters, such as the garbage dump which collapsed and caused the loss of several lives, expose the clear limitations and inadequacy of the NTS policy.

NTS issues in post-conflict Sri Lanka

The dimensions of internal conflicts in Asia have also become more complex due to the growing challenges posed by religious radicalism and terrorism. Internal conflicts continue to plague Asia. Sri Lanka was engaged in an almost three-decade war on terror against the LTTE Tamil Tigers.

Two police officers were killed by a rehabilitated LTTE[46] fighter in an attempt to stop several Mahaviru Day[47] celebrations. The terrorism expert, Prof. Rohan Gunaratna, in a recent interview[48] assessing this latest development, cautioned India and Sri Lanka that LTTE still posed a threat to their national security. The INSSSL, the national security think tank with the mandate to assess the threat environment in Sri Lanka, determined through analytical processes if such threats could emerge in the future. In applying the Risk Assessment Model (RAM) or Ethnic Rebellion Model (ERM) in the Sri Lankan case, there is not enough data captured to suggest that the conflict is likely to return and that the recent incidents will trigger another conflict. Since the LTTE has been completely dismantled in the Island, we found no accelerating factors that the terrorist outfit could regroup to fight against the military in the present environment; however, there exist threats of individual incidents. Therefore, I do not agree with Prof. Gunaratne's assessment.

According to Prof. Gunaratne, India lost three iconic leaders to terrorism: Mahatma Gandhi, Indira Gandhi, and Rajiv Gandhi. These political assassinations shocked the nation and the international community. Sri Lanka lost many political leaders, including a President and a Presidential candidate, to terrorism. Our nation has been crippled and destabilized by terrorism, sometimes creating leadership vacuums. Acts of terror now occur not only in South Asia but also in many other nations worldwide.

Although the LTTE outfit has been defeated by our valiant military, the shadow operators and proponents of this terrorist organization and its ideology are active outside Sri Lanka. LTTE was designated as a terrorist group under UNSCR 1373. By tactfully engaging with the Tamil National Alliance (TNA), the former coalition Government delisted the LTTE entities on November 20, 2015. Prof. Gunaratna clearly points out it was the then former Foreign Minister who delisted 16 organizations and 424 individuals listed by the Rajapaksa Administration on March 21, 2014. The terrorist entities delisted by the then government were Global Tamil Forum (GTF), British Tamil Forum (BTF), National Council of Canadian Tamils (NCCT), Tamil Youth Organisation (TYO), World Tamil Coordinating Committee (WTCC), Canadian Tamil Congress (CTC), Australian Tamil Congress (ATC), and Tamil National Council (TNC). Some of these entities have revived and reignited the separatist spirit in Sri Lanka by supporting LTTE activities.

The ideology is clearly visible in these groups, and there is a threat to destabilize the government from outside using political allies in their respective nations. But this does not imply that the LTTE will reemerge in Sri Lanka. Some of these groups openly celebrate the dead terrorists, including suicide bombers, on November 26 (Mahaviru day) to support activities to radicalize the Tamil community, but the Sri Lankan government could always suppress these activities or transform it into a day of reconciliation.

Security architecture in South Asia

While the global multilateralism order is threatened by Trumpism, with its nationalistic sentiments, in an extreme case where the liberal institutions are facing a direct threat, one could argue for the design and creation of a South Asian multilateral security architecture.

Since the military or traditional aspects of security are sensitive areas to all nations, due to the many cross-border issues, we could begin with the NTS architecture. NTS challenges are common to all South Asian nations, and a post-conflict nation like Sri Lanka could commence the process.

The need of the hour is the formation of a regional security architecture in South Asia to combat NTS threats. Weapons of Mass Destruction (WMDs) are seen as posing grave danger to humans, but small arms have taken more lives than WMDs in this region and elsewhere. If you look at gun-related killings in the US, the annual statistics show a shocking figure. One of the gravest threats to human security and international peace is Small Arms and Light Weapons (SALWs). Regulation and controlling the proliferation of SALWs should be a topmost priority for South Asia, and the importance of the NTS architecture should be strongly inculcated in all nations of the region. SALWs cause more conflict-related deaths than any other conventional weapon, resulting in the loss of an estimated 200,000 to 400,000 lives.[49]

While accounting for the severe constraints and impediments in overcoming deeply entrenched regional acrimonies, it is widely believed that a regional security architecture is an important step toward confidence building, preventative diplomacy, and conflict prevention, which would set the precedent for regional cooperation on traditional threats and NTS issues.

One of the fundamental steps in achieving cooperative security is the formation of a holistic security architecture which would espouse security cooperation between politically diverse nations through a wide network of institutions.

Viable security architecture in South Asia should be envisioned as independent of SAARC, as incorporating it within the organization would require modification of its charter.

National Security and Cyber Domain: Global Threats and Local Challenges[50]

Cybersecurity and its impact on national security is an important topic of discussion at the global high table. The former US President Barack Obama and Chinese President Xi Jingping both declared their governments will not engage in cyber-related attacks and that they will combat them.[51] In the backdrop of this statement, 5.6 million fingerprints and security clearance records of 22 million people was breached. Since 2015, cyberattacks have become a top national security issue for many nations. Russia and China also signed a comprehensive agreement on cybersecurity. Evidence of cyber-related interference by another country in the 2016 US Presidential elections have also been extensively reported in the news.[52]

After land, sea, air, and space, cyberspace, the fifth domain, has become the most complex when viewed from a national security perspective. Cybersecurity issues are contentious and proving to be difficult, even as the incidents of cyberattacks, cybercrime, and cyberterrorism grow exponentially, according to Arvind Gupta, former Indian Deputy National Security Advisor.[53]

Unlike nuclear deterrence, where the players involved in developing the arsenal scope and quantity can be identified due to the presence of few actors, the situation is completely different in the cyberspace arena. Multiple actors (both state and non-state) with complete anonymity are at play, and there are no clear cut definitions of the nature of cyberattacks. Every year, the attackers and their tools are expanding and evolving in their complexity. Some observers even suggest cyber-deterrence measures will fail because of lack of attributability in cyberspace, since anonymity is the key, a fundamental challenge posed to cyber-deterrence measures.

Placing cybersecurity at the forefront of the national security framework could help resolve the lack of consensus among the international community. A theoretical analysis can be used to identify how cybersecurity fits into the national security apparatus. Barry Buzan,[54] on observing the vulnerabilities of a state, describes a state as weak and strong, depending on its power and social cohesion. Forrest Hare[55] has applied the theory with inclusion of cyber vulnerabilities into the equation and thus measured the strength of a state depending on how power and social cohesion will affect cyber vulnerabilities. Therefore, irrespective of a state's power and its strong social cohesion, it is suggested that criminal activities can still flourish. A weak power with weak socio-political cohesion is vulnerable to destabilizing political actions in cyberspace. According to the model, a stronger power with weak socio-political cohesion, such as Russia, could still have destabilizing actions in cyberspace, and a stronger power with stronger socio-political cohesion, such as the US, will have to combat criminal activities in cyberspace.

The theory has its limitations, and a state might not exactly fit the description of a given quadrant. The states may shift from one quadrant to another, and these shifts may occur in a rapid and unexpected manner. The 2018 Kandy communal riots[e] can be taken as an instance where it shifted to an unstable quadrant from a stable one with the influence of social media.

According to an expert report from World Economic Forum, there are eight key issues in cyberspace faced by nations globally[56]: Critical Infrastructure Protection, Cyber Piracy, Systemic Risk and Resilience, Technology and Law, New Norms of Collaboration, Cyber War — 5th Dimension of Warfare, Cyber Crime, and Security of Things. They are discussed in detail in the following sections.

Critical infrastructure protection

The need to protect the cyber-integrity of critical infrastructure such as energy grids and sanitation systems is one of the paramount challenges faced by the present-day society. The proliferation of systems that fuse the cyber and physical worlds by blending physical infrastructure with computing power may increase functionality, but it also creates more targets for cyberattacks. An attack on even just one critical infrastructure sector, be it energy-related, the financial system, communications networks, or water services, could leave communities or even entire nations crippled. In 2016 alone, the US dealt with 290 such incidents.

But the real question is: Is Sri Lanka's critical infrastructure protected from cyberattacks? The answer is clearly no, and the security infrastructure lacks adequate investments in this area.

---

[e]A series of violent incidents was reported from Moragahamula, Udispattuwa, Teldeniya, and Ambagahalanda. The unrest spread to Digana, where a mob converged on the town and set fire to a mosque, shops, and houses. These acts were further fueled by hatred and tension on social media.

Cyber piracy

Use of online card payments is projected to increase, reaching US$70 billion by 2022 according to research by RBR, London.[57] Data sharing and collection has become a part of every electronic transaction. Calls to abridge privacy in the name of better security must be countered with solutions that strengthen both and still manage to create a climate conducive to economic growth. Therefore, rules for data sharing must be transparent and ensure protection of individual privacy with increasing data theft.

System risk and resilience

Just as a country with extensive borders must fortify a relatively greater number of potential points of entry, the growing expanse of digital networks has multiplied the amount of digital ground that must be placed under surveillance. Data fusion and automation could be used to identify cyberattacks and potential intrusion. However, this presents new challenges, as cybersecurity professionals now have to determine just how precise their warning systems are; automation that produces false alarms and fails to detect actual threats jeopardizes cybersecurity.

Technology and law

With evolving cyber threats, regulation of the cyberspace has become legal struggle and nightmare. Public officials must be up-to-date on the evolving cybersecurity threats, and collaborations must be undertaken with experts to minimize cyber threats. An inability to stay ahead of the curve creates the risk of abuses (through ignorance or malice) with no legal recourse — and may leave entire nations without the ability to make an informed response to cyberattacks.

New norms and collaborations

As the cyber world increasingly merges into the physical world, there is a hunger for new ways to collaborate. Consumers, for example, look for different ways to collaborate, both with one another and with the businesses they patronize. The European Union's Cyber Security Strategy is an example of measures that can be taken to secure and strengthen the cyberspace domain. Each industry is susceptible to different kinds of cyberattacks. There is a general lack of understanding on how states and organizations should conduct themselves in cyberspace. Hence, by connecting academic researchers, private sector organizations, non-profits, and government agencies, the transmission and shared analysis of big data can lead to more fruitful efforts in combating cyberattacks.

Cyber war

The cyberspace can be termed as the fifth dimension of warfare. While the internet was conceptualized as a military technology, cyberwarfare is actually a relatively new concept, with few people possessing experience in the area. Small-scale cyberwarfare already occurs on a daily basis. The American and British governments, for example, issued statements in early 2018, blaming the Russian government for the "NotPetya" cyberattack, which they said was intended to destabilize Ukraine. The US is already well-prepared to attack foreign infrastructure during future conflicts. The UN has shown concerns over the formulation of rules governing cyberwarfare as traditional international agreements cannot address these aspects of non-traditional warfare.

Cybercrime

Our lives have become easier with the advent of online connection of appliances via the Internet of Things and increasingly powerful mobile devices. However, these advancements also have their downsides: now there are more devices to potentially hack and more opportunities to commit cybercrimes. This has led to an arms race between the creator and cybercriminals. Cybercriminals have found it lucrative to target both individuals and businesses, by holding technological assets hostage not only via DDoS attacks, but also with the use of so-called ransomware to first block a person or firm from accessing their data, and then demand payment in order to unblock access. The "Wannacry" and DDoS attacks affected over 150 countries and brought large-scale harm to the UK National Health Services and Russian Interior Ministry.

Cybercrime is not limited to the internet that most of us are familiar with. It also extends to the darknet, where interactions remain anonymous. The darknet provides a large black market connecting nefarious dealers of illegal goods to anyone in the world and is a haven for criminals. It also serves as a place to recruit agents to further spread ransomware on computers at their schools or companies. It is particularly important to train employees of organizations on how to spot potential threats and to institute policies that encourage workers to report potential security failures so that action can be taken quickly. Backup files should also be kept and regularly updated.

Security and things

The so-called Internet of Things ties everything together, from our cars and phones to our medical devices and houses, through internet connectivity. The research firm Gartner has estimated that the total number of connected "things" will more than double to 20.4 billion by 2020 from 8.4 billion in 2017, while security spending related to the Internet of Things will reach US$1.5 billion in 2018, a 28% increase compared with the previous year. However, there are questions that arise concerning consumer consent, compensation, etc. Manufacturers depend on accurate shipping information, militaries depend on maintaining full control of armed drones, and patients depend on properly functioning, wireless insulin pumps. All could put privacy, money, and lives at risk.

When looking at the global context, other states have addressed cybersecurity in their national policy frameworks. For example, the UK has framed its National Cyber Security Strategy 2016 to 2021, investing £1.9 billion to make Britain secure and resilient in cyberspace. The National Cyber Security Centre has been established as a hub of world class and user-friendly expertise for businesses and individuals. India, our neighborhood state, has included cybersecurity in their policy plans. They established their cybersecurity policy in 2013.

Cybersecurity challenges for Sri Lanka

Although it is true that Sri Lanka's cyber domains have not witnessed large-scale cyberattacks compared to other nations, it does not mean that we are not vulnerable to future attacks. Sri Lanka's unique position and the influence of many global powers are visible and variable, and cyberspace, in this equation, is an important domain. Cyber espionage and intercepting data is now a widely discussed topic. For example, in the US, a Chinese telecommunication equipment provider was seen as a national security threat by a Pentagon report. The Chinese-owned undersea PEACE cable, which will connect Africa, South Asia, and East Asia, pose another concern for some nations.

Misinformation and disinformation has proven to be twin dangers to Sri Lanka's peace and stability. Incidents of communal violence that escalated due to misinformation through social media were evident. The recent disinformation on an article that appeared in *The Hindu*, an Indian newspaper, regarding press coverage on Mithra Shakthi[58] and Indian aircraft bringing Sri Lankan military personnel to Bodh Gaya[59] as exercises to counter China's influence could create confusion and instability with Chinese relations.

According to former Secretary, Ministry of Defence, Kapila Waidyaratne,[60] Sri Lanka is in the process of drafting a cybersecurity policy, and stated it is vital to identify mechanisms for implementation and policy execution. In 2017, INSSSL, the national security think tank, after a round table discussion with cyber experts on a cyberattack, came up with the recommendation of having a National Cyber Security Strategy. Subsequently, Mr. Wasantha Deshapriya gave leadership for this strategy to be developed, and it is certain that we will soon have a national strategy for cybersecurity for our nation after inputs from all stakeholders.

A multi-stakeholder approach is needed to address cybersecurity threats. It is pivotal to engage Armed Forces, Police, the public sector, and the private sector. The nation has to strengthen its law enforcement capabilities in the cyber domain. For coordination amongst various agencies, a National Cyber Security Coordinator (NCSC) and a National Cyber Coordination Center (NCCC) should be created.

A Cyber Security Research and Development Policy should be created to develop our in-house capabilities and capacity as a nation. A nation that does not develop its own capabilities will have to depend on other nations for protecting its cyberspace, which again poses a national security threat. Our own encryption algorithms have to be developed to avert cyber threats. It is pivotal we focus on the eight areas discussed in this section and invest in cybersecurity to protect any national security threat from this domain to our nation.

Aerial Fears[61]

The truth is that this technology really began to take off right at the beginning of my presidency.[f]

Barack Obama

Following the 4/21 Easter Sunday attacks in Colombo, Sri Lanka's civil aviation authority discovered a drone belonging to extremists, and then proceeded to ban drones owing to the security situation in the country.

From pizza delivery in New Zealand to assassinations in the Middle East, autonomous machines, especially drones, are transforming our skies. They have already influenced our daily lives. We will see more mind-bending, life-saving, and life-threatening applications of the autonomous technology in the years to come. Swarms of drones will work together to paint the exterior of your house in just a few hours, heat-resistance drones will fight forest fires with hundreds of times the current efficiency of firefighters, and other drones will perform search and rescue operations in the aftermath of natural disasters. In *AI Superpowers*, Dr. Kai Fu Lee explains that: "China will almost certainly take the lead in autonomous drone technology ... Shenzhen is the home to DJI, the world's premier drone maker."[62] China will surpass the US in research and development budgets for autonomous technology, and there is a clear danger in the competition. While drones could help humans, they could also bring destruction to our lives.

On September 14, 2019, two drone strikes on Aramco facilities in Saudi Arabia destabilized the global oil markets. The attack conducted by Houthi rebels from Yemen knocked out more than half of crude output from the world's top oil exporter in Saudi Arabia. It cut output by 5.7 million barrels per day. While a Saudi-led coalition launched airstrikes on Yemen's northern Saada Province, Houthi rebels claimed responsibility for the drone attack and sent a clear threat to Saudi Arabia that their targets "will keep expanding" in the future. The world's third-largest spender for military, with a staggering US$67.6 billion defense budget, could not prevent the drone strike by the financially tied rebels.

---

[f]Obama speaking on drone strikes to Ta-Nehisi Coates, *The Atlantic* interview, December 21, 2016.

In a similar drone attack on January 10, 2019, Houthi rebels assassinated Mohammad Saleh Tamah, Yemen's military intelligence chief, during a military parade.[63] The drone carried between 70 and 100 kilograms of explosives, which detonated while flying over the main stage of the military parade.

On August 4, 2018, Venezuelan President Nicolás Maduro was targeted by two drones which exploded while he was addressing a group of soldiers at a military event in Caracas. He survived unharmed.

Small-scale terrorist outfits and extremists now have clear access to technologies that magnify their ability to wreak havoc. In Sri Lanka, the 4/21 Easter Sunday bombers used bitcoin transfers to obtain a drone and used it for pre-attack information gathering. There is no guarantee that the next set of attackers will not have access to drone technology or tools of cyber warfare. According to Collin P. Clarke from RAND Corporation: "This trend will likely be further exacerbated by subsequent technological developments, with the ability of individuals and small groups to cause wide-scale disruptions to society — through cyberattacks or the use of drones."[64]

The drone technology has assisted the replacement of human suicide bombers. It is more accurate and travel far, and it is relatively cheap to stage a high-profile strike. According to Wim Zwijnenburg, a senior researcher on drones at PAX, the drones used by Houthis may have cost US$15,000 or less to build. Human suicide bombers will now be replaced by autonomous machines.

Nations under high security threat and which have faced ISIS attacks should ramp up coordination among intelligence agencies, civil aviation, customs, air force intelligence, police, and other authorities to counter future attacks. Proposals put forward by the air intelligence division in Sri Lanka are still not fully implemented, and the government needs to give these proposals top priority to ensure public safety.

The 4/21 threat has faded from security discussion with the 2019 presidential elections taking the center stage. It was unfortunate to hear from the Sri Lankan President at the Parliamentary Oversight Committee hearing on September 11, 2019, that "not a single regulation has been fully implemented after the 4/21 attack and it's been five months." Some of the proposals include the Fake News Act, the Madrasa Regulation Act, the Burqa ban, and SIM card regulation.

The state has to be extra-cautious when introducing such regulations into the mainstream society and must be prepared for indirect consequences, which may cause further problems. For example, the SIM card regulation, proposed by the Telecom Regulatory Commission to limit SIM cards to two per person will not resolve the problem. Rather, it will affect the telecommunications market. Instead of limiting the purchase of SIM cards, which will be an unfruitful exercise, the authorities should focus on "profiling and cross-platform intelligence sharing." Even on regulating madrasas, there is no guarantee that it will be possible to monitor what will be taught, since there is no one unified syllabus. Courses offered by Arabic colleges in the Arabic language are taught across 1,675 centers in 24 districts in the country. There is no serious oversight of madrasas, though they have mushroomed around the country in recent years.

While the government struggles to introduce new regulations to improve national security, it is vital to keep in mind future possible threats. Security lapses will damage economic infrastructure, increase security costs, disrupt markets, and spread fear in a manner not very different from the Middle East.

Sri Lanka's Onward March toward Reconciliation[65]

Absence of war does not guarantee that another war will not emerge in the future. In this context, it is essential for Sri Lanka to invest in genuine reconciliation. The polity in post-war Sri Lanka is further divided on ethnic and religious lines due to non-intervention of the state to take action against groups spreading extremist sentiments. Although seen as a beacon of hope, the youth of the island nation is polarized due to absence of a holistic approach, although one was clearly identified and spelled out in the National Reconciliation Conferences conducted during 2011–2014.[66]

The Sri Lankan military was seen as the last resort to end the Liberation of Tamil Eelam (LTTE) conflict due to the failure of several previous attempts to negotiate a political settlement. However, the military cannot and should not be seen as the solution for every social issue in Sri Lanka. The war against the LTTE ended in 2009 after nearly 30 years of violent conflict. The defeat of the Tamil Tigers on May 18, 2009, a day remembered as "Victory Day" was later renamed as the "Remembrance Day" by the Sirisena government.[67] Among certain military and civil society groups, a different counter narrative still exists against the reconciliation process exercised by the government. A strong sentiment from certain groups of society was to revert to calling it the Victory Day. While some groups in the society see the conclusion of the war as a victory against ruthless terrorists, some see this as a loss of their beloved freedom fighters. This was evident in the Northern Province, where the Tamil Tiger leader Velupillai Prabhakaran[g] was remembered as a freedom fighter.[68]

The renewed interest by the former Government in peace-building strategies and achieving social cohesion is seen as important by the society and the international arena. Yet there are many limitations and challenges. It is imperative to formulate and adopt a holistic approach in order for people to reconcile with the past and focus on the future. A transformation is necessary in all sectors of society, especially the military, from a fierce fighting force to a post-war military, to many direct and indirect victims who require a healing process, and the general public to understand the importance of investment toward reconciliation.

The transformation has not taken place due to many limitations and myriad of challenges from the government and civil society. Although there are a few positive actions, such as President Sirisena pardoning his own killer, a suicide bomber named Sivaraja Jenivan, who attempted to assassinate him in 2005. According to Jenivan, "if there were a leader such as President Sirisena 50 years ago, the national issue in the country and destruction caused to the country would have never taken place. You are the only leader in the country accepted by all communities and love all communities in an equal manner. I pray to God that you become the real Father of the Nation by resolving the national issue and the issues of political prisoners."[69] Thus, Sri Lanka is a very good example to the entire world to study and reflect, especially on the subject of reconciliation, as we have experienced the radicalization of LTTE youth as well as the radicalization of political extremist youth partial to the Janatha Vimukthi Peramuna (JVP) political party during the late 1980s.

Sri Lanka cannot implement the reconciliation process alone or without the assistance of international community and the Sri Lankan diaspora, as emphasized by the Canadian Prime Minister Justin Trudeau in his statement on the ninth anniversary of the end of the war in Sri Lanka, in which he stated that, "... Canada offers its full support to the Government of Sri Lanka and those working to ensure that efforts towards re-conciliation ..."[70] due to the large Sri Lankan diaspora in Canada.

---

[g] Velupillai Prabhakaran was the founder and leader of LTTE, waging war over 25 years for an independent Tamil state.

The holistic approach could be implemented by stakeholders in the six sectors identified in the National Reconciliation Reports[71]: Education, Youth, Business Community, Religious Leaders, Women, and Policymakers. In October 2013, a seminar with the participation of six renowned speakers from South Africa shared their experiences with the Sri Lankan participants.[72] The topics of discussion were centered on the meaning of reconciliation; history, role, and purpose of the Truth and Reconciliation Commission (TRC); and politics of amnesty. Several Sri Lankan speakers explained the country's situation and challenges ahead in transitioning from a state of prolonged conflict to sustainable peace. The discussion with eminent Sri Lankan scholars was conducted to understand if Sri Lanka could implement its own TRC. For a holistic approach, Sri Lanka should begin its own TRC process, a measure that is required and necessary.

The process of implementing such mechanisms should be monitored by independent actors, such as Interpeace, from outside the nation to bring more legitimacy to the process. Unfortunately, the recommendations have not yet been sufficiently implemented and, at the time of writing, the process has been slow.

Role of education in reconciliation

The role of education is a pivotal area that will support the transformation process. Justice C. G. Weeramantry, one of Sri Lanka's most eminent jurists and a visionary for peace, was instrumental in introducing peace education to the world. Although he was a recipient of the UNESCO Prize for Peace Education, he failed to introduce peace education system to his own country. As Justice Weeramantry rightly identifies, "if humanity was to see an end to violence, peace education was needed to break down the barriers between peoples." Sri Lanka has still not managed to introduce peace education, global dignity, and the meaning of reconciliation to schools, universities, and other education institutions. However, under the Sirisena government, the Office for National Unity and Reconciliation has launched a pilot program titled "National Unity and Reconciliation through Higher Education," which aims to introduce a new subject on Conflict Transformation and Reconciliation, effective 2018 for the university students. A society engulfed in an ethnic conflict for a long period should bring education to the top of their priority list when implementing the reconciliation process.

According to the World Economic Forum's Global Competitiveness Report,[73] Sri Lanka is one of the only nations in South Asia to progress from a factor-driven economy to an efficiency-driven economy. By consolidating as a lower-middle-income country, the primary socio-economic issue will be to maintain steady economic growth and capitalize on peace-building and to transform the conflict-ridden Sri Lankan society into one of peaceful coexistence, and establishing Sri Lankan identity among all ethnic groups. Without social stability, the nation will have to face indirect consequences to its economy, such as the recent communal violence witnessed in Kandy.[74] Investment in genuine reconciliation is essential, and for this to happen, the policy introduced by one government has to be continued by future governments as well. To ensure a consistent policy, a mandate should be given to an independent institution that is impartial to politics. While political blessing is required to implement policy recommendations, a strong, steel-framed bureaucratic institute could be established to avoid unnecessary political interference and policy changes.

At present, the task of reconciliation has been divided between one Ministry and high officials. The reconciliation mechanism in the government has been mainly carried out by the President,[h] Prime Minister,[i] and the former President of Sri Lanka.[j] Therefore, there are different narratives put forth by successive governments, which were made evident as one supports the hybrid court system with local and international judges, while another opposes the process. Consensus building among policy-makers is essential to work toward a holistic approach.

Sri Lankan identity

Creating a Sri Lankan identity is essential in the post-war context. On a national level attitude survey on social cohesion carried out by the National Education Research and Evaluation Centre of the University of Colombo in 2007, the researchers attempted to find the predominant identity (Citizenship or Ethnicity) with which the respondents prefer to

---

[h] The Ministry of National Integration and Reconciliation was the main Ministry that was under the former President Sirisena.

[i] The Secretariat for Coordinating Reconciliation Mechanisms was under Prime Minister Ranil Wickremesinghe's office.

[j] Former President Chandrika Bandaranaike Kumaratunga is the chairperson of the Office for National Unity and Reconciliation (ONUR).

identify themselves. According to the survey, out of the two options, Sinhalese tend to identify themselves by their citizenship (22.1%), and Tamils and Muslims tend to identify themselves by their ethnicity (20.7% and 36.6%, respectively). However, there are several differences among groups such as students, teachers, lecturers, and trainees.

Although the data provided here is not sufficient to make an outright judgment on the attitudes with regard to the dominant identity, the need for better integration is highlighted.[75] Investment by all stakeholders in the society to create a Sri Lankan identity is of paramount importance in the present context.

A holistic approach would be necessary in order to progress toward genuine reconciliation. The limitations of achieving reconciliation should be quickly addressed, and it is important to build a genuine reconciliation process to deliver tangible results to the post-war Sri Lankan society.

Sri Lanka: Toward a Foreign Policy Pivoted on Conflict Diplomacy[76]

The LTTE might well believe that it can win a separate state by force. If it does believe that, as it may well do, it is making an absolute horrendous mistake.

Lakshman Kadirgamar

Despite the Liberation Tigers of Tamil Eelam (LTTE) being militarily defeated, its ideology for a separate state (Eelam) remains steadfast among its many diaspora members outside Sri Lanka. This is one example of how conflict diplomacy in the 21st century is laced with complexity due to the nature of conflicts — which are no longer static — and the evolution of diplomacy to face new challenges. The UN refers to conflict diplomacy within the broad rubric of "diplomatic action taken to prevent disputes from escalating into conflicts and to limit the spread of conflicts when they occur ... the most common expression of preventive diplomacy is found in the work of envoys dispatched to crisis areas to encourage dialogue, compromise and the peaceful resolution of tensions." In this regard, one of the key roles of a diplomat is to engage in both the prevention and management of conflict and its aftermath.

Sri Lanka embarked on conflict diplomacy during its conflict with the LTTE as well as in the post-conflict era. The country's experience with conflict diplomacy is unique in that peace was not "brokered" despite several diplomatic engagements and mediation by the international community. Rather, it came from within the country and was not externally leveraged. Successive governments since the beginning of the conflict in the 1980s made an effort to end the conflict and garner peace by inviting the LTTE to a political solution. However, this method failed due to mistrust on both sides and ceasefire agreement violations.

Conflict diplomacy in Sri Lanka was always tempered by nationalist, extremist political sentiment. It prevented the moderate political leaders from the south and north of the country from arriving at a peaceful resolution to the conflict, such as the devolution of power. Instead, nationalist fervor led to the exploitation of ethnic identities, and moderates on both sides were labeled traitors. Political leaders such as Vijaya Kumaratunga were clear examples of moderate leaders who negotiated with the LTTE in the 1980s but were called traitors and eventually assassinated due to their allegiance and support for the 13th Amendment.

Conflict diplomacy continues to be relevant for Sri Lanka in preventing the reemergence of war. The root causes have to be addressed in terms of consolidating Sri Lanka's ethnic make-up and ensuring that it is not politically crafted. Since 2009, post-conflict diplomacy in the country has had many shortcomings. First, the war victory was leveraged to extend political lifespans through constitutional amendments. This was to make space for the president at the time to remain in power indefinitely. This move altered Sri Lanka's democratic fabric and led to the downfall of the president in 2015. A failure in conflict diplomacy by the Rajapaksa regime was a cause of this downfall. The former regime failed to effectively engage with the Tamil diaspora, who represented an alienated community after the defeat of their political dream of Eelam. Second, in the aftermath of the conflict, the Rajapaksa regime failed to implement its own "Lessons Learned and Reconciliation Commission Report," drawn up in 2011, which delegitimized the reconciliation process in its entirety. Thus, it is evident that conflict diplomacy must endeavor to be multi-pronged in its approach.

According to Philip Bobbitt, it is a necessity for diplomatic strategy, which is designed to produce a "preclusive victory" to include "conflict prevention, successful negotiation, deterrence, the preparation for conflict should all else fail, and efforts to establish order, ensure stability, and promote political and economic pluralism after conflict." The latter part of this statement — to promote political pluralism — evaded both the

Rajapaksa and the Sirisena governments due to ethnic coalitions and nationalist sentiment. Thus, for Sri Lanka, internal politics have, for too long, plagued prosperity, which illustrates a gap in the country's means of implementing conflict diplomacy. External actors have also played a key role not only in trying to manufacture peace deals during the war but also in its aftermath — with claims of human rights violations that were taken up at the UN Security Council. In this regard, Sri Lanka failed diplomatically in demonstrating to the international community the military and human sacrifices of the three-decade-long conflict.

In the end, the shunning of external actors from the civil war is what gained Rajapaksa his political clout in claiming victory — in terms of diplomacy, it showed the many invisible hands involved in the Sri Lankan conflict. Historically, the Indian sphere of influence with its geopolitical underpinnings manifested itself through the vocal Tamil community of the Indian state of Tamil Nadu. This ethnic base not only influenced the conflict in Sri Lanka but also had, and still has, strong influences on the government of India. It resulted in Tamil Nadu providing military assistance for the separate state of Eelam as well as establishing and operating training camps for the LTTE rebel group within its territory. This represented a total failure of diplomatic channels bilaterally between India and Sri Lanka in terms of conflict diplomacy.

Another external factor was the rounds of peace-talks and peace processes that did not operate within the conflict diplomacy mechanism. The peace negotiations were plagued by mistrust and parties seeking political gain, thus rendering them ineffective. In certain instances, the peace negotiations were seen as an opportunity for internal power play. Such was the case in 2004, which saw the defeat of the then Prime Minister Ranil Wickremesinghe, by the creation of a grand coalition by then President Chandrika Bandaranaike Kumaratunga,[k] to take control of the government via the collapse of the Norwegian peace deal. Kumaratunga, in 2004, dissolved the parliament and called for renewed parliamentary elections, which later saw Wickremesinghe lose power and the ceasefire agreement with the LTTE being revoked. Yet, this is not to say that the LTTE would have accepted a political solution to the conflict. The Eelam aspiration was for a separate state and the means to achieve it was through guerrilla

---

[k]Chandrika Bandaranaike Kumaratunga is the only female President in Sri Lanka. During her second term, she had to suffer major defeats against the LTTE. She even lost her right eye due to an assassination attempt by the LTTE.

warfare. This is why the LTTE stockpiled weapons during the time of the ceasefire and assassinated many of their own ethnic kin, such as Dr. Neelan Thiruchelvan[l] and Foreign Minister Lakshman Kadirgamar.[m] Thus, when speaking about conflict diplomacy, it is important to look at how one goes about achieving it, especially in instances where self-determination has militant underpinnings, as was the LTTE case.

A third external contributor to the framing of the war narrative was the strong influence of the Tamil diaspora community residing in ethnic pockets of the US, Canada, Australia, and Europe. Tamilians wielded political influence in these countries as they made up strong voter bases. This led to the West pandering to their claims of human rights violations in Sri Lanka. Colombo failed to meaningfully connect with this diaspora community and their alienation ultimately led to external intervention in the internal affairs of Sri Lanka, and the tarnishing of its international standing. The same diplomatic disconnect seems to persist in the Sirisena regime, although there has been some attempt to engage with the diaspora in terms of reconciliation.

It is important also to note that the Sri Lankan conflict must be understood in the correct context as there are multifaceted dimensions and many narratives that form the basis of the conflict as described thus far. A fight against a ruthless terrorist outfit with a political agenda, ethnic grievances, communal issues, civil strife, humanitarian operations by international actors, and counter-insurgency operations were all threads interwoven into the fabric of war. Thus, conflict diplomacy in the Sri Lankan context must be approached with an appropriate understanding of the contributing factors as well as the historical narrative. In this overarching framework, geopolitical influence also has a role to play, as now more than ever, Sri Lanka is drawing regional and extra-regional strategic interest.

The island nation, in this post-conflict era, has to work on three distinctive areas of conflict diplomacy. First, preventive diplomacy must be applied in the country and a reengagement strategy in the form of a substantive policy document that not only illustrates the government's

---

[l]Dr. Neelan Thiruchelvan was a Tamil politician in Sri Lanka and a renowned academic. He was assassinated by an LTTE suicide bomber on July 29, 1999, at the age of 55.
[m]Lakshman Kadirgamar began his political career at the age of 62, when he was appointed Minister of Foreign Affairs in 1994 by President Chandrika Kumaratunga. He was assassinated by the LTTE in 2005.

stance but also provides a platform for the disillusioned Sri Lankan diaspora should be devised. The Sri Lankan missions overseas could play a key role in executing such a policy; this exercise would be ideologically productive in denouncing the Tamilian Eelam trajectory. Second, by involving international stakeholders to advise and consult on establishing a mechanism for transitional justice, Sri Lanka can engage the international community in addressing the human rights violations during the war but on its own terms. As former President Sirisena correctly articulates on the matter, there should be no international judges in this process; a local mechanism needs to be in place to address the root cause of the problem. Finding evidence of missing persons to bring closure to many cases from the war period is an essential component in this regard. International engagement to provide the tools for reconciliation will allow Sri Lanka to implement conflict diplomacy more effectively. Finally, Sri Lankan diplomacy needs to be strengthened, particularly with reference to the country's relationship with India, and this in turn is essential to bridge the gap between the southern Indian state of Tamil Nadu and Colombo.

Moving forward, it is prudent that conflict diplomacy take center stage in post-war diplomatic practice and Sri Lanka's foreign policy formulation. Conflict diplomacy should not only comprise the lexical vocabulary of the country but be practiced internally and externally so as to mitigate any future conflict. By deriving policy and strategy in terms of conflict diplomacy, Sri Lanka can redefine its international image as a beacon of hope, reconciliation, and resolve after suffering under the yoke of a three-decade-long war.

Ensuring Justice for the Victims of the Easter Attacks in Sri Lanka: One Year Later[77]

We offered love to the enemies who tried to destroy us ... We forgave them ...

Cardinal Malcolm Ranjith

There are two catalytic events triggered by Islamic radicalism that took place in two locations at almost the same time. It carried the same footprint, one stemming from another. It was 8:46 am, two decades ago, when the first flight crashed to the Northern Tower of the World Trade Center, resulting in the largest coordinated terror attack ever in the US soil which took place on 9/11. Retaliating to the terror attack was Operation Enduring Freedom and expanded US counterterrorism operations across the Muslim world. The US government's War on Terror began from Afghanistan and later entered Iraq, Libya, and Syria, culminating in the defeat and dismantling of the so-called "evil axis of terror," indirectly inflicting pain to thousands and causing the loss of many lives in Islamic regions worldwide. Al-Qaida, which later morphed into the Islamic State of Iraq and the Levant (ISIS), was losing its ground in the last stronghold battleground in Iraq and Syria a few months before the 2019 4/21 Easter Sunday terror attacks in Sri Lanka. The attacks were initiated at around the same time, at 8:45 am in a crowded church. In less than half an hour, 7 suicide attacks were carried out, killing 279 and wounding 573, as the war-scarred Indian ocean island faced its largest terror attack in a single day.

The Sri Lankan military was never part of the "Global War on Terror," as they were engaged in an internal protracted conflict for almost three decades, ending in April 2009.The military was getting ready to celebrate the tenth anniversary of the bloody operation they carried out to defeat the Tamil separatists, but another form of terrorism was breeding in the postwar context, i.e. Islamic terror. Many Islamic leaders foresaw such a threat, and from 2015, warned Sri Lankan government authorities of the growing threat of extremism. However, the authorities did not take much action against the ring leader Zahran Hashim[n] of the National Thowheed Jama'ath (NTJ). NTJ was a group with no prior history of terror nor did they demonstrate the capability to mount such an intricately planned, ruthlessly well-executed act of mass murder. But it happened. Sri Lanka was chosen as the target for the ISIS-influenced terror attack. However, some experts claimed it was "staged."

Jonah Blank, an adjunct senior political scientist from the US Security think tank RAND, says: "There aren't a lot of groups with the expertise to carry out an operation like this. ISIS has a history of taking credit for attacks which it has merely inspired — but in this case, there was almost certainly a **highly professional external sponsor**. ISIS may have selected Sri Lanka this time, but it can be counted on to choose any target of opportunity."[78] While the geopolitical high table and power politics breed

---

[n] Zahran Hashim was the mastermind behind the Easter Sunday Attacks on April 21, 2019, that killed more than 250 people, with many other casualties. He was also the founder of NTJ, an extremist group that spread Wahhabism.

terrorism and extremism due to multiple axes of power alignment, terrorism requires funding and some needs to benefit from coordinated attacks. The 3,000 innocent lives lost in the US on 9/11 and in Sri Lanka were lives lost due to revenge and grievances of the terrorists.

When the Tamil Tiger female suicide bomber detonated her strapped suicide vest on October 23, 1994, which killed my father and many others, it was an act seen as brutal for some. It is also an act of courage to some others. I was born in a country engulfed by ethnic and religious tension and disharmony due to hardline ultra-nationalist and failed policies pursued by the state. Terrorism or extremism stems from social agitation and frustration from multiple systemic failures in our society. The many ills that afflict nations give rise to extremism, which contributes to economic and political failure.

The key element in terrorism is that although its beginnings point to social and systemic failures, once it reaches a certain proportion, there is hardly any turning back. Radical Islamic ideology did not emerge from a vacuum. Terrorist groups grow from feelings of political, cultural, and social humiliation. Even Osama Bin Laden, whose name is synonymous with terrorism, murder, and Islamic fundamentalism, at the age of 34, was engaged in farmwork; he bred horses and had a peaceful life. There was a trigger that led to their transition toward taking up arms. In Bin Laden's case, it was Sayyid Qutb, the intellectual father of the Islamist movement, and Ayman al-Zawahiri, who preached that violence and vengeance could transform the society, that influenced him. At one time, he was fighting to push the Soviets from Afghanistan, a counter encirclement strategy put forward by the US and China against the Soviets. Freedom fighters were used as proxies for covert military operations in many different parts of the world; some existed and mushroomed due to the continuous supply of arms by certain nations. Professor Bruce Hoffman, a terrorist expert who has studied terrorism for four decades, explains: "ISIS was able to deliver what Bin Laden only promised … alarmingly, ISIS has been able to have it both ways: On the one hand, they're very effective at inspiring, motivating, animating 'lone wolves' or lone actors ... But at the same time, they've also been very good at creating an infrastructure — a network to support terrorist attacks." It was clear from a video that Zahran Hashim, the Sri Lankan Easter Sunday attack ringleader, pledged his allegiance and support to ISIS. What were the thoughts that influenced Zahran Hashim to assume leadership and carry out the brutal 4/21 attacks? What were the external factors? Were there internal facilitators?

In an almost empty cathedral during the Easter mass in 2019, Cardinal Malcolm Ranjith, the Archbishop of Sri Lanka, expressed that instead of retaliation, the nation's Catholic minority had contemplated Jesus' message of hope and reduced tensions.[79] In an ensuing BBC documentary on the 4/21 attacks,[80] a mother who had lost her entire family, including her child, says: "I will not forgive the perpetrators." A year has gone, but the pain has not vanished. The most lethal terrorist incident that took place in the country's history has not been forgotten.

Having narrowly escaped from the bomb blast one year ago at the Shangri La hotel in Colombo, I vividly recall the brutal killings by two bombers, including the ringleader Zahran Hashim. The image of the blood-soaked exit stairway lined with dead bodies which my wife and two young children had to witness has not gone away. For months, my younger child was drawing pictures of dead bodies and bombs.

One year has passed, and justice for victims is not yet in sight. The authorities who failed to act on intelligence inputs regarding the attacks have not been brought to justice despite their negligence in heeding multiple warnings by the Indian authorities. There was a phone call to a Sri Lankan intelligence officer by an Indian officer saying "today is the day" at 6.30 am on the day of the bombing, which was ignored. How did such vital information go unheard? What prevented them from taking action despite multiple warnings? Why did no one share prior warnings received by India with the national security think tank which I was heading? Was it because it was seen as some unimportant entity under Ministry of Defence? The authorities did not act on available intelligence. Had we acted in a timely manner, we would have prevented the attack and neutralized the threat.

On February 17, 2020, I submitted a 13-page statement to the Presidential Commission on the Easter Sunday terror attacks appointed by President Gotabaya Rajapaksa. The statement included several attachments, including the Presidential Monthly Threat Forecast (MTF) written in January 2019 and compiled by me to the President through Secretary Defence. The document indicated the significant threat from the extremist group after 100 detonators were found. The reports went unnoticed by the previous government. Former President Sirisena blamed the Secretary Defence for not sharing the important reports sometime after the attack. "No one shared these reports to me," he said when I presented the reports to him. The documents were sent via an official channel through the Secretary Defence office. There are two clear assumptions here: either someone did not want to chase behind the available information and the prior warnings or there was a willful suppression of information due to bureaucratic inertia at the Ministry of Defence.

After meeting His Eminence Cardinal Malcom Cardinal Ranjith last month, I learned the pain and sorrow he is going through. "Who will speak in behalf of my people? Asanga, why were you not called by the previous Government PSC on Easter Sunday? I want the truth and justice," he said. The Cardinal was absolutely right in demanding justice for the innocent lives lost. The current Secretary Defence General Kamal Gunaratna has assured that he will punish the perpetrators and the facilitators who were involved and that justice will be meted. Since 2019, the police have arrested more than 190 people in connection with the bombings with affiliations to NTJ. The Police Chief and Former Secretary to the Ministry of Defence have been charged with murder for allegedly not acting on intelligence about the attacks. The brother of a former powerful Cabinet Minister was arrested on suspicion in connection with the bombing. A second wave of possible coordinated attacks was revealed from these arrests and subsequent investigations held by the police.

The public voted the previous Sirisena–Wickremesinghe government out due to serious incompetence and acknowledgment of negligence from their own PSC report[81] and for soft-pedaling a national security threat. With the new government in power, with one of the former military officers at the helm as the President, there is no doubt of bringing justice and closure. President Gotabaya Rajapaksa, addressing Presidential Commission of Inquiry (PCoI) said: "The lackadaisical attitude towards national security prevailed during the previous administration led to the gradual collapse of the intelligence mechanism. As a result, the spread of Islamic extremism could not be contained."[82] So far, authorities have displayed an inclusive approach, with the commission and effective process in place, compared to the previous efforts, which scratched the surface.

There is hope from the victims that justice will be served to those who are directly and indirectly connected to the Easter day attacks. Sometimes it is easy to forget the spate of terrorism that occurred a year ago, when present crises, such as the Covid-19 pandemic, take precedence. The conversation could shift from terrorism to pandemics to financial crisis. Still, Sri Lanka remains a dormant volcano, erupting at various intervals and threatening national security. If the internal processes are weak, national security will be threatened and terrorists will take advantage. As the BBC rightly states, "… Islamic State group will exploit weak states, flawed systems that fail to act on intelligence, wherever they maybe."

Chapter 2

China, BRI, and Sri Lankan Foreign Policy

I asked for it (Hambantota Port). China didn't propose it. It was not a Chinese proposal. The proposal was from us; they gave money. If India said, yes, we'll give you a port, I will gladly accept. If America says, we will give a fully equipped airport — yes, why not?

Unfortunately, they are not offering to us.

President Mahinda Rajapaksa[*]

---

[*] TIME's Jyoti Thottam's interview with President Mahinda Rajapaksa at the President's official compound in Colombo on July 10, 2009. http://content.time.com/time/world/article/0,8599,1910095,00.html.

Geopolitical Scales of One Belt One Road[1]

Let China sleep; when she wakes she will shake the world.

Napoleon Bonaparte

In the year 1271 CE, a young Venetian begins a 24-year trek to Emperor Kublai Khan's court in Cambulac — modern-day Beijing — and returned via a different route. He visited the Indian Ocean island of Sri Lanka on his way home. This historic route traveled was later named *Seidenstrasse* (Silk Road) by Ferdinand von Richthofen, a German geographer, in 1877.

Further back in "Western" history, during the reign of Emperor Marcus Aurelius (161–180 CE), Chinese silk was the most valued commodity in Rome. In a manner of history repeating itself, Robert Kaplan, a contemporary writer, aptly titled his latest book *The Return of the Marco Polo's world*. Argument and speculation surrounding a revival of this world rang true with a memorandum of understanding (MOU) signed between Italy and China, connecting Rome to Beijing and her network at the highest levels. Italy is the first G7 country to endorse China's Silk Road the One Belt One Road (OBOR). The Italian Prime Minister Giuseppe Conte opened the doors for the dragon to reenter Europe, just as President Mahinda Rajapaksa pledged its support for the grand strategic Chinese project to enter Sri Lanka in 2014.

On November 5, 2018, when I was visiting the NATO headquarters in Brussels along with some scholars from Asia, a question was raised at the meeting: will NATO ever bring China and South China Sea to its agenda? The answer was a clear no. It is far from its global agenda. Today, the Trump Administration has tabled the Chinese agenda in the NATO, especially with regard to Chinese infrastructure projects and telecommunications expansions in Europe. This is with particular reference to Chinese telecom giant Huawei's investment in Europe's fifth generation (5G) infrastructure network. It is seen by some as a Trojan horse for Beijing's digital espionage. Jens Stoltenberg, the NATO Secretary-General, made a comment in a speech stating that China's rise also presents a challenge with its investment in Europe's critical infrastructure, including its 5G wireless communications networks.

With the new development of Huawei seen as a national security threat in the US, the country has threatened to curb intelligence cooperation with allies that allowed Huawei to build new mobile internet infrastructure. More than 70% of Sri Lanka's mobile network is on Chinese infrastructure owned by Huawei and ZTE. It is important to observe how Sri Lanka will manage its relationship with the US when awarding the next tender to Huawei. The Chinese foothold is clearly gaining, as evidenced by its infrastructure projects in Sri Lanka and several other South Asian countries.

Looking at Italy's entry into OBOR and China's surrounding commercial influences at important ports, including Rotterdam, Antwerp, Hamburg, and Piraeus, China has already placed its strategic footprint in Europe. It could influence future policy decisions in favor of China. This clearly weakens the US liberal hegemonic grip on Europe. The Trump Administration will use NATO to curb rising Chinese influence in Europe. This will be in addition to an existing incomplete list of duties, including deterring Russia and wars in the Middle East and Afghanistan.

Marco Polo was described by President Xi during his visit to Italy as the "first bridge" between Italy and China. The modern version is more sophisticated, with network of ports, railways, tunnels, and other infrastructure spanning 60 countries over land and sea. In a lecture held at the Venetian University Ca'Foscari in 2016, I highlighted the significance of the OBOR and its influence on Sri Lanka, including the Hambantota Port, and how the US$1 trillion OBOR will influence the geopolitics of Eurasia. Professor Renzo Cavalieri at Ca'Foscari University of Venice says: "Everyone is somehow involved in the project but no other G7 country has signed an MoU of this kind … what Italy has done, in quite a disordered way, is take a step ahead to create something which, so far, is not that strong in content but is quite important symbolically."

Italy ignored Brussels' warnings, despite an EU Commission paper that branded China as a "systemic rival," threatening to regulate Chinese investment in Europe and highlighting the security risk over the Huawei 5G network. Italy did not consult with Brussels or Washington when signing the MOU; the geopolitical calculation was made to move ahead with China just like 12 other EU nations who had signed MOUs on OBOR before Italy. In the future, it is clear many other countries in Europe will follow Italy's position owing to China's expanding economic power and failure of Brussels to adopt a common policy on China that could benefit all EU nations. While some nations like France and Germany are benefiting from Chinese trade, Italy and southern European nations feel left out. This trade imbalance with China will open bilateral prospects for the southern nations and former soviet bloc nations in central Asia.

I witnessed the same during a visit to Astana, Kazakhstan, where the Central Asian country, with its hard steppe zone of black rich soil is testimony to Beijing's attempt to dominate its central Asian minority areas. Kaplan describes this situation as "smothering them [central Asian states] with development, even as the Chinese build urban nodes for a postmodern Silk Road of long-distance highways, railways, and energy pipelines linking China with the former Soviet republics nearby."[2]

With their connected geographies, Europe and Asia are the two most significant regions with regard to global trade. According to Parag Khanna, they account for US$1.6 trillion in global trade, more than the transatlantic at US$1.3 trillion, and US–Asia, at US$1.4 trillion (Figure 1).[3] The US power balance in Eurasia is witnessing a decline. Stephen Walt argues that this is due to the liberal hegemony order propagated after the Cold War, with a misleading foreign policy followed by one US leader after another, from Clinton, Bush, Obama, and now Trump.[4] US interference and entanglement in regime changes in the Middle East has not economically benefited the country. The US agenda of protecting and restoring democracy to win the local communities has failed due to its double standards.

China, on the other hand, prefers to only strengthen the economic and trade agenda of OBOR-supporting nations. In this equation, the US, the current global power, has accused the emerging power China on "predatory loans" or "debt trap diplomacy," quoting Sri Lanka as an

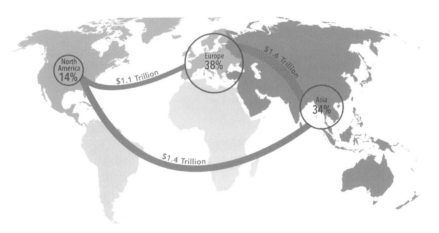

Figure 1.   Growing together: Europe and Asia form the most significant axis of global trade.

Source: Parag Khanna, *The Future is Asian* (2019).

example on many occasions. The US Secretary of State Mike Pompeo, citing Huawei in Budapest, said: "Beijing's handshake sometimes comes with strings, strings that will leave Hungary indebted both politically and economically." French President Emmanuel Macron has warned, saying Beijing "took advantage of our division." Irrespective of the criticism, China continues to win over one nation after another on its global agenda.

In Sri Lanka, the division on the Beijing factor is deep and polarized. This is reflected through our policymakers who are engaged with the two spheres of influence — the US and China. Our nation's policymakers lack in articulating a clear foreign policy and oscillate between the two increasingly divided factions of Washington and Beijing. The two factions are further supported by proxy nations such as India and Japan with the US and Russia with China. Not only does the pendulum swing with greater frequency between the poles, but the swings themselves have become more extreme and visible. It spins on security and power projection, a clear example was the US aircraft carrier John C. Stennis that navigated Sri Lankan waters in early March 2019, followed by 1,000 Australian troops with their 4 vessels that docked in Colombo and Trincomalee in April 2019, soon followed by the Chinese frigates in a few months' time. Another example of the pendulum's swing is on issues surrounding Sri Lanka's strategic infrastructure, including ports, airports, and power grids.

This short-term vision, which lacks strategic depth, poses a significant threat to Sri Lanka's national security. If the Government of Sri Lanka decides to award Mattala Airport[a] to India, who could be seen as a proxy pulling the strings toward the big power, it will be a move to counterbalance Chinese influence and clearly not an economic decision. The Chinese-built Mattala Airport, sitting 25 km from Hambantota Port, is now under discussion; since the Sri Lankan government lacks a clear strategic path, it has only a "leasing out" path, acting on short-term economic benefits.

According to Nathan and Scobell, "China sees its security environment in terms of four concentric circles" in the grand strategy of OBOR,

---

[a]Mattala Airport, also known as Mattala Rajapaksa International Airport (MRIA), is located in southeast Sri Lanka. This is the second international airport in the country and was a project by China, opening in 2013. Initially, several airlines flew to the airport, including Sri Lankan Airlines which established a hub. However, due to low demand, most of these airlines left Mattala.

first targeting the developing nations and then the developed nations. First, the innermost ring encompasses China's existing geography, while the second ring contains the land and water body directly adjacent to China. This periphery is most essential for the stability of China. The third ring consists of the entire Asia-Pacific region, and the fourth ring is everything beyond Asia. The report highlights the significant growing influence of China in these circles over time, particularly in developing countries. "China could set up more military bases, although may not call them bases" in these countries.

According to the report, Sri Lanka falls in the third circle; nations in the second and third circles have migrated from signing non-binding MOUs to entering into Pivotal Regional Partnerships (PRPs) with China. Nations in the fourth circle, such as Italy, will also follow the Latin American nations in establishing PRPs with China. China could establish PRPs but its pivotal Belt and Road Initiative (BRI) partner nations should understand how China might act economically, diplomatically, and militarily *vis-a-vis* the US in times of conflict or peace.

Many nations see the OBOR as a solution for economic prosperity only through an economic vantage point. The geopolitical prism must be addressed, for it holds more implications to the nation and its internal policies in the long run.

The Geopolitics of Ports and the Silk Road of the Sea[5]

The age of the west is at a crossroads, if not at an end.

Peter Frankopan

The expertise of a country's diplomats and the effectiveness of its armed forces are not the only variables determining its rise. Geographical factors must also be considered. Influencing the overall prosperity of a nation are its access to raw materials and trade routes, its climate, and — most critical in informing foreign policy — its strategic location.

In this light, it was no coincidence that the French Emperor Napoleon Bonaparte commissioned the translation of the works of the ancient geographer Strabo. The "subordination" of Asian countries to Western powers began in 1798, when Napoleon led a 40,000-strong French army into Egypt, ostensibly to protect French trade interests. Shortly afterward, issues concerning trade resulted in Western countries driving a wedge between China and India. Economic interests have similarly followed military interests on several occasions in the arc of history, and history could repeat itself. This time, though, the difference will be an Eastern power as the most significant player in the global arena.

Southern Sri Lanka has become a geopolitical hotbed after the construction of the Hambantota harbor and the recent relocation of the Galle Southern Naval Command next to Hambantota Port. There are more than 700 naval officers engaged in maritime security efforts who are based next to the harbor premises leased by China. The relocated post in Galle will be occupied by the Sri Lankan Coast Guard to further protect the oceans using its new military hardware. In doing so, scholars have suggested that Sri Lanka should opt for the P-3C Orion naval reconnaissance anti-submarine aircraft instead of Offshore Patrol Vessels (OPVs). This aircraft enables scanning a larger area and has been proven effective by many other countries. According to a statement by former Prime Minister Ranil Wickremesinghe, Sri Lanka should prepare for anti-submarine warfare.

On August 22, 2018, the Japanese Minister of Defense, Itsunori Onodera, visited the Hambantota Port and stated, "Despite the lease there was an agreement that the port remains free of military activities." This statement reflects concerns over the leasing of the facility to China for 99 years. Onodera was the first Japanese defense minister to visit Sri Lanka in a period in which the island finds itself entangled in the spheres of influence of India, the US, and China. Unfortunately, the expectation that Hambantota should remain free of Chinese military activities — as well as the other details of the lease agreement — has received little attention from the general public of Sri Lanka.

China's geopolitical presence is rapidly expanding under the aegis of the Belt and Road Initiative (BRI). Starting with ports such as Sittwe,[b] Gwadar, Djibouti,[c] Hambantota, and Dar es Salaam, China is testing a

---

[b]Sittwe Port is a deep-water port situated in Myanmar and constructed by India in 2016. This is aimed at developing transport infrastructure in southwestern Myanmar and northeastern India.

[c]The Port of Djibouti is located at the southern entrance to the Red Sea, at the intersection of major international shipping lines connecting Asia, Africa, and Europe. There is a military base operated by Chinese People's Liberation Army Navy (PLAN). This base is located close to the Chinese-operated Port of Doraleh to the west of Djibouti city.

strategy of using its economic influence to advance its security interests, much like Western powers have done in the past. To counter China's influence through BRI, the "Quad" (i.e. the US, India, Japan, Australia) was formed.

It has been argued that Sri Lanka has benefited from Japan's hedging strategies in the South Asia region. A tactic that could unfold into a larger strategy was the agreement signed on April 12, 2017, aimed at the "Deepening and Expansion of Comprehensive Partnership between Japan and Sri Lanka." The agreement covers three areas: first, Japan is to expand its maritime cooperation with Sri Lanka; second, Japan is to improve Sri Lanka's maritime capability by providing two OPVs in support of the bilateral defense partnership; and third, Sri Lanka is to participate as an observer in the next Japan–India joint exercise between coast guards. New alliances with nations such as Sri Lanka will further support and cement the core strategy between the US and Japan in the Indo-Pacific.

Djibouti is a former French colony with a small population and scarce natural resources. The country's GDP remains below US$1.8 billion, and it has only one significant geopolitical offering: its strategic location. Sitting at the eastern edge of the African continent and the western shore of the Indian Ocean, Djibouti has become a multi-military base and logistics operational hub. Even Japan's first overseas military base since World War II is found in this strategic location. Within Djibouti, a Chinese logistics base also sits, merely eight miles away from Camp Lemonnier, the US base.[d] There are 4,000 personnel from the US Combined Joint Task Force stationed in the Horn of Africa. From a realist lens, of the various countries who have leased property for military bases, China has a strategic advantage due to the billions of dollars of financial support it has offered continuously to Djibouti. One example is an infrastructural mega-project in the form of a railway connecting Djibouti and Ethiopia.

Outside powers pledging non-interference to the region and neighboring countries has significant economic and military implications. Other new ports emerging in the region could copy Djibouti's model in the years to come. Sri Lanka is not unique in this sense. Currently, Sri Lanka's Trincomalee Port is planned to be jointly developed by India, Japan, and

---

[d]Camp Lemonnier is a US Navy base located to the south of Djibouti city. This is home to Combined Joint Task Force of the US Africa Command.

Singapore; Hambantota Port is already leased to China, and the adjoining Mattala Airport will be operated by India, all in a bid to counter-balance China's influence. Merely moving a Sri Lankan naval post next to the plot leased by China for 99 years will not guarantee the ability to secure economic or military interests in the future.

Fluctuations in the frequency, scope, and intensity of diplomatic and military engagements are inherent to a volatile, multipolar world. China's rise in the Indian Ocean, made possible by its economic advances, is seen by many observers also as a result of it winning every move on the geopolitical chessboard. Djibouti was the initial victory in the Indian Ocean and presumably, other small states will give in to this tide.

China's Growing Influence in the Indian Ocean: Implications for Sri Lanka and its Regional Allies[6]

The Indian Ocean has become a friction point for tension between the US, China, and India. Such tensions intensify as each state takes measures to counter the others and project dominance within the region. Because of its central location, Sri Lanka often experiences the ripple effect of these regional power dynamics. Currently, Sri Lanka feels the impact of China's growth, particularly as a result of its Belt and Road Initiative (BRI). The effects are so significant that one cannot examine Sri Lanka's strained relationship with India without considering it in the context of China's rise.

Geostrategic significance of Sri Lanka

Sri Lanka's location is a major reason for its geopolitical significance. Over the years, many Sri Lankan governments have promoted the island nation as a maritime hub, an identity that extends back to ancient times. Even in the earliest maps, cartographers like Ptolemy and Henricus Martellus drew Sri Lanka in oversized proportions. Such representation of the island points toward its rich civilization and strong trade relationships with the rest of the world. Sri Lanka's foreign diplomatic relations date back many centuries, and recorded history speaks of emissaries between Sri Lanka and Rome in the 1st century CE. According to the historian Pliny, four members from Sri Lanka visited the Court of Emperor Claudius Caesar circa 50 AD.[7] An old map by Sir Halford Mackinder depicts two islands located in the outer rim of the mainland: the UK in the Atlantic and Japan in the Pacific, since each performs a pivotal role in its respective region.[8] Sri Lanka has a similar position as an island on the outer rim of Indian subcontinent and facing the Indian Ocean. Hence, Sri Lanka could one day play a role in the Indian Ocean similar to that of the UK and Japan.

Currently, scholars and leaders around the world are discussing Sri Lanka's geopolitical significance. In his book *Monsoon*, Robert Kaplan recognizes that Sri Lanka is "part of the new maritime geography, and that makes it very important."[9] Furthermore, the US Senate Committee on Foreign Relations, under the leadership of John Kerry, released a report in 2009 that highlighted the strategic importance of Sri Lanka and urged the US government to prevent it from drifting into the Chinese sphere of influence. Admiral Harry Harris, during his tenure commanding US Pacific Command from 2015–2018, remarked that "the Indian Ocean matters to the U.S., Sri Lanka matters to the U.S., and the U.S. matters to Sri Lanka."[10] According to Harsh Pant, China is rapidly catching up, and its ties with Sri Lanka are aimed at expanding its profile in this crucial part of the world.[11] He observes that Indian policymakers should realize that if they are not more proactive, they might lose the game for good. Historically, there have been rich cultural and socio-political ties between Sri Lanka and India. In particular, southern India has tremendous influence in the northern regions of Sri Lanka, and this is known as "Cauvery Delta Influence."

However, as Sri Lanka's erudite former foreign minister Lakshman Kadirgamar rightly observed, India–Sri Lanka relations are getting lost in the mist of time. Despite once having such strong ties, the relationship between Sri Lanka and India has been strained over the past 30 years.

China's sphere of influence and Sino–Lankan relationships

Recently, Sri Lanka has been caught in three overlapping spheres of influence, namely that of India, its closest neighbor; China, its largest trading partner; and the US. Thus, Sri Lanka has greatly experienced the effects of the increasing tensions in this region. In this context, it is necessary to understand the strategic position of Sri Lanka in order to assess the long-term consequences of such regional tensions. Foresight analysis is essential with this regard.

China's BRI, which is often compared to the "Marshall Plan," has identified six economic corridors across the globe. These economic corridors share a stark similarity with Mackinder's map and are a modern-day depiction of China's projection of power. BRI promises to boost the economies of the countries involved, and Sri Lanka was one of the first countries to support it. Under this initiative, the Chinese government is assisting countries through loans, and through this support, Sri Lanka was able to build many infrastructure projects. Chinese aid to Sri Lankan infrastructure projects is particularly evident in Colombo, the country's commercial hub. Hambantota Port, Mattala International Airport, Colombo Port City, and the Lotus Tower[e] are a few such projects initiated by China. Many analysts have warned Sri Lanka that these loans are predatory, and that China has created a debt trap for the island. Subhashini Abeysinghe, the research director of Verite Research, countered this notion, stating that Sri Lanka has more loans with other institutions, including IMF sovereign bonds, that exceed Chinese loans.

Comparatively, nations like Pakistan have borrowed five times more than Sri Lanka. Thus, claims that China has Sri Lanka in a debt trap are overstated. Sri Lanka will continue to borrow from China, and the bilateral relationship will continue to grow stronger in the near future. However, this does not mean Sri Lanka should not negotiate better terms for all commercial loans; nor should Sri Lanka rush into certain projects without public consultation and debate. In fact, the 99-year lease of Hambantota Port was hurriedly signed on a Sunday, despite former President Sirisena's advice to discuss the plan further in Parliament. The President's coalition ignored him, and former Prime Minister Wickremesinghe rushed to sign the agreement without much debate.

Indo–Lanka relationship vs. the Chinese sphere of influence

Swedish political scientist Rudolf Kjellen observed that spaciousness, freedom-of-movement, and internal cohesion are three main attributes of a "great power." In the recent past, China has essentially acquired

---

[e]The Lotus Tower is 356 m tall and is situated in Colombo, Sri Lanka. This is the tallest self-supported structure in South Asia and was constructed by China. The tower is lotus shaped and will be used for communication, observation, and other leisure facilities.

the above-mentioned attributes, which has significantly affected the Indo–Lanka relationship.

With respect to Sri Lanka, China's growing power has become somewhat problematic for India. For instance, China has expanded its international trade and has become the largest trading partner of Sri Lanka, overtaking India. Further, the position of the Mattala International Airport, which received financial assistance from the Chinese government, is particularly important. India has since come forward to take over the airport's operation. Some strategists opine that India was politically motivated to counter the growing Chinese influence in the island. Similar controversy has arisen regarding the antenna installed at the top of Lotus Tower, which is suspected have the purpose of intercepting Indian communications. Further, Hambantota Port has been at the center stage because it is situated at the southern tip of Sri Lanka; its position is just a few nautical miles from the busiest shipping lanes in the world.

Some experts view this as a Chinese strategy to establish a military presence in the Indian Ocean; both China and Sri Lanka deny this, stating that the port project is purely for economic and trade purposes. However, none of these assertions have been substantiated by evidence. Despite China's efforts to supplant India's influence in Sri Lanka, India's foreign policy decisions have been impactful.

According to former Indian Ambassador Shivshankar Menon's book, *Choices: Inside the Making of India's Foreign Policy*, India made "minimax" foreign policy decisions at the last stage of Sri Lanka's protracted civil war in 2009. The author defines minimax decisions as those aimed at minimizing the harm and maximizing the gain. Though the success of those decisions was not immediately apparent, Ambassador Menon asserts that no matter what one might think of its internal politics, Sri Lanka is a better place today without the Liberation Tigers of Tamil Eelam (a separatist group known as LTTE) and the civil war. And India contributed to making that outcome possible. However, Ambassador Menon also explains the limitations of India's foreign policy decisions in the Sri Lankan context. They are the same limitations voiced at a New Delhi conference organized by the Indian Council of World Affairs (ICWA) a few years ago, which coincided with India's vote against Sri Lanka at the Human Rights Council in Geneva on March 22, 2012.

Speaking at the ICWA conference, Salman Khurshid (India's minister of external affairs, an eminent lawyer, and a member of the Indian National Congress) explained to participants how a regional government can dictate terms to the central government, further adding that he is like the boxer Muhammad Ali, allowing his opponent to punch him but waiting for the right moment to strike him down. This is a clear example of how strong the Tamil Nadu factor is in Indo–Sri Lanka relationship.

The competition between China and India to influence Sri Lankan politics substantiates Sri Lanka's significance. This is on display in the words of former president Mahinda Rajapaksa. In a statement to the *South China Morning Post*, he asserted that Indian intelligence was behind his defeat in the 2015 presidential election. Further, he alleges that US and India used their embassies in Sri Lanka to bring him down. Of note, all the Chinese infrastructure projects mentioned above were initiated during the Rajapaksa Administration. This suggests that Sri Lanka's regional importance is affecting both the foreign policy and internal dynamics of the country. It also serves as an indication that India would do well to recalibrate and strengthen its relationship with Sri Lanka.

China and India are two players at a chessboard with different strengths and weaknesses. China has economic strength, but India's strengths are the historical and socio-cultural ties it has with Sri Lanka. India and Sri Lanka share a common colonial experience, post-colonial institutions, and political culture, all of which have ensured the mutual confidence of two strong democratic governments. Moreover, Sri Lanka is one of India's closest neighbors, a fact that also helps pave the way for the two countries to share a particularly unique bond. Hence, Indo–Lankan relations should improve at all levels, including political, economic, social, and cultural, even while Sri Lanka continues to engage in extra-regional relations with China and the US.

The way forward

Given Sri Lanka's geopolitical situation, the following recommendations aim to maintain ties with the great powers within and beyond the Indian Ocean region. Sri Lanka certainly has the potential of playing a pivotal role both regionally and globally, given its geostrategic position. Sri Lanka records the highest human development index in South Asia, with a literacy rate of 98%. Moreover, according to the World Economic Forum, Sri Lanka has progressed from a factor-driven economy to an efficiency-driven economy.

The US has observed that Sri Lanka is a contributor to the rules-based order and is a good example of a like-minded partner in the Indian Ocean. Furthermore, Sri Lanka should cultivate its role as a regional stabilizer in the Indian Ocean. Balancing New Delhi, Washington, and Beijing will be a priority for President Sirisena, who is rightly promoting a "balanced, Asia-centric" foreign policy. Clearly, Sri Lanka should pursue an equitable foreign policy with global powers. However, if Sri Lanka is to play the role of a regional stabilizer, it will require the assistance of countries such as India and Japan. The active participation of India is extremely important in this venture. Under the leadership of Prime Minister Modi, the Indian government's role in regional stabilization has appeared indolent, particularly given the failure of the South Asian Association for Regional Cooperation (SAARC); thus, it is essential for India to consider playing a more active role. India's lack of involvement can probably be attributed to the Monroe Doctrine mentality, or rejection of foreign intervention, perpetuated by President Nehru in the fight against colonialism. Such hostility toward foreign relationships was evident in 1977, when India was perturbed by Sri Lanka's open economic policy adopted by President J. R. Jayawardene's government.

In 1971, seven European members of the UN General Assembly formed an ad hoc committee and wrote the "Declaration of the Indian Ocean as a Zone of Peace." This declaration, which Sri Lankan Prime Minister Madam Sirimavo Bandaranaike helped shape, called for the great powers to curb further military escalation and expansion in the Indian Ocean. The document also stated the need for a system of universal collective security.

This declaration is especially relevant today, due to the tension among the great powers operating in the Indian Ocean — tensions that have made the region unstable. Therefore, ensuring a rules-based order in the Indian Ocean is of the utmost importance, as is balancing the relationships among India, China, US., and Sri Lanka, who may well be the lynchpin of this endeavor.

The Indo-Pacific Region and Geopolitics of BRI: A Sri Lankan Perspective[12]

Sri Lanka on the Easter Sunday April 21, 2019, lost more than 256 lives due to an organized terrorist attack by an extremist proxy to the ISIS, the National Thowheed Jama'ath (NTJ).[f] This was the largest terrorist attack

---

[f] National Thowheed Jama'ath was a Sri Lankan jihadist group founded by Zahran Hashim in Kattankudy, Sri Lanka. This group is believed to have had links to Islamic State (IS).

ever carried out in a single day in the island nation's history. Sri Lanka was peaceful without sounds of bombs after 2009 victory over terrorism, and today the nation is in a state of fear, fighting a different kind of terror.

The statement of the Archbishop of Colombo, Cardinal Malcolm Ranjith, that "powerful nations could be behind these attacks," shows that regional and global geopolitics play a significant role in Sri Lanka's internal politics and security.

This section will examine the Indo-Pacific region and the geopolitical tension in the region of South Asia from a Sri Lankan perspective and will discuss some surrounding arguments of the Belt and Road Initiative (BRI) projects in Sri Lanka. Critics label the Chinese loans provided for BRI projects as "debt traps" and "predatory loans," accusing Beijing of following a "strings attached" tactic to control these nations. From Delhi to Washington, BRI is seen from many different perspectives; some scholars and policymakers see this as a serious national security threat and paint a negative picture. I will argue why such speculations need to be viewed in a wider geopolitical lens and the importance of countering such negativity. It is clear to many nations that being part of the BRI will bring more benefits than otherwise. A closer examination shows that the existing power US, with its post-cold war liberal hegemony, has shown poor results in many parts of the world, while a more realist position taken by China, focusing on economic development without entanglement in military campaigns, has proven to be a right mix of domestic and foreign policy.

Since its inception in 2013, BRI has been the single largest infrastructure project launched by an Asian country for the entire world, a project that many nations including Asia, Africa, Europe, and Latin America has embraced to develop their economies and boost trade. This was evident with the recent MOU signing with the first G7 nation Italy, soon to be followed by many other nations. Beijing's drive to bring prosperity through infrastructure diplomacy from the BRI has already shown results in many parts of the world, altering geographical landmass cutting across mountains and harsh terrains, such as the China–Pakistan Economic Corridor and many other challenging projects. The Sri Lankan port project in Hambantota, which was identified many years ago for development, is now a reality, while the Colombo Port City is another vital project. These twin projects will definitely benefit the Sri Lankan economy in the near future. With 56 overseas economic and trade cooperation zones with an accumulative investment of US$18.55 billion, today BRI has filled the much-needed infrastructure deficit in many nations. As explained by the Chinese Ambassador to Sri Lanka, Cheng Xueyuan, "nearly 130 countries, regions and organizations had signed more than 150 agreements under the BRI and the trade value between China and BRI countries exceed US$5.5 trillion. China's direct investment in these countries exceeds US$70 billion, which have created 244,000 jobs for the local people."[13] The Sri Lankan Prime Minister, visiting the first BRI Forum in 2017, has given his fullest support while the Sri Lankan President Sirisena and the Opposition leader has commented positively, viewing BRI as a grand initiative which will bring prosperity to the nation and the entire continent.

Indo-Pacific

At the Shangri-La Dialogue in Singapore, the Indian Prime Minister Narendra Modi used the term "Indo-Pacific" 11 times. There was ambivalence in the usage of the term, according to Rahul Roy-Chaudhury at the International Institute for Strategic Studies: "the term would become popular with other countries, with the US referring to the region largely as Asia-Pacific or Indo-Asia-Pacific. It was only during US President Donald Trump's five-nation tour of Asia in late 2017 that he frequently used the term 'free and open Indo-Pacific region'."[14]

According to Dr. Satoru Nagao at Hudson Institute, "Over the past few years, infrastructure demand in the Indo-Pacific has surged, partly as a result of rapid economic development. Since 2012, China's Belt and Road Initiative (or One Belt One Road Initiative) has had the most potential to fulfill demand, both in terms of political will and overall national strategy. For want of a better phrase, China's BRI is 'the only game in town'. Despite the positive ability of Beijing to fill this need, a number of powers around China including Japan, India and US have begun to show serious concern about how China is engaging with recipients of its official development aid (ODA)."[15]

Dr. Nagao is right to call BRI "the only game in town," because there is no other infrastructure development project of the scale and magnitude of BRI. Viewing BRI from a geopolitical prism, there is a clear reason why Japan, India, and the US have shown concerns in the present geopolitical context.

Sri Lanka's neighboring country, the regional hegemon India, decided to openly boycott China's first Belt and Road Forum for International

Cooperation held in Beijing in 2017, followed by the second in 2019. India is the only South Asian country not part of this grand initiative.

South Asia lacks basic infrastructure for trade, including ports, railway, and roads, as well as investment for such infrastructure when compared to other region.[16] BRI addresses this missing gap and provides the necessary infrastructure for the region. Unfortunately, India is left out due to its present policy. According to Harsh Pant, "India has been the most vocal opponent of the BRI."[17] This hostility toward China's endeavor becomes clear when examined through the prism of geopolitics.[18]

In this context, some Indian and Western scholars see Sri Lanka and Pakistan's newly built infrastructure projects, Hambantota and Gwadar, respectively, as a strategic threat to India. This position is due to two factors: first, India's recent military alignment with US, and second, the decline of US as the global hegemon due to its policy of "liberal hegemony,'" as explained by two scholars, Walt and Mearsheimer. The US power balance in Eurasia is clearly at a decline.

Indo–US partnership

In July 2011, at the Anna Centenary Library in Chennai, India, the then US Secretary of State Hillary Clinton asked India, "not just to look east, but to engage east and act east as well"; following this statement, the US actively supported India's Look East Policy in the coming years. At La Martiniere School for Girls in Calcutta in May 2012, Clinton reiterated her belief in the centrality of "India's Look East Policy to the growth of the entire Asia-Pacific region." Encouraging India to focus on the entire security of the Indo-Pacific region has become a permanent feature of US diplomacy *vis-a-vis* New Delhi since the launch of the US "Pivot" and later "Rebalance" to Asia policy.

India was designated a Major Defense Partner of the US in June 2016; few months later, India signed the Logistics Exchange Memorandum of Agreement (LEMOA). LEMOA gives both countries access to designated military facilities for refueling and replenishment activities. In the same manner, the US signed Acquisition and Cross-Servicing Agreement (ACSA) with Sri Lanka, an extension to the previous agreement with amendments. The lack of a time frame in the agreement is a serious concern raised by the Sri Lankan national security think tank INSSSL. India and the US also signed a Communications Compatibility and Security

Agreement (COMCASA) that will facilitate access to advanced defense systems and enable India to optimally utilize its existing US-origin platforms.

These defense entanglements show India's support to the US liberal hegemonic foreign policy in the region. Some recent foreign policy decisions could be identified as "buck-passing" tactics used by US on India; "buck-passing" is when a state tries to get another state to deter or fight an aggressor state while it remains on the sidelines.[19] India, rather than seeing China's BRI as a threat, should move away from this policy and join the BRI just like all her neighboring countries. BRI should be seen by Indian policymakers as an opportunity for India and the entire region. The similarity of India and China being rising Asian countries and the economic factor of the BRI will eventually play a significant role for India to join the BRI in the near future.

Quad and counterbalancing Chinese influence

The "quadrilateral" grouping (Quad, comprising US, India, Japan, and Australia) formed alongside President Trump's formal enunciation of the term "Indo-Pacific." It was perceived that, whereas the Indo-Pacific was the new regional "geostrategic concept," the Quad was its "operating concept" — of a revived partnership between the four countries seeking to both counter China as well as offer other regional countries diplomatic options other than China.[20] However, there remain limitations from India's point of view to operationalize the Quad. It is not clear how Quad would evolve in the future and how the Quad nations will view BRI.

Frederic Grare, a French scholar who rightly identifies in his book India Turns East, quoting David Brewster, says that India is also trying to pre-empt the development of China's relationship in the Indian Ocean through the development of its own security relationships[21] (with countries such as Singapore, Indonesia, Japan, and Australia) within the framework defined by the Look East Policy.[22]

There are also counterbalance axes that have been created, such as Japan–India–US and UK, FOIP or Indo-Pacific against BRI. For example, Dr. Nagao explains a counterbalancing strategy, such as using Sri Lanka's Trincomalee Port: "Japan–India–US and UK might be able to use Trincomalee port as a naval port. Trincomalee is 25 m depth natural naval port used by the UK. A depth of 25 m means that US aircraft carriers can use this port. And it is well protected." The Mattala Airport project, built by China, to be given to India to counterbalance the Chinese sphere of influence in the Deep South is another example of a counterbalance strategy.

The pendulum of geopolitical power play spins on power projection through military visits and infrastructure projects in countries like Sri Lanka sitting at the geopolitical shadow of a larger Indian geographical mass. Sri Lankan geopolitics should be viewed by understanding its neighboring country India's position toward external powers.

Power projection through military visits is clearly visible, such as the US aircraft carrier John C. Stennis visit, navigating Sri Lankan waters, followed by 1,000 Australian troops with their four vessels that docked in Colombo and Trincomalee, and many other such visits expected in the near future.

China's predatory loans

The US Vice President Mike Pence's speech at Hudson Institute, where he warned about China's "debt diplomacy"[23] toward developing nations, highlighting Sri Lanka as an example, has no substance; when looking at the actual debt percentage with China, our sovereign bonds are much higher than the Chinese loans.[24]

According to a recent article by Dr. Harsh Pant titled "India, BRI, and Delhi's Indo-Pacific Strategy," "India has also expressed skepticism regarding several other infrastructure projects undertaken by Beijing in other countries. China has employed the BRI as a tactic for statecraft and attempted to influence foreign policy in some of these nations, Sri Lanka being a noteworthy case.[25] The construction of ports and highways by Chinese companies on the island nation has resulted in the accumulation of monumental amounts of debt at extortionate interest rates.[26] China waited for the concerned governments to sufficiently entangle themselves, and by the bribing of political leaders,[27] then influenced Colombo's foreign policy. The case of Sri Lanka in and of itself served as a major cause for the hardening of India's stance. While the development of the Sri Lankan port of Hambantota began in 2009, it was not until 2014, when Colombo allowed the docking of Chinese nuclear-powered submarines at the same port, that Indian concerns were validated."[28]

This is completely false and speculative information: (1) the submarines were not nuclear-powered and (2) it was not a kneejerk measure to accommodate Chinese submarines by Sri Lankan policymakers. The two submarines that arrived in September 19, 2014, were Chinese Navy type-039 (Song class) conventional submarines and not nuclear powered. The Chinese Government and Sri Lankan Government both informed the Indian Government. As a sovereign nation, Sri Lanka has all the rights to receive and conduct friendly port calls at its ports without informing another nation but we did inform. This hegemonic approach of India needs to change. Going out of the way, Colombo did inform India but India sees this as a security threat.

In the same manner, a Japanese scholar visiting Sri Lanka noticed the Hambantota Port lease as a national security threat since Sri Lanka's economic condition has deteriorated in the last several years and China would eventually convert the commercial operations into a military outpost. These are all speculative information, bringing in a negative perspective but we should always provide facts to validate that it is not the case. The Sri Lankan Government has clearly articulated its position that it will not allow any foreign military bases in Sri Lanka.

CPEC

CPEC has also faced many criticisms, and there is no evidence to back these allegations, such as the following comment published in a paper: "India argued that the proposed corridor would run through a territory in Kashmir that it claims. Red flags were raised higher, when it became clear that large proportions of the funds supposedly devoted to infrastructure projects were being routed to the Pakistani military establishment — an entity that New Delhi believes is responsible for a sustained campaign of state-sponsored terrorism in Kashmir and for propagating figures in Pakistan that are openly hostile to India.[29] Further, India sees the CPEC as an extension of the already robust physical axis between China and Pakistan, accentuating New Delhi's existing concerns over Gwadar Port. The port, which strengthens China's foothold in the Western Indian Ocean, is also a part of the maritime leg of the BRI."

This again is clearly a false and misleading, CPEC will benefit Pakistan and the surrounding nations, including the entire region, and India needs to see this as a positive endeavor focused only on trade and economic prosperity.

Declining US power

Stephen Walt argues the US power decline is due to its policy of liberal hegemony spelled out after the Cold War with a misleading foreign policy followed by one leader after another from Clinton, Bush, Obama, and now Trump. US interference and entanglement in regime changes in the Middle East has not economically benefited the country. US pursuit to protect and restore democracy to win the support from local communities has failed due to its perceived double standards.

This is further explained by President Jimmy Carter, who, after a recent phone call with President Trump, stated the concern that "China is getting ahead of us [US]" was discussed. The reason was explained by Carter as military adventures engaged by the US in the last few decades and the cost of these expeditions: "Since 1979 do you know how many times China has been at war with anybody? None. And we have stayed at war."[30]

These unfruitful exercises in Afghanistan, Syria, Iraq, and Libya to restore democracies and regime changes have cost the US rather than gain any benefit. Mearsheimer[31] very clearly explains in his book Great Delusion why the US needs to change its present foreign policy of liberal hegemony. Now the US is entangled in Venezuela, which will be another huge cost. The US position was explained by its Southern Commander Admiral Craig S. Faller in a recent interview, who said: "President Trump is determined not to see Venezuela fall under the sway of foreign powers. Beijing is using disinformation and debt diplomacy to dig in as Maduro clings to power.... I think the biggest threat to democracy and the way of life around the world is the trend that we see in China."[32] This is the liberal hegemony trying to forward and implement a regime change strategy in Venezuela by blaming the Chinese sphere of influence. This was the same strategy used to remove leaders of Iraq and Libya. What US should engage is offshore balancing,[33] a much healthy foreign policy than regime change.

Eurasian trade

While China is engaged in promoting global trade, today the Eurasian trade relations have become a significant component in terms of volume. With its connected geography, Europe and Asia are the two most significant regions in global trade. According to Parag Khanna, they account for

US$1.6 trillion, which is more than the transatlantic trade, pegged at US$1.3 trillion and US–Asia, at US$1.4 trillion.[34]

China, on the other hand, prefers to only strengthen the economic and trade agenda of OBOR-supporting nations. In this equation, the existing global power US has accused the emerging power China of engaging in "predatory loans" or "debt trap diplomacy," quoting Sri Lanka as an example on many occasions. The US Secretary of State Mike Pompeo, citing the entry of Huawei as a potential 5G service provider in Budapest, said "Beijing's handshake sometimes comes with strings, strings that will leave Hungary indebted both politically and economically." The French President Emmanuel Macron has warned, saying Beijing "took advantage of our division." Irrespective of criticism, China continues to win over one nation after another in its global agenda.

China is filling the large infrastructure vacuum, which is an underdeveloped sector in South Asia and many parts of the world. There are many success stories in Africa, Asia, Latin America, and Europe. But there are speculative arguments that surround these projects as some scholars see it as a first threat to the existing global liberal hegemonic order.

Sri Lankan foreign policy: Oscillating between two poles

The Sri Lankan President Sirisena clearly articulated his foreign policy in his election manifesto that he would continue on a "balanced Asia centric foreign policy," with the triple spheres of influence of India, China, and the US. It has been a challenging exercise due to Sri Lanka's geostrategic position in the Indian Ocean. Sitting at the center of major sea lines of communication (SLOCs), Sri Lanka is a "Super-connector."[35] The island nation's geographical position could be compared to two other nations: UK facing the Atlantic and Japan facing the Pacific, with reference to the geopolitical thinker Halford Mackinder's map. Sri Lanka's struggle has been that, even with its nonaligned past, it is evolving today into following a more "multi-aligned" foreign policy, which creates both opportunities and challenges.

Sri Lanka's strategic partnership alignment with China during the Rajapaksa regime was seen by India as a threat and a drifting away from the India/US orbit toward the Chinese orbit. Although a reassessment of Sri Lanka's foreign policy seems to have been done by the current President Sirisena regime, with the Prime Minister opening the US door to balance the Chinese sphere, there seems to be a recalibration, when revisiting the Rajapaksa regime's foreign policy, towards China in the present day.

In Sri Lanka, the division on the Beijing factor is deep and polarized. This is reflected through our policymakers, who are engaged with the two spheres of influence — the US and China. Our nation's policymakers are deficient in articulating foreign policy and oscillate between two increasingly divided fractions of Washington and/or Beijing.[36] The two fractions are further supported by proxy nations such as India and Japan (supporting the US). Not only does the pendulum swing with greater frequency between poles, but the swings themselves have become more extreme and visible.

Sri Lanka just celebrated her 72nd year of independence from British colonial rule, but even after 72 years, policymakers have failed to realize their promises of economic prosperity. What we have today is an underdeveloped nation with less than 4% growth. At the end of this year, Sri Lanka will face the Presidential elections followed by Parliamentary elections next year. The domestic elections will hopefully bring political stability to execute strong policies. Sri Lankan policymakers need to craft its security and foreign policy looking at the national interest and the geopolitical environment surrounding Sri Lanka. Sri Lanka, being one of the initial South Asian countries supporting the BRI and hosting the first BRI Conference in Colombo,[37] clearly shows we have taken the right steps toward achieving prosperity and creating an "Asian century," as Prime Minister Ranil Wickremesinghe says: "The Belt and Road Initiative is really creating an economic system, which is helpful to us in Asia. I would call it innovative."[38] With the new challenging security environment faced by many other South Asian nations as well, Sri Lanka will need to engage in the dual challenge of fighting extremism and engaging in its development path.

Sri Lanka and Maldives: The Chinese and Indian Influences[39,40]

China's economic security and Indian Ocean ambitions are deeply ingrained in the Indian Ocean's littoral states. Maldives and Sri Lanka are clearly two island nations within the Chinese sphere of influence. For example, the Maldives President Ibrahim Mohamed Solih has taken steps to restore democracy and balance the Indian and Chinese regional presence in the archipelago.

The geopolitics affecting small island nations needs a detailed study in the 21st century. To small island nations, China and India represent a rising power from the same continent. India is positioned 32 km from Sri Lanka and 700 km from the Maldives. To assume that internal instability is caused only by internal politics badly underestimates the complexities of the existing global geopolitical relations.

N. Sathiya Moorthy analyzes the Indian position on Sri Lanka as follows: "Unlike in shared neighbour Maldives, where India played all its cards in the name of democracy, on the current crisis in Sri Lanka, New Delhi has been holding the cards close to its chest. The return of traditional Indian pragmatism seems to have influenced not only post-Cold War European friends, at least up to a point, of whom some were seen as scaling down their criticism of the Sirisena-Rajapaksa duo, until rumours of imminent dissolution of Parliament began doing the rounds on Friday, November 9th."

In the Maldivian case, Solih's predecessor Yameen was labeled as an autocrat who signed MOUs to strengthen the relationship with China and support the Belt and Road Initiative (BRI), thereby departing from an India-first policy. This is similar to Rajapaksa being portrayed as seeking Chinese affiliation and support. The question is whether President Solih will renegotiate the Chinese projects, and if so, to what extent he will succeed. In the Sri Lankan case, it was clear that the renegotiation efforts of Prime Minister Wickremesinghe failed, resulting in the leasing of the Hambantota strategic port for three generations. I opine that this is connected to Wickremesinghe eventually losing his own portfolio, perhaps not only because of the leasing of the port to China but also his strategy of rebalancing China with other powers, which threatened the national security of the nation. In a related geostrategic incident occurring on Sri Lankan soil, a feasibility study was to be conducted by the Indians to lease out a strategic military air strip belonging to Sri Lanka.

How did the previous government's election promise of investigations into Chinese projects end up as a futile exercise? In an article in January 2018,[41] I expressed that the dragon cannot be contained. Will the same situation unfold in Maldives?

President Solih's new government's plans for democratization could be weakened from within by his coalition allies who are neither democratic nor progressive, similar to that of Sirisena, whose government was weakened from the inside and failed to balance the spheres of influence from outside.

Sri Lankan domestic politics

The internal instability of a state provides opportunities for external powers to have an upper hand and intervene in the state's affairs. Most nations that opened their doors to Western powers to restore democracy descended into further political instability and economic decline, Libya and Iraq being the best-case studies.

In 1913, Argentina was world's tenth richest country, but from 1930 to the mid-1970s, the country experienced six military coups, alongside political instability, and three separate bouts of hyperinflation that exceeded 500% per year while economic growth rates sank below zero for several years. The Argentinian Government failed to think in the long term. Among the factors contributing to a country's growth, clearly, political stability and short-term thinking are among the most important. This is a lesson to many nations in the present day that are wrestling with political instability and short-sighted policy, as explained by Dambisa Moyo, the internationally renowned economist, in her book Edge of Chaos.

Sri Lanka is no exception to this and is already at the edge of chaos. The unity government with the new bipartisan model was a failure as the two ideologies, center left and center right, did not create the required space to accommodate diverse opinions. Consensus within the coalition Yahapalanaya government[g] failed at many turns since its inception in 2015. What resulted was a constitutional gridlock between the executive and the legislature.

In a shocking move, the Sri Lankan President Sirisena ended up making his opponent Mahinda Rajapaksa as the Prime Minister. President Sirisena, perhaps accused of constitutional disruption and disloyalty, has acknowledged national interest and the cry for political and economic stability in installing a Prime Minister with the same political ideology.

---

[g]Yahapalanaya or Good Governance was the slogan of the government that came into power with the election of President Sirisena in November 2015. The coalition promised to reestablish good governance and democracy, hence the term Yahapalanaya was their rallying slogan.

What Ranil Wickremesinghe failed during the three years was to work his strategy. His Prime Ministership has been ceased twice on national security grounds. His Foreign Minister was dismissed for investigation on corruption; his own Minister, working as a consultant who wrote a book on Central Bank Bond Scam, was found guilty accepting funds from the bidders of the bond scam; and his closest friend, the former central bank governor, went missing after the bond scam of LKR11 billion, dealing serious blows to his office.

A divided house with Wickremesinghe majority will attempt to claim his legitimacy while the Executive will dismiss this claim, sticking to the appointment of President Rajapaksa. This position of the President will not change, and the Legislature will need to give in to the President's decision at one point or the house will be in continuous turmoil as one faction will surround the Speaker's Chair and another will surround Prime Minister's chair to secure the position. The son of the former visionary leader, Ranasinghe Premadasa, is a popular choice of many as the next UNP leader.

Sajith Premadasa[h] is also clearly seen in this picture, perhaps waiting patiently just like his father, who came to power after President Jayawardena. It is time for all party leaders come to a consensus and reach out common masses to cast their ballot to choose the new Prime Minister.

Yet again, the people of the small island nation of Sri Lanka await stability. Grand geostrategies of powers looking seaward weigh in, thus entangling the local to the global, to a measure it cannot be fully understood without one another.

Sri Lanka's Role in BIMSTEC at 20[42]

The Bay of Bengal, the world's largest Bay, is a funnel that connects over 1.6 billion people and is rich in natural resources. In terms of trade, it is an ideal platform for South Asian nations to look east and East Asian nations to look west. The Bay of Bengal Initiative for Multi-Sectoral, Technical, and Economic Cooperation (BIMSTEC) will be the regional integrator of this complex geopolitical environment, and June 5, 2017, marks 20 years of its establishment.

---

[h]Ranasinghe Premadasa was the second executive President of Sri Lanka and was assassinated by the an LTTE suicide bomber on the May 1, 1993.

Understanding the present complex geopolitical environment and the great power tension looming in Asia is essential in the context of China expanding its presence, with the BRI aimed at increasing China's north-to-south access routes to the Indian Ocean, especially via Bangladesh, Myanmar, and Sri Lanka.[43] In response, New Delhi now seeks to develop alternative east-to-west connectivity plans between South and Southeast Asia across the Bay of Bengal.[44]

From its inception in 1997, Sri Lanka has played a significant role in BIMSTEC. At the time of writing, His Excellency the President of Sri Lanka has assumed its chairmanship. Sri Lanka, situated at the East–West trade routes of the Indian Ocean, is a geostrategic "super connector" and a hub that could bring prosperity to the entire region. The role of Sri Lanka shall be deemed important not only in the field of trade and economics but also in security cooperation in combating terrorism, transnational organized crime, and illicit drug trafficking. According to former President Sirisena, "Illicit drugs have become the most serious challenge and we require more advanced technology and training for our coast guard to fight drug smuggling at sea."[45] BIMSTEC is an ideal platform to strengthen mechanisms in enhancing the security domain. BIMSTEC recognizes terrorism as the most significant threat to peace and stability in the Bay of Bengal. Hence Sri Lanka, as one of the nations that have completely defeated a terrorist outfit, can share its rich experience among the BIMSTEC member states.

As the Indian Prime Minister Narendra Modi said at the 2018 BIMSTEC Summit: "Each of our countries seek peace, prosperity and happiness, but in today's inter-connected world, we cannot achieve this alone."[46] In order to achieve peace and prosperity, regionalism is essential and the collaboration among the most powerful members in the BIMSTEC would be essential. The optimism about BIMSTEC's future is mainly due to the Indian Prime Minister Modi's absolute commitment to strengthen the organization. This section will examine a few areas which should be improved to achieve the goals set by BIMSTEC during the chairmanship of Sri Lanka. As observed by late Dr. Saman Kelegama, "empowering the BIMSTEC Secretariat should become a priority of the member countries to keep the BIMSTEC Work Programme moving and producing gains to the people of the Bay of Bengal region."[47]

Internal political challenges and promoting multilateralism

During the 4th BIMSTEC Summit concluded in Nepal, the Sri Lankan President His Excellency Maithripala Sirisena, assumed the Chairmanship. This should be identified as a golden opportunity for Sri Lanka to promote multilateralism and integration in one of the least integrated regions of the world. Such integration is essential in order to harness economic, trade, technological, and security cooperation among 1.6 billion people living in BIMSTEC.

Sri Lanka's greatest contribution to BIMSTEC will come from its ability to lead with values of democracy and the liberal economic policies the nation.

This section addresses the concerns relating to improving multilateralism in two areas. The internal political instability of South Asian nations and lack of political will toward multilateralism in the region are identified as the two key challenges.

Sri Lanka had a bipartisan Government created by former President Maithripala Sirisena and then Prime Minister Ranil Wickremesinghe, and the two opposition parties with different ideologies were working together, facing many challenges. Despite the fact that the Sri Lankan economy has been identified as one of the few South Asian economies to progress from a "factor-driven economy" to an "efficiency-driven economy," its performance has not improved. In fact, it has undergone a certain degree of deterioration owing to the recent currency depreciation, reduced FDI flow, and 27% poverty rate. According to Kamaya Jayatissa, the Sri Lankan political environment is characterized by multiplicity of actors involved in multiplicity of agendas. She points out the fact that "While President Sirisena receiving the Chair, PM is in WEF Vietnam and former President Rajapaksa is in Delhi with support from BJP." She argues that "this multiplicity of actors is not necessarily disadvantageous, and it could even turn to be beneficial if handled strategically." The issue, however, arises when a multiplicity of actors involves a multiplicity of approaches. However, if not handled strategically, this may create political instability within the country, a most probable situation in 2019 since there are no working commonalities among the three actors. The opportunity and time available to Sri Lanka to create and promote multilateralism through BIMSTEC will depend on the internal political dynamics, and we might lose an important opportunity first as a Region and second as a Nation.

By advancing cooperation in working groups chaired by India, such as Transport/Communication, Tourism, Environment and Disaster Management, and Counter-terrorism and Transnational Crime, the country has performed a commendable role. Drafting and circulating texts for agreements on motor vehicle and coastal shipping connectivity by New Delhi was an important diplomatic initiative to sustain the organization's positive momentum.

In the same manner, Sri Lanka could focus on the following important areas during its Chairmanship. The need for a clean vision and direction was articulated by the leaders attending the 4th BIMSTEC Summit. Sri Lanka could provide this by rationalizing the BIMSTEC by restructuring existing areas of cooperation to ensure tangible results in a short time.

Strengthening economic cooperation

The BIMSTEC's littoral states account for 22% of the world's population and have a combined GDP of around US$3 trillion. BIMSTEC intra-regional trade in goods was valued US$44 billion in 2017, which is an increase from US$29 billion in 2007.[48] BIMSTEC was created with the vision to strengthen economic ties among the Bay of Bengal nations.

According to Kithmina Hewage, while holding the chairmanship of BIMSTEC, Sri Lanka should move forward opening trade avenues and be economically proactive in the region. He highlighted the importance of Bilateral Agreements as opposed to the Free Trade Agreements (FTA) currently proposed by BIMSTEC. BIMSTEC could become the platform in creating value chains, which Sri Lanka has failed to plug into, and it could be pursued as an alternative for SAARC in creating trade relations. In the process of building trade relations, the Regional Comprehensive Economic Partnership (RCEP) was mentioned as a positive coalition and a response to Trans-Pacific Partnership (TPP) by the developing world. He concluded his remarks with a skeptical note on BIMSTEC, particularly on its FTA which has been in process of negotiation since 2004 but has not yet been concluded or implemented.

The BIMSTEC Development Fund, proposed by the member states, is an important step and should be immediately established before the 5th Summit in Sri Lanka. The fund could be used for institutional developments discussed earlier and to ensure the smooth execution of the BIMSTEC agenda.

Counter-terrorism, transnational crime, and intelligence sharing

BIMSTEC is no longer a development forum; it also has a security component. The integration of a military agenda into BIMSTEC is a clear departure from India's existing security agenda, which is tied down with its neighbor Pakistan and has stagnated. BIMSTEC is not a replacement or substitute to SAARC in relation to security, and should never be in the future as well.

Now security has become a part of BIMSTEC's agenda, with or without the formal consent of all members. Prime Minister Modi's proposal during 2018 summit for a joint anti-terror military exercise in India is a clear indication of the penetration of security concerns into the BIMSTEC agenda. The prioritization of "anti-terrorism" by the member states in the 4th BIMSTEC Summit, gives Sri Lanka a clear space to step in with its experience of nearly three decades of war against terrorism. The Sri Lankan military has been one of the few countries to defeat such an insurgency. Hence it could play a major role in sharing its experience amongst the member states.

A Track-2 security dialogue among the BIMSTEC member countries could discuss the issues pertaining to regional security, and Sri Lanka as the Chair could initiate this dialogue. This exercise would be an important step toward sharing the common experience among member states on counter-terrorism and transnational crime.

President Sirisena[i] rightly identified the illicit drug trade faced by all nations, including Sri Lanka, with the customs seizure of large container loads carrying drugs. Hence, a mechanism to counter illicit drug trade within the BIMSTEC nations shall be deemed essential.

Commodore Sanjeewa Dias identified the increased occurrences of non-traditional security threats, such as maritime terrorism, piracy, illegal migration, illegal and unregulated fishing, trafficking of narcotics, marine pollution in the region, has affected maritime security. Further, he pointed out the risks of weapon smuggling and the dangers of hybrid threats (e.g. ships being used as bombs) that can affect not only the seas but also the shores. Such occurrences were identified as a threat to the tourism industry of the country as well. He also highlighted the need to consider maritime security as a top priority in BIMSTEC.

---

[i]Outgoing President of the Democratic Socialist Republic of Sri Lanka.

An article by Anishka and Divya suggests that Sri Lanka could also work to establish a hotline among littoral states of the Bay to facilitate coordinated patrolling. In 2016, Indonesia, Malaysia, and the Philippines agreed to establish a hotline to combat piracy and kidnappings and to coordinate patrols in waters of common interest.[49]

At present, India has given Sri Lanka a full grant to establish a Maritime Rescue Coordinating Centre (MRCC), which the Sri Lankan Government is evaluating at the time of writing.

Intelligence sharing

In addressing the security issues of the region, such as terrorism and transnational crimes, the necessity of an authoritative and legal institution which lists the comprehensive specifications in sharing intelligence in BIMSTEC has been identified.

Certain member states have entered into separate bilateral agreements with extra-regional nations. Therefore, there is no guarantee that the information shared by the member states of BIMSTEC shall remain within the region. The India–US security collaboration provides a good example. With regard to intelligence sharing in order to control and mitigate the traditional and non-traditional security threats to the region, INSSSL proposes the establishment of an infusion center in Sri Lanka, enabling intelligence sharing among the members of the BIMSTEC.

Democracy: Rule of law

Indian Ocean peace zone to Bay of Bengal peace zone

BIMSTEC could demonstrate its commitment to upholding the high standards of rule of law by developing common criteria that emphasize financial responsibility, socioeconomic inclusiveness, and environmental sustainability.

Recently, INSSSL, together with Munasinghe Institute of Development (MIND), conducted a workshop on the Sustainability of Belt and Road Initiative Projects. When establishing connectivity, sustainability must be the topmost priority.

India has spoken of alternative standards for implementing connectivity projects, "based on universally recognized international norms, good governance, rule of law, openness, transparency and equality."

In 2008, leaders of the BIMSTEC member states agreed to establish a Technology Transfer Facility (TTF)[50] in Sri Lanka. The TTF aims to expand the technological knowledge and skills of micro-, small-, and medium-sized enterprises in the Bay of Bengal, and thereby build knowledge-based economies, which should be identified as an important initiative.

BIMSTEC should strive to help keep the waters of the Bay of Bengal open, free, and peaceful, by managing them as a regional commons. The Sri Lankan Prime Minister Ranil Wickremesinghe's proposal for an "Indian Ocean Order" with "accepted rules and agreements" should be implemented in the Bay. In order to achieve this goal, BIMSTEC must encourage its member states to embrace maritime multilateralism.

BIMSTEC should also focus on regional mechanisms for the peaceful settlement of disputes, on borders and fisheries, under the United Nations Convention on the Law of the Seas (UNCLOS). It could develop codes of conduct that preserve freedom of navigation and apply existing law of the seas regionally. In addition, BIMSTEC could stem the region's creeping militarization by instituting the "Bay of Bengal Zone of Peace" similar to the "Indian Ocean Zone for Peace," proposed by the late Sri Lankan Prime Minister Sirimavo Bandaranaike, to create a mechanism to limit unaccepted behavior of extra-regional powers.

BIMSTEC is a natural platform through which its member states can develop the best practices and establish institutions to ensure that the Bay of Bengal is governed cooperatively under the rule of law. BIMSTEC should focus on articulating how such liberal and inclusive normative standards inform its organizational mandate in four domains.

When establishing a dispute resolution mechanism, mediation should be deemed a priority. It is also important to ensure that BIMSTEC should not be reduced to the status of SAARC. The experience of Myanmar and Bangladesh in 2017 indicates how bilateral issues may quickly escalate to impede cooperation through regional institutions.

Leadership of the Secretariat

It took 14 years for the establishment of a BIMSTEC Secretariat in Dhaka. As observed by Dr. Kelegama, back then, strengthening the secretariat was crucial for the overall success of BIMSTEC. Among the institutional challenges identified by Dr. Kelegama, "empowering the BIMSTEC Secretariat should become a priority of the member countries to keep the BIMSTEC Work Programme moving and producing gains to the people of the Bay of Bengal region." Therefore, the necessity of a strong, well-staffed, and adequately resourced secretariat was indisputable. At the moment, none of this is visible, and putting words to practice is essential by the leaders who pledged to strengthen the secretariat. As identified by Xavier, India's role as a regional leader "to match words with deeds and, more importantly, inject hard capital into the organization" is important.[51] Former Indian ambassador Rajiv Bhatia identifies that India's leadership must be "exerted with a mix of sensitivity, generosity, astuteness and determination."[52]

India must respect the sensitivities of small states — leadership should not be confused with domination. To strengthen BIMSTEC's multilateral and cooperative nature, New Delhi will have to walk a thin line between control and passivity. Playing a driving role will require diplomatic skill and the willingness to delegate by letting smaller states take the lead on both symbolic and substantive issues.

Challenges to Multilateralism in South Asia[53]

Standing in the way of realizing the vision of a "South Asian Union" at present is largely the rift between India and Pakistan. According to India's Foreign Secretary S. Jaishankar, the South Asian Association for Regional Cooperation (SAARC) "is an organization which has been made ineffective due to insecurity of one member." Yet, one cannot imagine multilateralism without the presence of Pakistan, a large player in the South Asian arena. Unfortunately, multilateralism in the SAARC has failed due to this weak regional political leadership, and its inability to work toward resolution mechanisms when disputes are triggered. Poverty, weak governance with high levels of corruption, and inconsistent policies have further weakened the region, curbing the establishment of a "rules-based order" within South Asia. The Indian hegemon, with overspilling nationalism, will make the task of promoting multilateralism even more difficult.

The European Union (EU), with a very different geopolitical context, has managed to resolve disputes in the region, for example between Germany and France. This was a key milestone for the development of a multilateral order; ripening the fruits of multilateral integration for many nations in the region who sought to adopt the "rules-based order." Although it is not valid to compare South Asia directly with the EU due to historical and geopolitical differences, the key weaknesses of the region that is hindering it from prospering economically should be identified and clearly understood. South Asia's intra-regional foreign direct investment (FDI) is only 3%, compared to that of the Association of South East Asian Nations (ASEAN), which is at 25%.

Even after nearly 70 years of independence, many South Asian nations are still engaged in internal conflicts within the periphery, for which many governments have failed to find sustainable solutions. Although the colonial past has some lingering effect, it cannot be blamed for the entirety of the past, since sufficient time has passed for the individual nations to find political solutions to create a better rules-based order, and thus a harmonious region.

Multilateralism in South Asia: A possibility?

Insecurity in South Asia has threatened economic cooperation and contributed to the failure to recognize the benefits of multilateralism. For one to understand the limitations and difficulty in implementing multilateral cooperation, it is important to understand the region, the regional power dynamics, and the internal issues the nations are grappling with from the past to the present day.

A sustained regional integration with multilateralism in economic and security cooperation could transform South Asia into a major economic growth zone. With the largest youth population the world, as well as the largest population concentration in the world, there are enough opportunities and resources for economic growth. Unfortunately, the region is engulfed with half of the world's poverty, political rifts, border disputes, natural calamities, and ethnic and religious disturbances.

Poverty and education

South Asian politics has failed miserably after colonial independence in terms of economic development and poverty eradication. Out of 1.8 billion people in South Asia, close to 256 million live in poverty. According to the Poverty and Equity Data Bank,[54] about 43.6% of people in Pakistan live on US$1.90–3.10 a day. In India and Bangladesh, the figure is over 50%. Sri Lanka, which celebrated its 70th independence day this year, has a 27% poverty rate. Poverty is thus the common enemy of the region, and for this very reason, the Sri Lankan president rightly declared 2017 as the year of eradicating poverty in Sri Lanka.

Over the past decade, South Asia has focused on improving the overall health and primary education levels and upgrading infrastructure. As the World Economic Forum's 2017–2018 Global Competitiveness Index report[55] notes, there are only two economies in South Asia that have moved from the factor-driven stage to the efficiency-driven stage: Sri Lanka and Bhutan, both of which have got stable scores compared to the other nations. Education remains Sri Lanka's main strength, according to the report, compared to other countries in the region. To eradicate poverty, education plays a key and sustainable role in terms of allowing social mobility and enhancing the living standards. The region should focus on advancing the steps that have already been taken in this venture in overpowering our common enemy, poverty.

Limitations in promoting multilateralism

South Asia occupies 3% of the world's land surface. It shares 1% of the world's trade, yet intra-regional FDI is 3%, compared to ASEAN's 25%.

In addition, South Asian regional trade is dismally low at 4% compared to the regional trade of the European Union at 67%, the North American Free Trade Agreement (NAFTA) at 62%, ASEAN at 26%, the Common Market for Eastern and Southern Africa at 22%, Gulf Cooperation Council at 8%, and Latin America and Caribbean at 22%.[56] Regional trade among the SAARC countries was valued at US$5 billion, out of which India's share was 76% (US$3.8 billion).[57] India, as the regional hegemon with its large population of over a billion people and huge geographical land mass, is the key player to bring the South Asian nations together to move toward regional integration. If India displays the necessary leadership, regional multilateralism can be achieved and this will create many exciting opportunities for new synergies based on comparative advantages, ranging from investments in cross-border infrastructure projects to coordinated programs and addressing challenges in areas such as governance, security, environment, social development, and other fields that stretch over national boundaries.

The hostility and tension between India and Pakistan over border disputes have unfortunately affected regional multilateralism and SAARC, the only regional integration with all nations of South Asia involved, is now at a standstill. Since there is no dispute resolution mechanism built into the SAARC charter, it is difficult to envisage how the SAARC process can be restarted. This is a major limitation, and due to the absence of SAARC, the regional nations are divided into groups led by India and Pakistan; this is a very unfavorable situation to promote multilateralism.

Another factor is the extreme asymmetry of power among the South Asian countries. While India accounts for 75% of the SAARC's population and about 80% of GDP, the second and third largest member states account for only about 10% and 7%, respectively.

The military power asymmetry between India and the rest of the South Asian nations is another factor limiting multilateralism. India's Monroe Doctrine mentality to take action against extra-regional powers getting closer to India's neighboring nations is a major geopolitical variable in play. The Chinese submarine visit to Sri Lanka became a political and security concern to New Delhi. Bangladesh's acquisition of Chinese submarines was also a huge security concern to India, as was Nepal allowing China to build the Lhasa–Kathmandu road; the latter was interpreted by India as Nepal's acquiescence to China's presence and involvement in South Asia and a serious threat to India's security. There is furthermore no multilateral security agreement or discussion forum among South Asian nations to address the security concerns of the region.

At the regional level, India has resisted inviting Pakistan to join the Indian Ocean Rim Association (IORA) or allowing China to become a full member of the Indian Ocean Naval Symposium (IONS). On the other hand, India is building a massive naval fleet, with 48 warships under construction, including one aircraft carrier, one nuclear and six conventional submarines, and a variety of destroyers, frigates, and corvettes. By 2027, the capacity will be expanded to hold 198 warships. The need for a security discussion forum in the Indian Ocean region is clearly evident. IORA for Regional Cooperation is for economic cooperation and not for security. The Galle Dialogue, a popular Sri Lankan initiative, and the IONS, an Indian initiative, bring together the naval chiefs of a large number of littoral countries for a discussion on the security challenges in the Indian Ocean. Unlike Southeast Asia, which hosts the ASEAN Regional Forum

(ARF), in the Indian Ocean region, a ministerial-level forum that explicitly addresses maritime security issues and involves both regional countries and extra-regional major powers is lacking. Without such a discussion forum in place, multilateral security agreements will be unachievable.

Another factor is the geography and the geographical dependency of most South Asian nations on India. Distrust, hostility, and apprehension, as seen among the SAARC members from the initial stage, could be analyzed as a geographical factor. Probably seeing this factor, India joined SAARC with the condition that security issues would be kept outside the purview of SAARC. India shares borders with a majority of the South Asian states. When examining the Indian border, it can be noted that except for Pakistan, no other member state shares a border with any SAARC country other than India. Bhutan and Nepal are landlocked between India and China and depend on the former. Bangladesh has direct access to international seas on one side but is surrounded by India on all other sides and remains dependent on West Bengal, which continues to be part of India. These factors have caused India to be perceived as a threat by certain countries in South Asia. A close examination of the river basin of India, Nepal, and Bangladesh will illustrate clearly why regional integration should happen. According to Dr. Uttam Sinha, "India's hydrological experience with Nepal and Bangladesh in sharing the waters and the benefits of the Ganga has been a positive experience providing opportunities for closer regional integration but also provide an outcome to help resolve political issues. The Ganga, thus, becomes a catalyst for transforming bilateral friction to tangible gains."[58]

Apart from the geographical dependency between India and its neighboring nations, a common external security threat to the region is missing. The European Union had a common threat to galvanize the creation of an alliance among the western European nations. The growing power of the Soviet Union in Eastern Europe and the emergence of the US after World War Two were two major considerations pushing Western Europe toward increased integration. In East Asia, the increased power and influence of China and communist regimes caused the smaller Southeast Asian nations to come together to form ASEAN.[59] The absence of a common security threat to the South Asia region could be limiting the interest among regional nations to promote multilateralism.

Time before SAARC

Many South Asian nations came out of the clutches of the British imperial rule and gained independence somewhat around the same period. The divide and rule policy by the colonial empire was clearly visible in the region. The tension between the periphery and the center (government) was evident in almost all the nations of South Asia. These could be due to ethnic concerns, religious issues, or federalist power-sharing struggles. For instance, in Sri Lanka, the quarter-century war after independence, the Indian intervention to resolve the war through a power-sharing agreement, and the 13th Amendment to the constitution, which was to devolve power so as to ease tensions between the center and the periphery, are discussed even in the present day. A 13+ Amendment with more devolution of power was promised by subsequent governments that came to power after 2005 but failed to deliver due to the political instability that could arise from the majority Sinhalese Buddhists, who were suspicious of and feared the terrorist group LTTE's primary goal of a separate state, the Tamil Eelam. Furthermore, Sri Lanka had always been viewed as the land of the Sinhala Buddhist majority, given the records of the dominance of this ethnic group for over 2,500 years in history. Many of the South Asian nations are unstable due to such internal political challenges that were unresolved after independence. The colonial past cannot be blamed for this malaise, as the governments have had sufficient time to resolve internal political issues and bring economic prosperity to the respective countries.

In the post-independence period, before SAARC was created as a permanent institution and the discussion forum for multilateralism, there were many regional conferences. Therefore regional multilateralism is not alien to South Asia, and the region can look back at several attempts at regional cooperation, both small and large scale. There were eight pan-Asian regional conferences that eventually determined India's austere position *vis-à-vis* regional multilateralism.[60]

SAARC

Given the absence of a permanent institution for multilateralism, especially in the sphere of economic cooperation among the regional countries, SAARC was initiated through a proposal by former President of

Bangladesh Ziaur Rahman in May 1980. This was endorsed by Nepal, Sri Lanka, the Maldives, and Bhutan, with a view of achieving stability, security, and peace in the region. The SAARC charter was accepted by all the seven founding members in mid-1985. SAARC became the main vehicle for moving toward greater integration and for building trust in the region.

The India–Pakistan border dispute, however, has put an end to the SAARC process, which has not met since 2014, at the time of writing. In addition, its institutional ineffectiveness, vulnerability to regional politics, and inadequate capacities were other major undermining reasons. Despite many attempts to restart the SAARC process by the regional countries, it has failed to reconvene. Even Prime Minister Modi's initial approach to promote SAARC through the symbolic gesture of launching a SAARC satellite to be shared by all member states, as a means of recognizing the importance of regional multilateralism, was articulated but in practice has failed miserably.

As a consequence, the multilateral platform is fading away from regional policymakers' attention since internal challenges in the realms of ethnicity, religion, terrorism, corruption, and poor economic conditions have become the top priority on the policy agenda. The absence of a multilateralism platform has allowed new avenues of bilateralism to be promoted. For example, bilateral ties between Pakistan and Sri Lanka in the form of a Pakistan–Sri Lanka Free Trade Agreement (PSFTA) came into force in 2005. Since then, the total trade between Sri Lanka and Pakistan has tripled to US$462 million in 2013 from 2005's US$158 million. Bilateral trade will soon reach US$1 billion between the two nations. This further aggravates challenges to regional unity as each nation is working closely with other powers in the region and beyond, thus further threatening the regional hegemon India. Pakistan and Sri Lanka's strategic relationship with China, as evidenced by the Gwadar and Hambantota ports recently built by China in the two countries, respectively, has been seen as a security threat by some Indian scholars.

Even the creation of "regional economies" (geographical units such as Hong Kong and Southern China, Silicon Valley and Bay Area, and growth triangle of Singapore and Johor, Malaysia)[61] at the sub-regional level has been overshadowed by the inward-looking policies of the South Asian nations. For the nation states and their leaders, the primary issue remains protection of territory, resources, jobs, industries, and even ideology. The largely protectionist policies in South Asia have pulled the entire region away from creating regional integration. According to Kenichi Ohmae, "region states welcome foreign investment. They welcome foreign ownership. They welcome foreign products. In fact, they welcome whatever will help employ their people productively, improve their quality of life, and give them access to the best and cheapest products from anywhere in the world. And they have learned that such access is often best and easiest when the products are not produced at home. Singapore, for example enjoys better and cheaper agricultural products than do the Japanese although Singapore has no farmers and no farms of its own."[62]

In South Asia, the creation of such regional harmony between states, especially within two nations, is near impossible given the political tensions and insecurity. The creation of zones of regional economies, such as between Nepal and India or between Bangladesh and India, continues to be difficult due to the protectionist measures adopted by their respective governments.

The East Asian miracle and the strong regional integration achieved through ASEAN has allowed Southeast Asian states to move away from the national states mentality to creating region states that are integrated in the global economy. For example, trade between ASEAN and China has exceeded US$1 trillion. In ASEAN, a series of multilateral agreements for trade, services, and investment have been concluded, including the "Agreement on the Common Effective Preferential Tariff Scheme for the ASEAN Free Trade Area (CEPT-AFTA) signed in 1992, the ASEAN Framework on Services (AFAS) signed in 1995, the Basic Agreement on the ASEAN Industrial Cooperation Scheme signed in 1996 and the Framework Agreement on the ASEAN Investment Area (AIA) signed in 1998."[63] Such multilateral agreements will shift the existing bilateral issues to a regional level and bind signatory countries to a timetable for implementation. For greater integration in the South Asian region, similar levels of institutional support and initiative will be required. The key success factor of ASEAN, when comparing it to SAARC, is the ability of its member states to set aside their political differences and focus on economic prosperity. South Asian nations, unfortunately, have a greater trust deficiency among its member countries due to political differences and India's suspicions, which has led it to try to isolate the region from extra-regional powers working around India's vicinity. Until this hostility among the South Asian nations subside, a strong regional integration will not materialize.

Conclusion

It should be understood, in conclusion, that FTAs in the BIMSTEC, between India–Sri Lanka, India–Nepal, India–Bhutan, Bangladesh–Pakistan, and India–Bangladesh, alone will not help to establish regional multilateralism. It can, in fact, potentially create a chaotic situation if not properly coordinated by the member countries. Other regional blocs such as ASEAN have made significant progress in promoting multilateralism while South Asia has no similar platform due to the political differences, border disputes, and internal issues that have created further instability in the region. The absence of SAARC has a profound impact on the South Asia region. To bring back regionalism to the South Asian agenda, a significant structural transformation in terms of capacity building at the political level is required. To bring back multilateralism to the national agenda of every South Asian nation and to build competitive strength through regional integration at an accelerated pace, internal issues have to be resolved. Ethnic, religious, and political tensions have fully occupied the agenda, and at present, there is little space to discuss regional integration. This space has to be created in order to reenergize organizations such as SAARC. The EU and ASEAN are great examples of regional integration, the former for its long-term-oriented agenda and the latter for its member states putting aside political differences. If the South Asian countries learn from these examples, the vision for South Asian regional integration can be achieved.

Military–Political Dimension among CICA Members[64]

This section will outline the military–political environment and the challenges faced and role played by CICA[j] to strengthen the Asian military–political dimension. Three areas of confidence-building measures (CBMs) that Sri Lanka could offer to other members and partners are discussed.

This is my second occasion speaking at CICA after my presentation at the CICA Non-governmental Forum in Beijing on June 28, 2017.

---

[j]The Conference on Confidence-building Measures in Asia (CICA) is an intergovernmental forum established in 1999 by Kazakhstan for enhancing cooperation towards promoting peace, security, and stability in Asia. See: http://www.s-cica.org/

During my speech in 2017, I spoke of the importance of Sri Lanka becoming a full member, and today with the great visionary leadership of our President, Sri Lanka is a full member from August 2018. From its observer state in 2012, Sri Lanka is now the 27th Member. It is indeed a great honor for me to deliver the inaugural statement after Sri Lanka has become a full member of CICA.

This is my first visit to Central Asia, and I have navigated Central Asia from maps and geopolitical literature with my university students at the geopolitics class in the United States. An entire chapter was left for this ancient and mostly landlocked hub of the ancient Silk Road connecting Asia and Europe. As Robert Kaplan explains, Central Asia constitutes the world's most fascinating geopolitical experiment, and its legal borders make little sense. Rich in hydrocarbons and minerals and metals, Kazakhstan will become the world's largest producer of uranium and possesses the second largest chromium, lead, and zinc reserves. The map is already crisscrossed by energy pipelines in all directions.

Sri Lanka, known as the "Pearl of the Indian Ocean," is also geographically well-positioned and is a "super connector," situated at the crisscrossed East–West trade route on the Maritime Silk Road. Many scholars have highlighted the pivotal role of the island nation in the Indian Ocean region.

At the beginning of the 20th century, Sir Halford Mackinder rightly identified that the Eurasian landmass will be the significant center of military–political power play in his "Heartland Theory," in the present day; with the geopolitical axis of power shifting from the West to the East, the rise of Asia is clear and felt by the entire global community.

Centrality of central Asia and centrality of Sri Lanka at the center of the Maritime Silk Road touching the Sea Lines of Communication (SLOC) will be vital for the existing and rising powers in the global order.

In this background of geostrategic importance for both Kazakhstan and Sri Lanka, and many other nations, a multinational platform such as CICA will be essential to discuss military–political dimensions in our larger surroundings.

Interaction and confidence-building measures among the varied and multicultural nations in Asia to enhance cooperation toward promoting peace security and stability in Asia should be at the top of all Asian nations' agenda. A destabilized Asia will create ripple effects on our economic, political, and security order.

CICA, the grand initiative was proposed by H.E. Mr. Nursultan Nazarbayev, President of the Republic of Kazakhstan; on October 5, 1992, at the 47th Session of the United Nations General Assembly for Asian states for enhancing cooperation toward promoting peace, security, and stability in Asia. I would like to commend his far-sighted vision of seeing the importance back then and initiating this multinational forum, which has grown to 27 members as of today.

CICA has developed into an open and inclusive multilateral security institution as well as a venue for substantive consultations and dialogues on regional security challenges, capable of building a broad-based consensus among regional countries. Bearing in mind diverse security concerns of the countries in the region, CICA is well-positioned to meet the shared security demands and advance a common security agenda for all stakeholders in the region.

Nations such as Kazakhstan has pursued a multi-vector foreign policy seeking equally good relationships with Russia, China, and the US. The Sri Lankan foreign policy, according to former President Sirisena, is balanced and Asia-centric, balancing mainly the triple spheres of influence of India, China, and the US.

The complexity of security surrounding the island nation Sri Lanka, with its proximity to the Indian subcontinent and the Indian Ocean, is clearly visible. Sri Lanka wishes to spearhead a peaceful agenda and bring stability to the region since the island nation suffered a nearly three-decade war, losing many lives and resources in the process. Sri Lanka's efforts to bring regional peace is clearly articulated from early days by our visionary Prime Minister Sirimavo Bandaranaike's 1971 UN resolution 22:38 declaring Indian Ocean as an "Indian Ocean Zone for Peace"; this was to leave the region away from great power rivalry.

But militarization is seen in the subcontinent in the backdrop of the Indo–Pakistan rivalry, two nuclear-armed states in the South Asian region. In October 2018, India signed an agreement to purchase the S-400 missile defense system from Russia; the same procurement was done a month earlier by China as well. The Asia we live in today has complex security architecture, as rightly identified by President Nursultan Nazarbayev, who highlighted this emerging security threat in his inception speech at the CICA.

Nations like Sri Lanka and Kazakhstan which was part of the ancient Silk Road can bring stability and promote peace to achieve economic prosperity through trade, political–military dialogue. Being part of the modern-day OBOR, the two nations and the two regions, Central and South Asia, could resurrect the ancient ties of trade to bring prosperity to our people. Kazakhstan spent US$30 billion during the last ten years on the transport and logistics sector; by 2020, an additional US$8.4 billion is expected to be spent to revive the ancient silk road. Khorgos SEZ[k] was established as a transit conduit between China and Europe.

When looking at Sri Lanka's support and its role in the OBOR, Sri Lanka was one of the first countries to support from South Asia, when President Xi announced this grand initiative. The southern port Hambantota will play a pivotal role in the MSR in the near future. China is one of Kazakhstan's primary trading partners, and China and Kazakhstan has set a target to reach US$20 billion in trade volumes. India was the largest trading partner of Sri Lanka for many years, and now Sri Lanka's largest trading partner is China. China's influence is clearly visible in both nations.

In this backdrop, one of the biggest challenges is the lack of a common "Asian awareness" or "Asian identity." While European countries share similar cultural and religious origins, Asia is more of a geographical concept imposed on the nations of the region by Western narrative.

In such a vast land with striking distinctions and immense diversities in terms of geographical condition, ethnic composition, religious belief, and ideology as well as their historical development, the difficulties in evolving a common recognition of Asian entity will be tremendous, let alone the acceptance of a shared community of Asia.

The Confidence-Building Measures (CBMs), spelled out on January 15, 2013, by the CICA member states who agreed to implement four CBMs in the military–political dimension could be referred in the present day. They are: (1) importance of mutual visits by the military authorities and representatives of defense colleges; (2) mutual invitations among armed forces for participation in national holidays, cultural and sport events; (3) information exchange on CVs of top military personnel; and (4) exchange of information on the status of their accession to or ratification of multilateral instruments on arms control and disarmament as well as conventions on the outer space.

---

[k] There is a dry port and special economic zone at Khorgos on the border between China and Kazakhstan. This paved the way for the easy transportation of goods from China to Western Europe.

Sri Lanka as a new member state would support the CBMs, considering its capacity to commit and support for peace building in South Asia and Asia.

There are three areas in military–political dimension Sri Lanka could contribute.

First, Sri Lanka with its experience on fighting a three-decade war with terrorism: Our military is known to be one of the few military forces that have defeated and completely eradicated terrorism. We possess expertise in this sphere, and we can share our experience with the CICA members. Sharing experience and learning important lessons on countering-terrorism could be done at two levels. Firstly, at the academic think tank level, since the CICA has think-tank–level sharing of expertise already in place, the Institute of National Security Studies Sri Lanka (INSSSL), the national security think tank, could play a role in sharing at the academic level in the area of counterterrorism and other security-related challenges with similar think tanks in other member states. INSSSL also wishes to invite a CICA representative from the secretariat in this regard to Colombo for its annual conference "INSSSL Shangri-la Colloquium 2018" held on December 16, 2018, as an initial step. The next stage will be military-to-military exercises, which could be designed among member states and Sri Lanka.

The second area is threats posed by transnational organized crimes, maritime security, drug trafficking, human trafficking, terrorist financing, and money laundering. CICA members can work together to secure and guard against the threats to territorial integrity of each other's borders, and Sri Lanka could assist in this regard.

The third dimension is cybercrime. Domestic unrest and cybercrime is threatening the national security of many nations. The younger generation has been targeted and has become the pawn of misplaced agendas. I highlighted the importance of nations to give their highest attention to cybersecurity at the National IT Conference held in Colombo. Protecting critical infrastructure and considering cybersecurity as a top national security threat is pivotal. The importance of building a "Unified Mechanism to Improve Cyber Security" should be considered, as highlighted at the 2017 CICA Non-governmental Forum in Beijing, where I discussed the importance of CERTs to work together to design and achieve a unified mechanism to counter cybercrime. A unified understanding of cybercrimes has to lead to a unified concept of criminalizing cybercrimes in order to deter such crimes as well as to normalize the concept of a safe cyber domain. Consequently, a common cyber security policy can very well become a turning point, where all new strategies will become integrated and comprehensive, approaching cybersecurity in a holistic manner, encompassing economic, social, educational, legal, law enforcement, technical, diplomatic, military, and intelligence related aspects.

With this, let me conclude wishing all success to CICA for its future endeavors to achieve the CBMs and strengthen the military–political dimension of Asia. I am certain Sri Lanka as the new member of CICA will play an important role in the years to come.

Chapter 3

Geopolitics

The historic Western and the more recent American dominance of the Indian and Pacific Oceans is likely to be tested by the rise of Chinese and Indian maritime power in the coming decades.

C. Raja Mohan*

---

* C. Raja Mohan (2012). Samudra Manthan, Carnegie Endowment for International Peace.

Strategic Stability in the New Decade: Ports of Asia in a Period of Escalation[1]

The Sirisena Government gave it [Hambantota Port] on a 99-year lease, and even though China is a good friend of ours and we need their assistance for development, I am not afraid to say that was a mistake.

Gotabaya Rajapaksa[2]

The year 2020 dawns with a US airstrike. The significance of this strike, killing the head of Iran's elite Quds Force Qasem Soleimani and Abu Mahdi al-Muhandis, the Deputy Commander of Popular Mobilisation Forces, presents a turning point in the geopolitics of the Middle East. Soleimani himself had once said to President Trump: "You will start this war but we will be the ones to impose its end." US–Iran tensions will escalate and so will Tehran retaliate with its asymmetric capability. According to RAND scholar Ariane Tabatabai, it will be a "more strategic, more careful, planned approach,"[3] by Iran.

As a trading partner and largest buyer of Iranian oil, China's reaction must be monitored. China is also Iran's ally as a part of the Belt and Road Initiative (BRI), which gives it a clear reason to secure Chinese–Iranian interests in the long term. The Gate of Supreme Harmony in the Forbidden City in Beijing is guarded by a pair of bronze lions of the Ming era: the female plays with a cub, and the male who holds the world in his paw symbolizes power. Does China wish to hold the world in its paws? China is seen as a rising revisionist power.[4] The ancient Silk Road introduced many symbolic and cultural values, including the statues of lions, to China from Central Asia and from the Buddhist traditions closer to Ming Dynasty. I learned this during my recent visit to the Forbidden City during the New Year. The modern-day Silk Road, i.e. the BRI, has facilitated Chinese economic inroads in many nations, however, certain scholars believe China's footprint in many developing nations is aimed at global dominance, just as the symbolic gesture of the male lion.

China's Vice-President Wang Qishan highlighted the importance of multilateralism at the Davos Forum in 2019. The year before, President Trump declared at the same forum that "We support free trade, but it needs to be FAIR and RECIPROCAL, the United States will no longer turn a blind eye to unfair economic practices, including massive intellectual property theft. "The US trade war with China has escalated and its ripple effects have been felt in many nations, especially those with Chinese large-scale infrastructure projects. This includes US ally Israel and the Indian Ocean island nation of Sri Lanka, seen as a strong partner of China.

The Chinese are altering a static nanometer to understanding geopolitics — i.e. geography. It is altering geography across the world unlike any other nation, from CPEC[a] in Pakistan to the coastal regions of Sri Lanka. Recently, Chinese projects effectively altered Sri Lanka's western coastal geography by adding 269 hectares reclaimed from the sea for the Colombo Port City.[b] Newly elected Prime Minister Mahinda Rajapaksa, who elevated the Sino–Lanka relationship to a strategic height during his tenure is back in power and visited the project site he inaugurated along with the Chinese President Xi Jinping in 2014. Rajapaksa along with Chinese Ambassador to Sri Lanka, Cheng Xueyuan, officially declared the newly reclaimed land by the Chinese as part of the Colombo district last month.

The Hambantota Port — another Chinese project in Sri Lanka — was leased out for 99 years by the Sirisena government. It was a discussion point when the newly elected President Gotabaya Rajapaksa commented that he would revisit the agreement to ensure national security.

It is the first time in the island nation's recent history that a Sri Lankan leader prioritized national security in negotiations on foreign projects — this is required and commendable. As the previous Sirisena government's rush for a bailout due to difficulty in repayment of the Chinese loans came to the forefront with the President's comment, this was further explained by Prime Minister Mahinda Rajapaksa, who termed the media's coverage of the Sri Lankan President Gotabaya Rajapaksa's remarks on Hambantota Port deal as "quoting out of context. The President didn't mean there is any problem with sovereignty. What the President meant was that our government, unlike the previous one, has a principle of not privatizing assets." Furthermore, the Prime Minister fully dismissed the notion that China's BRI was a "debt trap," refuting the allegations by the

---

[a]China Pakistan Economic Corridor (CPEC) is a framework of regional connectivity, that is financed by China. This will improve road, rail and air transportation.
[b]Colombo port city is a project financed by China Harbour Engineering Company (CHEC). This is spanning over 269 hectares of reclaimed land from the sea. The development will comprise of 5 different precincts including the Financial District, Central Park Living, Island Living, The Marina and the International Island.

Western media: "We are very confident that Sri Lanka can very clearly repay the loans for the Hambantota Port and other development projects. Today, the economy has collapsed but when we rebuild it, paying back loans won't be a question," Rajapaksa said.[5] What President Gotabaya said on "national security" will be an interesting comment when one carefully examines another "silent" port project unfolding in a different geography, which has become a security concern, i.e. Haifa.

When the eastern border of Israel was blocked, the strategic port of Haifa along its western shores was the only gateway to the rest of the world. Conquered by the Crusaders in the year 1100, Haifa became the main port for the ancient city of Tiberius. As rightly predicted by Theodore Herzl in 1902 in his book *Altneuland*, Haifa was to become a strategic port in the future for the nation of Israel. We see this prediction unfolding particularly in this century. Haifa in naturally endowed with 700,000 sqm of natural bay along the Mediterranean coast. It is a blessing with its natural deep-water geography. A new container terminal, "Bay Terminal," was built to handle 800,000 TEU container movements annually by 2021. The terminal will be operated by the Chinese-owned Shanghai International Port Group (SIPG), who won the international tender to operate it for 25 years. This adds Haifa to the Chinese BRI. When the US Sixth Fleet is docked at the same port, the Chinese will be in charge of the port operations, which has raised a significant security concern for the US and Israel security experts. Israel's top intelligence agency Shin Bet's chief Nadav Argaman warns: "Chinese influence in Israel is particularly dangerous in terms of strategic infrastructure and investments in larger companies."[6] He further requested the Knesset (Israel's Parliament) to pass legislation to monitor foreign investment in Israel. The same fear was articulated by the US Congress report on National Defense Authorization Act 2020, Section 1289,[7] stating: "The committee recommends a provision that would express the sense of the Senate that the United States has an interest in the future forward presence of the United States naval vessels at the Port of Haifa in Israel but has serious security concerns with respect to the current leasing arrangements of the Port of Haifa. Therefore, the provision would express the view that the United States should urge the Government of Israel to consider the security implications of foreign investment in Israel."

However, despite US fears, Israel has increased its trade with China to 73% in 2018 to US$2.8 billion. This shows the importance placed on bilateral economic interests, regardless of US sensitivity to Chinese acquisitions and infrastructure diplomacy, in Israel. It appears Israel is moving ahead and strengthening its Chinese relations. In the same manner, Sri Lanka has increased its trade with China, despite the external security concerns and fear, especially from its neighbor India.

China has become the largest donor and trading partner of Sri Lanka. Economic attractiveness and the availability of Chinese loans leave other nations with limited space to win large-scale infrastructure projects. Viraj Solanki from IISS rightly observes that: "New Delhi cannot match the level of spending offered by Beijing for infrastructure projects in Sri Lanka — these include US$1.4 billion in backing for the ambitious Colombo Port City project8 — but it clearly views security cooperation ($50 million offered during President Gotabaya's inaugural visit), and in particular counter-terrorism cooperation, as an area in which it does have scope to strengthen relations with the new Rajapaksa government."[9]

Highlighting the importance of Chinese investments, the Sri Lankan Prime Minister's Economic Advisor, Ajith Nivard Cabraal, who was the former Governor of Central Bank during Mahinda Rajapaksa's Presidency, said that: "Hambantota Port, which reported 60% growth in shipment volumes in 2019, is one of the most important and strategic assets for the country and that the Government is keen for the port to play a leading role in the economy in 2020."[10] While there is a higher expectation of return from the Chinese projects, the Sri Lankan experience is often highlighted as an example of the dark side, depicted by many Western analysts and media as a "debt trap" diplomacy or "predatory loans" to lock in strategic assets.

Jean Francois Dufour, Economist and Director of DCA China Analysis, comments that "the sums invested by China are not donations but loans with consequences. The opponents of China, like India painted the entire operation as deliberate plan to acquire strategic positions in the region,"[11] warning the same could happen to Italy's Trieste Port as Italy is already a partner of BRI.

However, this critical view is not accepted by many nations that receive Chinese funds, such as Sri Lanka. BRI is seen as an ambitious foreign policy strategy to bring the developing world under the Chinese orbit. One of the fears in the developing world is that BRI would likely institutionalize a Chinese authoritarian model, undermining the existing democratic and economic model in many nations. These nations could disregard these fears if the respective governments adopt a transparent model. In the case of Sri Lanka, the 99-year lease agreement was not discussed at the parliament and signed in a rush without receiving any strategic inputs from the previous Government.

In light of the comment of the newly elected President Gotabaya Rajapaksa, we can anticipate the present Government will follow a novel process to reign in a strategic dimension in assessing the long-term implications to national security before leasing out strategic assets.

Sri Lanka, the Indian Ocean, and the New Era of Great Power Competition[12]

We must not return to the age of great power rivalries. Asia in rivalry will hold us back; Asia in cooperation will shape the century.

Pankaj Saran[c]

How will Sri Lanka manage a new era in the Indian Ocean?

As the sponsor of the 1971 United Nations Resolution 2832 for an Indian Ocean Zone for Peace, introduced by the visionary Sri Lankan Prime Minister Sirimavo Bandaranaike, Sri Lanka watches, with cautious optimism, the hope of witnessing the reality of a Zone of Peace. While the Deputy National Security Adviser of India, Pankaj Saran, has advised the region to keep away from great power rivalries, a realist perspective would suggest that, in the present geopolitical environment, rivalry is inevitable.

The 2017 US National Security Strategy describes a new era of "great power competition" as foreign nations have begun to "reassert their influence regionally and globally…contesting [America's] geopolitical advantages and trying to change the international order in their favor."

Realists like the University of Chicago's John J. Mearsheimer and numerous geopolitical thinkers argue that China's rise lies with its geographical advantage. To keep the dragon at bay, the US will use a defensive strategy of containment in three ways, they argue.

First, the US will seek to bar China from turning toward its military forces to conquer territory and expand its influence in Asia. Second, Washington will build an alliance structure along the lines of NATO,

---

[c]Deputy National Security Adviser of India, at "The Indian Ocean: Defining our Future" conference in Colombo, 2018.

which proved highly effective to contain the Soviet Union during the Cold War. Third, the US will look to dominate world oceans, making it difficult for China to project power in distant regions of strategic significance, such as the Persian Gulf and the Western hemisphere.

As explained by Mearsheimer, today, all three strategies are at play. There is no reason the US cannot have substantial economic relations with China while it simultaneously implements a containment strategy. Historically, this would be much like Britain, France, and Russia trading extensively with Wilhelmine Germany two decades before World War I while creating the Triple Entente for the very purpose of containing Germany.

China is becoming militarily stronger today. In September 2018, the US imposed sanctions on Beijing for its purchase of the S-400 surface-to-air missile defense system. The S-400 is a cutting-edge security tool that will protect against any missile attack by enemies. It is manufactured and designed by Russia. In October 2018, another S-400 deal was sealed in New Delhi during the visit of Russian President Vladimir Putin to India; for now, it appears that the same US sanctions will not apply to India and may perhaps be fully waived.

Such sanctions are required under the Countering America's Adversaries through Sanctions Act, which codifies sanctions against Russian arms manufacturers in national security interests. However, the 2019 National Defense Authorization Act (NDAA) gives the US president the power to waive these sanctions. A "free pass" given by the US to Beijing's fearful neighbors may be described as Washington's strategy of lingering in the background and letting the surrounding Asian nations bear the brunt of containing Beijing.

This was observed a few weeks ago by the Japanese scholar Atsuko Kanehara, who visited Colombo University in Sri Lanka and spoke of the importance of the Shinzo Abe government's strategy of a Free and Open Indo-Pacific (FOIP). FOIP is a construct by the Japanese to assist their ally, the US, to maintain order in the two oceans surrounding Asia, i.e. the Indian and Pacific Oceans.

China's aggression, in the meantime, was on display when a Chinese naval vessel came within 45 yards of the USS Decatur as it conducted a freedom of navigation operation in the South China Sea. An aggressive maneuver by a Chinese destroyer coerced the US ship to quickly move to avoid a collision. As US Vice President Mike Pence stated at his speech on China at the Hudson Institute in early October 2019: "Despite such reckless harassment ... we will not be intimidated; we will not stand down." Pence further explained: "China now spends as much on its military as the rest of Asia combined, and Beijing has prioritized capabilities to erode America's military advantages — on land, at sea, in the air, and in space. China wants nothing less than to push the United States of America from the Western Pacific and attempt to prevent us from coming to the aid of our allies."

Managing tensions between established and rising powers

The established power in Asia, the US, will most likely engage in two strategies to counter China's aggressiveness. First, it will use its economic power to slow down the Chinese economy. This has already started through the implementation of US President Donald J. Trump's trade wars with China. The second will be to use a rollback strategy to peacefully encourage regime changes in Chinese-allied nations. Mearsheimer highlights this maneuver in his book *The Tragedy of Great Power Politics*. He compares regime changes and the operations carried out by the US during the Cold War with the nations within the Soviet sphere of influence.

The same strategy could be adopted today against nations with governments that are willing to sit within the Chinese sphere of influence. This was seen in Sri Lanka's previous change in government, with the ouster of President Mahinda Rajapaksa's pro-Chinese regime. Some opine that the Rajapaksa regime was toppled by India, which acted as an agent for the US to install a pro-Western government.

For the US, slowing down the Chinese economy is certainly more attractive than a direct confrontation or war. Forcing an economic slowdown in China will also hurt US interests as many nations might be eager to fill the void created by the US and be willing to trade with China. While US takes on a broadly isolationist position, China works with a globalist approach. Trump was clear at the 2019 United Nations General Assembly that the US has chosen patriotism and not globalism; this approach assumes an inward-looking position.

Meanwhile, Mike Pence, in his speech, explained China's "debt trap diplomacy," directly referencing the island nation of Sri Lanka, which is situated in an Indian Ocean geopolitical hotspot and is a participant in China's Maritime Silk Road. Pence used Sri Lanka as an example of a country "which took on massive debt to let Chinese state companies build a port with questionable commercial value." He continued: "Two years ago, that country could no longer afford its payments — so Beijing pressured Sri Lanka to deliver the new port directly into Chinese hands. It may soon become a forward military base for China's growing blue-water navy." Pence is not alone in this view, as Sri Lanka is widely referenced in this context in the media and academia.

China is offering hundreds of billions of dollars in infrastructure financing to governments where the terms of these loans are opaque and the benefits flow overwhelmingly to Beijing and not to the borrower. Despite being accepted as predatory loans, all of these nations continue to borrow from China as there is no good alternative. This is the case for Sri Lanka, even as its economy weakened to an historic ebb, with the highest-ever recorded depreciation of the Sri Lankan currency. With this, the US projection of taking Chinese loans by other Asian, African, and Latin American nations — cautioning they are predatory debt traps — will not work either. Many South Asian nations are going through similar Chinese debt issues due to heavy borrowing, Pakistan being another such example. It is often argued that nations in Asia should not follow Sri Lanka's fate of the debt equity swap model used to lease out the strategic port Hambantota in the south of Sri Lanka.

Sri Lanka has of late become the host of many Indian Ocean conferences to promote a free and open Indo-Pacific agenda, with particular attention given to the importance of a rules-based order in the region. It is worth considering the inner dynamics of such agendas, which are sponsored to instill strategic influence to the island nation's foreign and security policy. It is worth to keep in mind too that the internal characteristics of states do not determine their behavior, but rather the anarchic structure of the international system — and how nations interplay in the present geopolitical tapestry.

Scholars at an Indian Ocean Conference held in Colombo on October 12, 2018, spoke of the importance of peace. This included the Indian Deputy National Security Adviser, who said that "based on the principles that India has highlighted most recently in the Shangri-La dialogue, you will see in the years ahead that India will be more engaged as a maritime nation with the Indian ocean community in a manner that enhance collective prosperity, peace, and security, and in this endeavor we regard Sri Lanka as a specially valued and important friend and partner." In this light, the recent S-400 weapons system purchased by India from Russia violates the demilitarization agenda pledged by regional nations.

Finally, in an unexpected move in the South Asian political landscape, Sri Lanka's internal political coalition was reset by former President Maithripala Sirisena on October 26, 2018. The former president, Mahinda Rajapaksa, was appointed directly by Sirisena to take the seat of the prime minister. Both Sirisena and Rajapaksa are political figures groomed by the late former Prime Minister Sirimavo Bandaranaike's political party. If both leaders choose to continue her center-left political positions and visionary foreign policy, including an Indian Ocean Zone for peace, Sri Lanka may be a leader in charting turbulent waters to leading discussions toward stable security measures and diplomatic cordiality in the Indian Ocean region.

Brewing Tensions: Talking Tea and Terror from the South [13]

Trade friction [were] started by the US, if the US wants to talk we will keep the door open. If they want to fight, we will fight until the end... bully us? No way.

General Wei Fenghe,
Chinese Defence Minister at Shangri-La Dialogue 2019

Geography can provide safety and prosperity. It can also leave a country's citizens exposed and struggling. Sri Lanka is located at the busy center of East–West Sea Lines of Communications (SLOCs) in the Indian Ocean. It is a strategic maritime hub. Her people have become prisoners of location, increasingly defined by external spheres of influence from powerful nations.

Trade wars between the US and China have heightened, hurting global trade. Chinese companies are accused of cyber-espionage and labeled as a direct national security threat to the US. Singapore will need to take a different perspective on their 5G network if Chinese telecommunication products are seen with suspicion. Quoting his father Lee Kuan Yew, the Prime Minister of Singapore, Lee Hsein Loong, said at the Shangri La Dialogue: "When elephants fight, the grass suffers, but when they make love, the grass suffers also." The US–China rivalry has caused multiple effects, and many nations are already paying the price.

The US President Donald Trump's thirst for a trade war with China is wholly misguided. It will likely hurt American consumers just as much as it does the Chinese, explains Peter Frankopan, Professor of Global History at Oxford University in his book entitled *The Silk Roads: A New History of the World*. The US has extended the trade war from China to the Middle East through sanctions on Iran. A recent statement by President Trump declared, "US air force was cocked and loaded to attack three Iranian targets ... but called off the strike with 10 minutes to spare after being told that the airstrike might kill as many as 150 people in Iran." A direct military confrontation will take much more than 150 lives. An asymmetric confrontation is already in place between US and Iran. It is carried out by proxies who destabilize the region and its surroundings.

A destabilized Middle East region has experienced multiple waves of security and economic threats. It echoes and enters across seas into islands such as Sri Lanka. The Middle East origin of ISIS and effects of trade sanctions on Iran have hit Sri Lankan tea exports, a primary export commodity.

The Trump Administration has tightened the noose on Iran, with her oil-exporting ability directly affected. Ships are advised to avoid Iranian territorial waters. Located between Oman and Iran, the Strait of Hormuz is vital for transporting over one-sixth of global oil production and one-third of the world's liquified natural gas (LNG). A total of 40% of the world's seaborne oil and roughly 60% of crude oil pass through the 39-km-long Strait and goes to China, Japan, South Korea, and India. The tensions at the strategic choke point have escalated after multiple attacks on oil tankers. President Donald Trump has directly accused Iran for the attacks, while the US Fifth Fleet is securing the sea lanes. Strangling Iran is seen as the only strategy to stabilize the Middle East region. The escalation of tensions and resentment at the social and political levels will lead to a further unstable region. The geopolitical ripple effects will be experienced worldwide.

Global energy security requires a stable Middle East region. Nations cannot be expected to downgrade their profile in the region and coerced into stopping concessional oil imports from Iran. Heavy-handed US tactics have led to a sharp rise in the oil import bill. US attempts to undercut the strategic ties of many nations with Iran are going to pose serious challenges for their internal foreign policy. Short-term US unilateralism will bring instability to the entire Middle East region and the surrounding nations. It is inevitable that many nations, including Sri Lanka, will have to face the indirect economic consequences. The impact to Sri Lankan tea exports is already felt due to sanctions on dollar transactions with Iran by the US. Iran is one of the top five markets for Sri Lankan tea. In 2018,

Sri Lanka sold 23,914 metric tonnes (MT) of tea to Iran compared to previous year, which was much higher at 27,418 MT.

In the backdrop of US trade sanctions to Iran and trade war with China, the then-US Acting Secretary of Defense, Patrick Shanahan, released the first comprehensive strategic document on the Indo-Pacific at the Shangri-La Dialogue. The Indo-Pacific Strategy Report (IPSR) opens to identify the Indo-Pacific — the massive geographic construct — as the Department of Defense's "priority theater." Sri Lanka is referenced 13 times in the IPSR, from the importance of her strategic location, to building military partnerships, political instability, and the Chinese debt repayments.

The IPSR highlights the People's Republic of China, under the leadership of the Chinese Communist Party, as seeking to reorder the region to its advantage by leveraging military modernization, influence over operations, and predatory economics to coerce other nations. The report identifies China as a "revisionist power," accusing the country of undermining the "International System by exploiting its benefits while simultaneously eroding the values and principles of the rules-based order." On Chinese investments, the IPSR points out its one-sided and opaque deals are inconsistent with the principles of a free and open Indo-Pacific and are causing concern in the region. IPSR references three nations: Bangladesh, Maldives, and Sri Lanka in this regard.

The Indian Prime Minister, at the 2018 Shangri-La Dialogue, referred to Indo-Pacific 11 times in his keynote address. While his previous tenure witnessed a series of defense-related agreements, including the 2016 Logistics Exchange Memorandum of Agreement (LEMOA) allowing the Indian and US forces to use each other's facilities, the next agreement to follow was Communications Compatibility and Security Agreement (COMCASA), allowing the US to transfer communication equipment to India for the secure transmission of data and real-time information, which was signed in 2018. Finally, the Basic Exchange and Cooperation Agreement (BESA), the last of the three agreements, is likely to be signed soon.

In a similar manner, the US has put forward renewal of several defense-related agreements to Sri Lanka the ACSA (Acquisition and Cross-Servicing Agreement) and SOFA (Status of Forces Agreement), which is at the center of discussions at many levels in Sri Lanka due to the dual position taken by Sri Lanka's Prime Minister and President. The ACSA was concluded in 2017 without considering the inputs provided by the national security think tank under Ministry of Defence, and SOFA is now on the table. These agreements need to be discussed and amended according to the Sri Lankan regulations and laws. The narratives from certain critics are highly politicized and would stain the relationship between the two countries if such observations are believed to be accurate. SOFA has been signed in many countries after careful consultation with their respective legislatures. Sri Lanka should do the same and amend accordingly and proceed. The former President Sirisena has taken a strong position rejecting the SOFA in its present state, pointing it out as a threat: "I will not allow the SOFA that seeks to betray the nation. Some foreign forces want to make Sri Lanka one of their bases. I will not allow them to come into the country and challenge our sovereignty," he said, while the Prime Minister denied the SOFA would lead to a permanent US presence on the island.

In the midst of US military agreements and the cancellation of the recent visit by the US Secretary State Mike Pompeo to Sri Lanka, a Chinese built P-625 vessel with fire power was donated by China to enhance the patrolling capabilities of the Sri Lankan Navy and arrived at the Port of Colombo on July 8, 2019. A month earlier, General Wei Fenghe, the Chinese Defence Minister, at the Shangri-La Defence Dialogue in Singapore, made his remarks clear to the entire audience that China will not be bullied. After Sri Lanka signed the ACSA, a Chinese officer was also clear to articulate his position to this author that one should not be surprised if China also sends a similar agreement to the Sri Lankan Government in the future.

Each year the Chinese footprint expands in Sri Lanka and its Indian Ocean vicinity. The US, witnessing the Chinese influence as a strategic threat, will invest in Sri Lanka and enhance the regional maritime security and collaborations to secure bilateral military agreements. The great power struggle between US and China has affected Sri Lanka's security, economy, and foreign policy. While the US administration is vocally concerned about 150 Iranian lives, it is also essential to understand the global effects of unilateral sanctions to China and Iran, and their clear effects on other nations.

The Liberal Order, Critical Technologies, and Small States: The Case of Sri Lanka[14]

While globalization was seen as a path to bring prosperity in the Western hemisphere, the UK, who was championing the idea of the globalization, has officially exited from the European Union and disappointed its closest ally, the US, on its decision to work with the Chinese 5G network provider Huawei, which will undermine US national security interests. The UK will allow Huawei 5G equipment in their network, limiting access to sensitive areas. "Nothing in this review affects this country's ability to share highly-sensitive intelligence data over highly-secure networks both within the UK and our partners, including the Five Eyes," explained Foreign Secretary Dominic Raab to the British Parliament.[15] The problem of these technologies is whether the nations who acquire this equipment have the capabilities to separate and identify the core from the edge of the millimeter wave technology used in the 5G network. While the core is protected with encrypted algorithms for sensitive information sharing, will the Chinese break into the core area where sensitive national security information is communicated? The US identifies that Huawei, a company established with a PLA affiliation, which carries the largest number of patents for the 5G technologies, will have the advantage to carry out espionage for the Chinese government and have full control of the network.

"Can you imagine Reagan and Thatcher having a conversation in the 1980s saying: Let's have the KGB build our telecommunications systems because they're giving us a great discount?" commented Matthew Pottinger, US National Security Advisor at the Raisina Dialogue in New Delhi.[16] The discount offered by Huawei has won every stage of its mobile network expansion in developing nations like Sri Lanka. During the last decade, Huawei has become the leading network equipment provider due to its attractive prices, while sometimes offering cushion fees to developing nations to grab the tender. Sri Lanka is a clear victim in this regard. Recently interviewing a Huawei official, one was shocked to hear the confidence of the officer in winning the 5G network tender due to the Huawei's footprint in the island nation, who said: "Sri Lanka has missed much opportunity, look at the Maldives who is now on 5G network with us, we gave proposal to Sri Lanka before the Maldives." India is undecided on the idea of the Huawei 5G network similar to most East Asian countries. It is essential to understand and assess the long-term national security concern before acquiring such technology; specifically, a viewpoint from the signals intelligence officers of the nation is essential.

As these events unfold, three scholars, including a Harvard professor in the US was charged with being foreign agents of China.[17] Since 2011, this academic has been part of the Wuhan University of Technology as a scientist receiving large sums of funds from China as part of the "Thousand Talents Plan." It is a program that has flagged the national security concerns of the US for stealing and conducting espionage by the Chinese. The other researcher who was accused of being part of the PLA worked at the Boston University Robotics department, while a cancer researcher was found with 21 vials of biological samples in his bag at the Boston Logan International Airport. Michael Pillsbury, in his book, *The Hundred-year Marathon* identified that, "for decades the US government has freely handed over sensitive information, technology, military know-how, intelligence, and expert advice to the Chinese, so much has been provided for so long that Congress complained in 2005 that there is no full accounting, and what we haven't given the Chinese they have stolen." At present, the US will take full account and will want other nations to respect its decision in being cautious of the Chinese so-called unidentified espionage. The US decision and that taken by other nations in the future will have a drastic impact on the new world order. The liberal order is threatened by these incidents and decisions made by governments in the developed and the developing world.

Governments should adopt certain processes and values to certify the critical infrastructure projects of the Chinese. The Blue Dot Network (BDN) — a certification program[18] which sets international standards and is the right response to the Chinese BRI projects — supports recipient nations, ensuring that the aid they get is an effective and sustainable response to their needs. Ensuring more transparency will guarantee a better process when dealing with critical infrastructure. This was a point made by the Sri Lankan President Gotabaya Rajapaksa on leasing out national assets during his election campaign. The president clearly emphasized that: "Sri Lanka doesn't wish to be engaged in the major power game taking place in the Indian Ocean." Leo Tolstoy wrote that one would not need to be interested in war for war to be interested in them. In the same manner, the major powers are already in the Indian Ocean, and Sri Lanka is a part of the major power game despite its unwillingness. Four top officials — the Minister of Foreign Affairs of Russia, Sergey Lavrov; Wang Yi, the Chinese Foreign Minister; Alice Wells, the US Assistant Secretary of State; and Ajit Doval, National Security Advisor — visited Sri Lanka in January 2020, not to speak of collective interest but to speak of their own national interest. As Henry Kissinger[19] refers to one leader, Klement von Metternich's intent to maintain stable international relations required leaders to acknowledge the true interests of all actors, however, realpolitik of 19th century Western Europe saw nations focused on their own interest, ignoring others. While US–UK and the like-minded liberal intelligence platform will go through significant changes, will Sri Lanka and UK, two strategically positioned island nations facing the two oceans, maintain stability in their vicinity to preserve the liberal order or have they drifted toward China? For Sri Lanka, although, "There is a need to decouple security cooperation from economic relations in small power-great power engagement,'[20] do we have the capacity to decouple while unidentified tactics has already coupled security and economic relations?

Patterns to Politics: Entering 2019[21]

To understand is to perceive patterns.

Isaiah Berlin

In 2020, Sri Lanka remains at crossroads. As before, the island nation requires carefully calibrated statecraft from policymakers to choose the path toward prosperity. The political, constitutional, and parliamentary crises over the last months of 2018 were a waste of time. Possibly, the President never was fully in control of the crisis-riddled turbulent political alliance strategized by him.

More Machiavellian than his appointment, a lightning strike introduced a model which was a legally proven impossibility. What came out of it was that the President should be consulted in national affairs. In the months ahead, the polity will decide which road to take from casting their ballot from local election to parliament and finally the presidential by 2020.

External influences play a pivotal role in statecraft. Two roads ahead are shaped by external forces. Perhaps, these roads can be seen as diverting at a point to a perhaps simplistic East–West binary. It is also visible in internal polarizations of nations. Western or Chinese influence is the case in Sri Lanka, but this debate and international tug extends far beyond the island nation. International relations and its effects on nations should be understood through time, space, and scale. There are moments in history when natural order is disturbed by leaders breaking the natural patterns doing the impossible, mobilizing and bringing the people together to achieve the space and scale imagined by the leader. Such was the moment in 331 BC in the dusty plains of Gaugamela, a town near Iraqi Kurdistan, which changed history. According to Plutarch, the young General Alexander was sleeping so deeply that his commanders had to shake him awake before the battle; dressed in his favored outfit with a bright helmet made from most refined silver, he grasped a trusted sword in his right hand and led his troops to a crushing victory defeating Darius III's vastly superior Persian empire.[22] It was the moment which opened the West to the East, a moment of confluence of Western and Eastern cultures and values touching the Silk Road, explains Peter Frankopan. Alexander was the first to combine a sweeping approach with gigantic scale, reaching the distant Asian space embracing the richness of Asia, and realizing the value of the Silk Road. He respected cultures and even his defeated enemies while marching toward the Hindu Kush; time was the only barrier in between achieving the space and scale of his ambition, death at a young age of 32. The empire he built was scattered after his time. A powerful will of a great and strong man may bring grand visions, but time will capture and recalibrate the world order and, as explained by the German geopolitical thinker Karl Haushofer, "sinked back to its accustomed ways: its lasting earth bound traits will eventually win out."[23]

This is applicable to all empires, including the modern-day superpower US; the nation is now engaged in withdrawal of its troops from Syria, Iraq, and Afghanistan. The scale and space of the US power built in the past had to be reduced with time due to economic slowdown and massive spending required to sustain the geographical spaces captured for power projection. While the US is trying to sustain its existing spaces and retain the power projection it had a decade ago, another Asia power, China, is seen gaining momentum of building its own empire with its own characteristics. For the US, it was a massive effort to capture the central artery of Asia, i.e. the Silk Road across the two oceans of Atlantic and Pacific, setting up bases, listening posts, trade hubs, and allies. US does not wish to play the global policeman, according to Donald Trump quoting President Kennedy, who explained the US position during the Cold War.

The US is busy recalibrating its security strategy and rechristening its terminology from "Asia-Pacific" to "Indo-Pacific" to regain and sustain its geopolitical space. What we see is US withdrawal and pullout from the central artery of Asia, i.e. the Silk Road. The quadruple alliance with India, US, Japan, and Australia, another form of christening to emphasize the likeminded allies should look elsewhere. India, an emerging

South Asian power, should realign its position with China, a rising and expanding Asian power, rather than count on the US, which follows a withdrawal strategy. Sri Lanka, sitting at crossroads between the two powers, should have a balanced approach rather than veering off balance due to its internal political disarray.

Like all other empires, the proposed scale of the BRI is massive. Can China achieve this initiative or will it slow down and scale back? Dr. Françoise Nicolas from the French Institute of International Relations (IFRI), a leading French think tank, speaking at the Colombo Shangri-la Colloquium 2018 held by Sri Lanka's security think tank, opined that OBOR is a "systemic project, and a strategic plan rather than an 'initiative.'" There are three possible scenarios which could unfold. First, the project develops and succeeds in promoting a new form of globalization, which is gradually referred to as new globalization with Chinese characteristics (or "Alibaba world"). Second, the project develops but is faced with increasing resistance and problems and thus gradually slows down. The third scenario is the OBOR develops successfully, although not perfectly smoothly, and it is in conflict with other forms of globalization, leading to the emergence of two rival poles, one led by the US and the other by China, each having their own infrastructure networks.

Going back to geopolitical thinker, who clearly understood the importance of the island nation Japan's geography in the Pacific, Dr. Karl Haushofer explains in 1925 "Powerful new states emerged because their creators, with the sensitivity of the true statesman, understood the geopolitical demands of the hour. Without such insight, violence and arbitrariness would have charted the course of history. Nothing with lasting value could have been created. All structures of state which might have been created would sooner or later have crumbled into dust and oblivion before the eternal forces of soil and climate." If China fails to understand the geopolitical demands of the hour, it would fail to achieve its grand OBOR strategy.

Given these scenarios and the grand project spelled out by the rising China, a nation such as Sri Lanka will experience several effects of the global power transition. First, the internal polarization of political parties and society between the two camps (the third scenario explained earlier) could also lead to internal political instability. Second are economic projects from China and the West demanding for strategic assets and investment to secure the sphere of influence in the Island, as some nations prefer to play one against the other to demand better economic offers.

Regionally, the internal political instability in Sri Lanka has deeply affected the nation's economy. The recent parliament elections in Bangladesh, with Prime Minister Sheikh Hasina's clear majority victory, is a sign of political stability to sustain the country's economic growth of the last quarter (2018) at 7.6% GDP. In comparison, Sri Lanka, with its recent political instability, would find it challenging to sustain or improve from its last year's economic growth of below 4%.

Balancing the global and the local, the need of the year is to continue building and strengthening internal policies in small nations such as Sri Lanka.

Gotabaya Rajapaksa's Leadership in Domestic Politics amid Geopolitical Conundrum and Regional Instability[24]

A political society does not live to conduct foreign policy; it would be more correct to say that it conducts foreign policy in order to live.

George F. Kennan

Sri Lanka held its Parliamentary elections on August 5, 2020. The efficient leadership of President Gotabaya Rajapaksa was demonstrated in managing the recent COVID-19 health crisis. Proven leadership will be a significant factor to ensure a landslide victory in the elections for the Rajapaksa front. There are two other factors which will determine a Rajapaksa victory. First is the fracturing of the main opposition party, the United National Party (UNP). For the first time in its history, UNP is split into two camps, which will divide and erode their voter base. Second, the loss of several years of economic growth and political instability due to Sirisena–Wickremesinghe policies resulted in the loss of hundreds of lives and threatened national security. Perhaps predicting the upcoming defeat at the elections, one-time political spin doctor and the former Foreign Minister of the Sirisena–Wickremesinghe Government, Mangala Samaraweera, withdrew from the parliamentary race. Hopefully after the 2020 parliamentary elections, the long-eluding political stability will be restored in the island nation.

There are currently two major ongoing inquiries, one on corruption and the other on negligence. The Central Bank bond scam and the Easter Sunday terror attack inquiry findings will impact the domestic political

landscape. Both inquiries are in full swing, revealing shocking information such as a previous Central Bank Governor accused of the bond scam
who is now residing in Singapore having changed his name. On the Easter
Sunday inquiry, more previously unheard and unattended information
were revealed and exposed to the public on the extremist activities by the
perpetrators. Further, discussing the Easter Sunday attack at a recent interview to BBC, former President Sirisena explained: "Why should I accept
responsibility for the Easter attacks? Responsibility should be taken by
those responsible."[25] As the commander in chief with direct responsibility
on national security, there should have been acknowledgement of the failure of authorities. In comparison, after the Norway terror attack by Anders
Behring Breivik on July 22, 2011, Prime Minister Jens Stoltenberg apolo-
gized to the nation[26] for failings in his duties, even though the attack
occurred without any prior warnings. The Sri Lankan situation was a
systemic failure at different levels, and the system was headed by no other
than the Sirisena–Wickremesinghe duo.

On the economic front, Sri Lanka and several other developing
nations will face the brunt of COVID-19 and the ensuing global economic
recession. Japan's JICA suspended funding for a new project until the
financial policies and debt position of Sri Lanka were clarified, raising
concerns on the current debt situation of the country.[27] However, China
recently extended its assistance, standing strongly by the island nation.
As a symbolic gesture, the acting Chinese Ambassador in Sri Lanka, Hu
Wei, handed over an official letter from President Xi to the Sri Lankan
President Gotabaya Rajapaksa on his 71st birthday, praising his leadership
in managing COVID-19.[28] Medical assistance during the pandemic has
transformed into financial assistance as China takes the helm in assisting
many nations.

Containment strategies: Sri Lanka's role in regional stability

The COVID-19 pandemic has made the world a more dangerous place,
with pressure surmounting within nations from internal and external
sources in the political, economic, and security spheres. Assessing China's
aggression, the former Indian National Security Advisor, Shivshankar
Menon explains: "it seems to me that it's part of a general pattern and a
general shift in Chinese behaviour in the way they deal with the world.
What I supposed the Chinese themselves have called wolf warrior
diplomacy."[29] This "shift" in China's behavior could be attributed to the

pressure exerted on China from the recent containment strategies at the geopolitical high table. Nations use other nations for their strategic advantage. Long before the Cold War, using Russia's geographical position, the US formed an alliance with Russia to act as a wedge and not a bridge between Nazi Germany and Imperial Japan. In the same way, has the US has taken advantage of India's geography to drive a wedge between China and her strategic allies surrounding India? With the brewing Indo-China conflict, how would Sri Lanka manage its defense and foreign relations with both nations?

China is directly facing geopolitical challenges arising from multiple issues at multiple geographies at the same time in the surrounding Indian geosphere at Galwan and Pangong Tso, Ladakh, Senkaku islands, South China Sea, and Taiwan to the Hong Kong streets. According to JNU Prof Srikanth Kondapalli, "all of these Chinese assertive and aggressive responses have been put down to a new 'wolf warrior' diplomacy and is a bid to cover-up the Covid-19 disaster."[30] While China's presence in the multiple geographies is visible, it does not reflect that its actions are intended to cover up the pandemic. More than a cover-up, it is symbolic and strategic, depicting Beijing's military might at multiple locations simultaneously. A clash triggered at the Galwan Valley between Indian and Chinese troops resulting in casualties on both sides was explained by the Chinese Foreign Ministry spokesperson Zhao Lijian as: "on June 15th Indian troops seriously violated our consensus and twice crossed the borderline for illegal activities and provoked and attacked Chinese personnel." The direct accusation by China has intensified and reset the China–India confidence-building mechanism (CBM) exercises during the last three decades, while both sides accuse each other of violating the unmarked border, the 3,440-km-long Line of Actual Control (LAC). Threats at the harsh geographical terrain are linked to the larger geopolitical context. There has been a threat looming from the militarization of strategic alliances in which India has played an active role.

While the pandemic environment has the potential to severely erode military budgets and minimize the military projection of many nations, there seems to be silent military alignments and infrastructure expansions taking place in South Asia. The US President's decision to reformat G7 grouping of the advanced economies to G11 inviting India, Australia, South Korea, and Russia[31] is a significant step impacting the Indo-Pacific geopolitical space. Two scholars from India, Mansheet Singh and Megha Gupta, suggest "Indo-Pacific requires an urgent need for a coordinated strategy to mute China's swaying strategies in the region. Leadership for this should come through mooting a proposed Indo- Pacific Treaty Organization (IPTO)."[32] IPTO must be patterned on the lines of NATO which have been a successful and effective association even after the disintegration of the USSR. Only through an alliance like this can we hope to avert further security turbulences inflicted by China in the Indo Pacific region."[33]

The Mutual Military Logistics Support Agreement, which facilitated reciprocal access to military bases, was signed on June 4, 2020, by Prime Minister Narendra Modi and his Australian counterpart, Scott Morrison.[34] This logistics support agreement would further strengthen the quadrilateral partnership that includes Japan and the US. The agreement adds to India's already existing agreements with the US, Japan, Singapore, Vietnam, and Indonesia. These agreements would assist in securing India's role as a net security provider of the region and to contain Chinese influence in India's marine sphere. Australian scholar David Brewster highlights: "Australia will need a sober understanding of India's likely future abilities to act as a regional security provider across our shared oceanic space." While the agreements would provide strength, it also drags India closer to the US orbit and western sphere, departing from its South–South agenda, away from Iran in India's western shores. The Sri Lankan government did not proceed with the similar US military logistics agreement SOFA (Status of Forces Agreement) and financial assistance MCC (Millennium Challenge Compact), seeing it as detrimental to its national security. This position could push Sri Lanka closer to the Chinese orbit, despite its neighbor's alliances with the US.

Thus, the entire focus is on India's north, i.e. the LAC. There is less focus on India's south, the Indian Ocean and its littorals. Abhijith Singh, in his analysis, states: "China at the Line of Actual Control is not the only thing India needs to worry about … China is growing its military presence in the Indian Ocean too. Satellite pictures in May this year suggest China's military base at Djibouti is being modernised. The facility, set up in 2017 as a logistics support unit, is being upgraded into a full-fledged naval base with a 1,120-feet pier that can berth Chinese warships, including the Liaoning aircraft carrier. This follows China's expansion of an artificial island[35] in the Maldives, a development with seeming strategic overtones, leading some to claim that China is encroaching on India's sphere of influence."[36] Seeing the growing security threat from China in India's vicinity, there will be strong reaction to counter and strengthen

India's role as the net security provider of the region. At the beginning of the year, India started to reorganize its military command structure, introducing the first Chief of Defence Staff (CDS) since 1947, General Bipin Rawat. Sri Lanka introduced its CDS many years back, providing a single point of view to the government on the three-armed services bringing under a unified command. Perhaps the reason India took so long was to keep military at limited engagement with bureaucracy at the center. The shift and internal reorganization would assist its process to take swift coordinated action.

The tense situation in the Sino-India relationship will have a significant impact on regional nations that maintain a cordial relationship with both countries. The recent conflict has forced the Indian foreign policy circle to revisit their view on China, and long-term economic barriers on Chinese products are already being discussed. India would need a mediatory partner to ease the tension in the region, while conflict would minimize the strategic space for nations like Sri Lanka to gain and maximize its gains while not antagonizing either. There is no harm in Sri Lanka playing a mediatory role, such as that by Prime Minister Sirimavo Bandaranaike in 1962 December, where she was trusted by both nations to minimize the tension and draw up the "Colombo Proposals" which India accepted, and China accepted in principle. Although the context is different to 1962, Sri Lanka, has its unique geography in the Indian Ocean, being the closest neighbor to India, and a strong strategic partner to China. In revisiting and resuscitating its foreign policy legacy, President Gotabaya Rajapaksa perhaps could play an active role in regional stability in the geostrategic and the maritime spheres of the region.

Chapter 4

Sustaining Democracy and Facing a Pandemic

Between being loved and being feared, I have always believed Machiavelli was right. If nobody is afraid of me, I'm meaningless.

Lee Kuan Yew

Leviathan in an Island Democracy[1]

*Mankind has a perpetual and restless desire for power, a desire that
ceases only in death.*

Thomas Hobbes

India is concerned by the growing Chinese influence in the North and East
of Sri Lanka. Part of this concern stems from a housing project awarded
by the Sri Lankan Ministry of Resettlement, Rehabilitation, Northern
Development and Hindu Religious Affairs to a Chinese construction company to build 40,000 houses in the northeast of the island. This infrastructure project — reflecting the Sri Lankan state's development agenda, but
to be carried out in significant part by China — will be a security concern
for India.

Fueling this concern was a speech delivered by the Chinese
Ambassador in Colombo in May 2018. At a symposium titled "From
Millennium to the New Era: Jointly Build the Belt and Road and Embrace
the Sri Lankan Dream," he had stated China's aims to boost Sri Lanka's
infrastructure as part of the former's long-term global initiatives.

According to Vinay Kaura's recent commentary, as part of an attempt
to offset China's presence in the island, the Indian government has used
the Indian C-17 Globemaster aircraft to bring Sri Lankan military personnel and their families to the Indian Buddhist site Bodh Gaya in Bihar.
A local political commentator noted that this act of military–cultural
diplomacy is aimed at drawing Sri Lanka back toward India's traditional
sphere of influence. Given this, the importance of Sri Lanka's delicate
balancing of these spheres of influence will be part of its idealist foreign
policy. However, a realist lens suggests balancing will be a challenging
task and sometimes unachievable.

China's efforts to project power through infrastructure development
and mega projects also extend underwater. For 60 years, it has developed
strategic nuclear submarines, nuclear attack submarines, and conventional
submarines organized into submarine bases and flotillas. It has also constructed PEACE (Pakistan East Africa Cable Express), a submarine cable
that reaches Djibouti, Gwadar in Pakistan, many African cities, and ends
in France. Laid by a Chinese company, the cable carries up to 60 terabytes
per second, creating a new information super-highway. The first stage to
this ambitious plan was to enhance connectivity between the Western

Indian Ocean and Europe. If a second stage comes to pass, it will likely connect the Eastern Indian Ocean — encompassing Sri Lanka, Bangladesh, and Myanmar — with East Asia. The ring of the Chinese development reverberates through continents and oceans, from East Asia to Europe.

According to international security analyst Ewen Levick, "Beijing is seeking new ways of intimidating or spying on other states." This could occur through targeting vulnerable telecommunications cables crisscrossing the ocean bed that carry 98% of global internet and phone data and 95% of American strategic communications.

While China is expanding its global footprint by developing infrastructure, across the world, internal political struggles are rife. The liberal values and norms upheld by US hegemony which undergird the international order are being questioned. The withdrawal of the US from the United Nations Human Rights Council (UNHRC) revealed a sinister ethos behind the global decisions taken by the Trump Administration. In response to tariffs imposed by the US on EU goods, EU import duties on US products have also opened another dialogue between China and the EU, which have agreed to form a group to update global trade rules. Trump's weak policies recall Noam Chomsky's 2006 characterization of the US as a "failed state" due to deficit of democracy. Chomsky refers to President Bush, who redefined what a failed state looks like, "the failed state include all aggressive, arbitrary or totalitarian states those with democracy deficit, lacking the institutions that work to fulfill the principles of democracy which Chomsky argues that the description fits US itself due to deficit of democracy."

In Sri Lanka also, deficit of democracy got the previous government under Mahinda Rajapaksa out of office two years before the tenure. The change to the previous regime was based on not adhering to well-defined limits of power and not respecting the limits of power. During the 2015 Presidential Election, the polity was in favor of policies geared toward recalibrating the Executive, Legislative, and Parliamentary powers and clearly defining its boundaries to reset the centralized authority of individual power toward the institutions. The same polity has decided to revisit what was lost and resurrect the centralized authority, shaming the executive who pruned his own power as a failure of delivery. Political discourse is shifting toward the next presidential election. Local voters may then create an enforcer, in the manner of Thomas Hobbes'

17th century *Leviathan,* in the hope that life will be better with more centralized power than is presently the case.

The willingness of people to move to a stronger centralized authority could turn into a nightmare within a token democracy. In an expression of politics through religion, a Buddhist monk in a private religious ceremony called upon former Defence Secretary Gotabaya Rajapaksa to resurrect the authoritarian role he once carved out for himself and delivered results. This statement drew national attention and criticism from many camps. Many speak of the possibility of a presidential bid by Gotabaya Rajapaksa's for 2020, but a decision is yet to be made formally by Rajapaksa himself.

Apart from geopolitical influence, Sri Lankan polity in the next presidential race is certain to grapple with the twin thoughts of creating a centralized leader or a leader who believes in separation of power between the executive and legislature. As Locke's *The Second Treatise of Government* states, it is also worth to remember that, due to human fragility, abuse of power is certain if powers are vested in one individual. The island nation has experienced this in the past. In the pursuit of authoritarianism through the ballot, is a section of Sri Lankan voters actively consenting to the rise of a Leviathan?

Sustaining Democracy[2]

It is better to be feared than loved, if you cannot be both.

Niccolo Machiavelli, The Prince (1532)

St. Augustine's *City of God* was perhaps the book Sirisena was following since the beginning of his Presidency in 2015. A kind and calm leader from humble beginnings was seen trying to be righteous yet appeared cornered, isolated, and perhaps pushed to the wall by his coalition partners. That is why, it seems, he decided to borrow political ideas from another book, which was banned since as soon as it came into print. This book is another Italian masterpiece, Machiavelli's *The Prince*. This book had once helped Queen Elizabeth to create a golden age while assassinating the people who went against her; a terror far worse than her father Henry VIII's time.

Machiavelli advised in *The Prince* to be a lion and a fox at the same time; former to frighten wolves, the latter to detect snares. Elizabeth was a combination of both, turning adversaries against each other while keeping steady on the tightrope she walked with patriotism. In the same manner, President Sirisena appointed Rajapaksa — a move that the entire nation or the coalition partners never contemplated — and dismantled and stripped the power of the former Prime Minister Wickremesinghe in the same way he treated Sirisena, according to a Presidential adviser, and completely ignored the advice of the President when making decisions in the bipartisan government. Matching to the last trick, in 1571, the most elaborate plot was to assassinate Elizabeth and install Mary Stuart to the throne. A Florentine banker Roberto Ridolfi was planning this plot connecting Pius V, King Philip, and Duke of Alba which Elizabeth's spymasters tracked and exposed at the right time.

In the same way, the assassination plot of Sirisena was revealed with recorded conversations and investigations taking place at the same time where another nation appeared involved, indirectly. The investigation will tell if there was such real plot to assassinate the President. Just like in the ancient time, Sirisena will use the exacts words of Machiavelli to crush all his adversaries with the help of the man who he contested against in 2015 and perhaps use the same nation that supported his election victory, calling and requesting assistance on the assassination plot. So in an article titled "Laviathan" (Sea Monster), I had appealed to the leader to follow the work of Hobbes,[a] who wrote of a central figure with authority rather than a weak figure at the center who was seen by many as a puppet on strings.

Sirisena, like Elizabeth, was a strange leader who perhaps never took advice. The Ambassador to Philip of Spain in England, Count de Feria, wrote "Elizabeth is a very strange sort of a women ... she is determined to be governed by no one." She was calm in public even at times of much rebellion and chaos, in the same way Sirisena was seen as calm and watching the success of his pet project Moragahakanda Dam project,[b] opening the sluice gate while one of the gatekeepers of democracy,

---

[a] Thomas Hobbes was an English philosopher and one of the founding fathers of modern political philosophy and is renowned for his book 1651 book *Leviathan*, where he formulates the social contract theory.
[b] The Moragahakanda Dam project was the last of the great Mahaveli projects, which is a gravity dam built to contain the Moragahakanda reservoir for agricultural use in Sri Lanka.

the Parliament[c], was in chaos and trending on social media and television screens. The entire nation saw the fist-fights between the honorable representatives of the highest democratic institution. Perhaps a question could be raised if political parties who are an essential gatekeeper of democracy had given election nominations to the right kind of candidates to become people's representatives?

While many leaders from history practiced Machiavellian philosophy, another document keeps leaders from engaging in authoritarian acts. National constitutions represent that document with long history from the ancient times of Hammurabi's code, which codified 282 laws to govern Babylon, to the modern-day English Protectorate introduced after the English Civil War by Oliver Cromwell. But all constitutions also have had their flaws. The US constitution does little to prevent the President from engaging in undemocratic behavior such as filling the FBI or other independent government agencies with obedient subjects or acting by decree, issuing executive orders. President Trump is seen today exercising all these undemocratic practices and further interfering with the judiciary by calling the US Supreme Court Chief Justice "an Obama judge," even though the judge denied this allegation.

So how does democracy sustain its credibility? What keeps democracy going is an adherence to the unwritten rules, and it thrives on two things, which are: mutual toleration and institution forbearance, according to Steven Levitsky and Daniel Ziblatt's book *How Democracies Die*.

Mutual tolerance means participants of a democratic system, i.e. political rivals to power are not branding each other enemies, traitors, or criminals. In recent past, this axiom has been repeatedly undermined in the Sri Lankan Parliament. For example, in Chile, during the 1960s, mutual toleration began to erode between the two political camps. In August 1973, when the chamber of deputies declared the then Chilean government unconstitutional, it triggered a military coup led by right-wingers, and for the next 17 years, Augusto Pinochet was in power. There is a grave danger when mutual toleration is lost and the political opponents are seen as traitors or part of a plot to assassinate the Executive. In a similar manner, autocracy could creep into the system with gradual erosion of democracy. In Peru, when Alberto Fujimori failed to deliver

---

[c]President Sirisena ousted Prime Minister Ranil Wickremesinghe in an undemocratic manner and installed the Opposition Leader Mahinda Rajapaksa as his replacement, which was considered *ultra vires* by the Supreme Court of Sri Lanka.

economic progress through democratic means, he took the law in his hand, ignoring the courts and the constitution. On August 5, 1992, he dissolved the Congress and suspended the constitution. Fujimori's transformation from a democratic leader to a dictator was by piecemeal approach.

Institutional forbearance means refraining from actions that would undermine the spirit of democracy — even if the act is technically legal or not prohibited by the constitution. For example, George Washington exercised this by limiting his term, serving only twice as President even when there were no set term limits in the US Constitution. In Sri Lanka, institutional forbearance was lost when the past regime scrapped the Presidential term limit and took control of all independent commissions — an act which made the former President unpopular. However, President Sirisena's move to remove Prime Minister was done on many grounds, according to the President, but there was one point which made his case acceptable. This was breach of national security by the former Prime Minister during his conduct at office, seen by some as being an agent of another nation and not working for Sri Lanka's national interest. Chandrika Bandaranaike Kumaratunga[d] fired the same Prime Minister on the grounds of national security since he signed an agreement with another nation without her consent in 2004.

Hope perhaps likes in going back to the people to unlock the present gridlock between the executive and the legislature. In the long run, political culture of mutual toleration and institutional forbearance need to be restored to preserve South Asia's oldest democracy. Else, Sri Lanka could drift toward a worse form of government, a dictatorship with its main gatekeeper of democracy, the Parliament, crippled and judiciary undermined.

President Sirisena should shelve Machiavelli and revisit the work *City of God* by St. Augustine. It is important to understand that dismantling of democracy can be a gradual imperceptive process that may elude our day-to-day priorities. But once it began, this drift can take a long time to restore and redo what is lost, which may take a real long time to rebuild.

---

[d]Chandrika Bandaranaike Kumaratunga is a Sri Lankan politician who was the fifth President of the Democratic Socialist Republic of Sri Lanka, serving from November 1994 to November 2005.

Disruptions and Democracy: The Sri Lankan Political Crisis through Geopolitical Lens[3]

The pattern of history cannot be changed. We are the progeny of progression across time and space that shift from small scales to big ones and back again.

John Lewis Gaddis, On Grand Strategy[4]

The masterpiece, *The Rise and Fall of the Great Powers* by Paul Kennedy, clearly identifies the shift from the US imperial overstretch and its position to remain as the bastion of global democracy, and its decline. Kennedy explains, "it has been a common dilemma facing previous number one countries that even as their relative economic strength is ebbing, the growing foreign challenges to their position have compelled them to allocate more and more of their resources into military sector, which in turn squeezes out productive investment and, heavier taxes, deepening domestic splits over spending priorities and a weakening capacity to bear the burdens of defense."

In 415 BC Athens, a maritime power, Pericles strengthened democracy and built a wall to defend the city state. He underestimated its relative decline of strength. It was an overstretched Athenian power that attacked Sicily and took a hard lesson in defeat. It was the beginning of the decline, recorded Thucydides. The expedition was launched on the pretext of the danger of being ruled, if they ceased to rule others.

In late 2018, the power of the US is not in calculation with its strength. Furthermore, its own democratic structure is in question. President Trump has decided to go against the very foundation and norms of the nation. His rhetoric of nationalism, protectionism, and disruptive foreign policy threatens world order as we know it. US hypocrisy is clear in most places they intervened to install democratic values in the recent past, including the Middle East. Western intervention was clearly seen after end of the Sri Lankan Civil War in 2009. This was seen as interfering with the sovereignty of the nation during Rajapaksa's regime. Later, the West was disturbed by President Sirisena's move to dissolve the Parliament and call for elections. On the other hand, the Executive had completely lost confidence to work with the former Prime Minister Ranil Wickremesinghe — who has in turn requested international assistance to restore democracy. One should also not forget that in January 2015, Wickremesinghe was sworn in as Prime Minister in a politically amoral way, despite not holding the majority in the Parliament.

Meanwhile, China gives a clear signal that they will not intervene in Sri Lankan domestic political issues. The Chinese Ambassador to Sri Lanka, H.E. Cheng Xueyuan,[e] visited and congratulated Prime Minister Mahinda Rajapaksa when he was appointed by Sirisena in 2018. According to local media, out of the 43 foreign missions based out of the island nation, diplomats from the US and Europe stayed away from a meeting with the Sri Lankan Foreign Minister. This move was said to be in protest of President Sirisena's decision to dissolve the Parliament. The US Ambassador to Sri Lanka, H.E. Ambassador Teplitz attended the Parliament to observe the proceedings the day after the Supreme Court ruling and tweeted that she was glad the institution was functioning according to the constitution.

Looking at the Sri Lankan situation, a senior US Administration official said, "I would say speaking about countries generally, not just the country we're talking about, generally speaking one of the key tenants of President (Donald) Trump's Free and Open Indo-Pacific (FOIP) concept and our Indo-Pacific Strategy is to protect the sovereignty of countries all across the region." The FOIP concept, introduced by the Japanese Prime Minister Abe Shinzo and now supported by Trump, will be used to contain the Chinese influence in the Indo-Pacific. FOIP targets nations such as Sri Lanka and Maldives that have pledged support to China's grand strategy of One Belt One Road, according to some scholars.

Managing Systemic Risks during a Pandemic[5]

The oldest form of systemic risk, which is that arising from viruses and pandemics...

Ian Goldin and Mike Mariathasan,
The Butterfly Defect (Princeton, 2014)

---

[e]His Excellency Mr. Cheng Xueyuan is the Ambassador of the People's Republic of China to Sri Lanka since 2018.

Geopolitics and interdependence

Pandemics have no respect for borders or individual social status. Pandemics killed world leaders, including Pharaoh Ramses V of Egypt, Emperor Marcus Aurelius of Rome, Ferdinand IV of Spain, Emperor Fu-Lin of China, Queen Mary II of England, King William II of Orange, Tsar Peter II of Russia, and King Louis XV of France. In the present context, COVID-19 has infected close to a million, including the British Prime Minister. Pandemics can infect anyone, anywhere.

The 21st century has faced four pandemics. The first was in February 2003, as SARS was reported in Guangdong province in China. SARS spread in four months to 26 countries with 774 deaths and 8,000 cases. The second was the H5N1 Bird Flu triggered in 1997 during a poultry outbreak in Hong Kong. The third near-pandemic was the H1N1 Swine Flu, which emerged in April 2009 in Mexico City and New York, spreading to 30 countries in weeks. Unlike the previous two, the Swine Flu pathogen originated in the West rather than in East Asia. This was a clear early warning to how dangerous super-cities and airport hubs can be in terms of health risks — it was a warning ignored. The virulence and severity of H1N1 influenza killed 570,000.[6] The fourth is the Coronavirus that has killed more than 40,000 people around the world as of April 2, 2020, according to the World Health Organization (WHO).

Larry Klayman, a former federal prosecutor under the administration of President Ronald Reagan, said in an interview that he was willing to work with Sri Lankans and others to build international pressure on China. He accused that the novel coronavirus was designed to be a "biological weapon of war ... creation and release, accidental or otherwise, of a variation of coronavirus known as COVID-19 by the People's Republic of China and its agencies and officials as a biological weapon in violation of China's agreements under international treaties, and recklessly or otherwise allowing its release from the Wuhan Institute of Virology into the city of Wuhan."[7] These are baseless allegations. It will create geopolitical tensions and disunity at a time of human distress.

One may wonder who was behind or which nation released the past outbreaks in our human history. It is a time for transnational cooperation and coordination, since national governments alone will not be able to manage the magnitude of this global challenge. While the exchange of physical goods and services will be reduced due to the pandemic, you cannot halt globalization and the globalized interdependent world that have been created. According to Robert Keohane and Joseph Nye, "complex interdependencies"[8] is what the world has experienced during the past few decades. If managed insufficiently, it will lead us to overly complex interdependencies and will trigger systemic risks such as the present pandemic.

Interdependence in such times is evident even from the past. One of the first epidemics in recorded history, which ravaged Athens in 430 BC, did not start in Athens, but came from Ethiopia via Egypt. Spanish Flu did not start in Spain; Spain was open to reporting the cases. Globalization is not a new phenomenon. It has transported pathogens to many nations. The Spanish Flu in 1918 came in three increasingly deadly waves with nine-month intervals between them, killing 50 to 100 million people world-wide. This deadly outbreak killed 17 million in India alone.

Butterfly effect to butterfly defect

American mathematician Edward Lorenz's[9] work in Chaos theory discovered the "Butterfly Effect," explaining how a hurricane formation is influenced by minor perturbations such as flapping of the wings of a distant butterfly several weeks earlier. A small change in one place can lead to major differences in a remote area. In the same manner, the negative unintended ripple effects of coronavirus that started in Wuhan, China, ended up affecting many nations, including Iran, Italy, Spain, and the US, which has the highest number of infected cases at the time of writing.

I was introduced to the concept of the "Butterfly Defect" by Prof. Ian Goldin at the University of Oxford.[10] It is a remarkable work of scholarship co-authored with Mike Mariathasan, published by Princeton University, which predicted in 2014 that the next financial crisis will arise from a pandemic. His book examines how globalization creates systemic risks from micro-distresses from the closely-knit systems and connections we have built and the importance of significant investment in mitigating the risk factors arising from such a system.

Professor Goldin explains, "Systemic risks cannot be removed because it is endemic to globalization. It is a process to be managed, not a problem to be solved." Out of the risks, he identified pandemics and the health risk from globalization. What triggered in Wuhan rapidly spread to many countries due to globalization. Despite the immense health benefits reaped through globalization, the global healthcare officials did not anticipate the systemic risk from a pandemic such as coronavirus. According to Goldin and Mariathasan, "Globalization, population growth, and urbanization have facilitated the transmission of infectious diseases." The complexity of global travel and global integration means there is but a few degrees of separation from patient zero to formerly isolated communities, as is clear from the COVID-19 pandemic. There are three lessons to be learned for systemic thinking regarding the health risks arising from globalization, according to Prof. Goldin. First, to identify risks, mechanisms for early detection are essential. Second, once a pandemic is detected, mechanisms for early response must be enacted. Third, systemic risks require systemic responses. COVID-19 was picked up too late, the communication was late, and systemic responses to fix were late. This is a wake-up call to the WHO and global leaders.

Multilateralism during the pandemic

While national borders are shut, each nation has adopted their way of containing the coronavirus. After Italy's death rate, virtually all of Europe went on curfew and lockdown. According to Judy Dempsey, Senior Fellow at Carnegie Europe, "Whenever there is a crisis, European Union leaders have the habit of saying that the bloc will emerge stronger. They have been repeatedly disproved of this slogan, which has lost all meaning."[11]

The importance of multilateralism is magnified from Europe to South Asia, where leaders who have dismantled multilateral organizations such as the South Asian Association of Regional Cooperation (SAARC), are now finding ways of discussing activating health funds and strengthening regional cooperation. The ultra-nationalist narrative is weakened by the pandemic. Showing directions toward cooperation and promoting multilateral efforts are the only ways forward. Ambassador Rajiv Bhatia, who is a Distinguished Fellow from Gateway House, identified four main points which are relevant and timely. First, COVID-19 is a global challenge and needs to be addressed on a national and international level. Second, the Government of India has been studying the approach of affected countries and assimilating elements that apply to India in its strategy of containment. Third, India is adopting a sober view *vis-à-vis* China, maintaining a constructive spirit, sending assistance where required — rather than falling prey to disputes — as the pandemic has affected all of mankind. Finally, Prime Minister Modi is proactively initiating multilateral cooperation through SAARC and G20.[12] Appreciating the multilateral directive taken by "Prime Minister Modi's prompt convening of a video summit of SAARC countries for a more coordinated containment response to the pandemic was, therefore, a bold diplomatic step: other countries are now replicating this in combating the geopolitical, economic and health dimensions of the disease."

At the video conference, as a blanket security measure, PM Modi pledged US$10 million while Sri Lankan President Gotabaya Rajapaksa contributed US$5 million, the second-highest contribution from South Asia even at a time when the Sri Lankan economy is the lowest-performing in the region. Sri Lanka's exports and tourism sector have been affected by multiple risk factors starting from the Easter Sunday terror attack in April 2019.

With an economy that experienced a double whammy, from the Easter attack and the pandemic — Sri Lanka will need to navigate a global recession this year. Hopefully, we will not see another wave of the pandemic in the coming months. While developed nations such as Singapore will prepare for the next several waves, the developing countries with their squeezed health budgets will find their limitations in facing the next several waves of the pandemic.

Local to global leadership to manage systemic risks

Sri Lankan authorities started taking strict measures to contain and manage the virus from March 19, 2020, after soft-pedaling until election nominations were submitted for the upcoming Parliamentary elections. As explained by S. Ratnajeevan H. Hoole, a member of the election commission, "Mr. Deshapriya was insisting that April 25 is possible. It seemed that he was afraid to disagree with the President. Here is the strategy that was finally agreed upon. It was decided to accept nominations as announced, and then gazette the names of candidates and polling booths as required in Section 24(1) of the Parliamentary Elections Act of 1981 ... The country is functioning with Votes on Account without a Parliament."[13]

If we had the Parliament functioning, we would have many stakeholders, including the opposition discussing the mitigating strategy, and perhaps would be able to recalibrate a better strategy than the curfew in place.

How long does the Government wish to continue the curfew strategy? What are the short- and long-term impacts to the economy from a lock-down or curfew strategy? What is the importance of a mitigating strategy rather than a suppression (curfew) strategy? How do we protect the elder community and the most vulnerable? How can we sustain as a nation if there are multiple waves of the pandemic in the future? How do we have better sustainable debt management practices during and post pandemic? These are some critical questions that could have been discussed in the Parliament by enabling and echoing multiple expert stakeholder advice from our society.

The number of infected cases was at 143 by March 31, 2020, and curfew was declared with the international airport shut. The Sri Lankan citizenry is now aware of the significant threat, even as some senseless politicians started distributing face masks in public for popularity and certain individuals began violating curfew laws. What people should understand is the effort taken by the authorities to bring the numbers down. People typically think of a linear sequence of growth, but corona-virus has displayed a slow exponential growth, which needs to be under-stood by the public. Human beings are social creatures who like to group in packs and crowds, naturally rejecting social distancing, especially during the month of April, where they get together for religious holidays, including Easter, followed by Sinhalese and Tamil New Year obser-vances and Ramadan. It is the first time in this century that every faith will be practiced in isolation and quarantine. Practicing social distancing and the quick adapting of the polity toward best practices will be a key factor for the success to bring down the curve of the outbreak in the island nation.

Sri Lanka is far behind testing when compared to nations like Australia, as noted by a Sri Lankan medical expert, Dr. Ravi P. Rannan-Eliya. Sri Lanka has done nearly 2,280 tests as of 30 March, and of these tests, 115 persons were positive, which is 5.5% of tested cases found posi-tive. "This is a relatively high rate compared to other countries such as Australia which has a population similar to ours and has done 160,000 tests and found 3,966 positive cases — a positive case rate of 2.47%."[14] Sri Lanka and many South Asian nations need to get the testing capacity increased to efficiently manage the spread of the outbreak; curfew and lockdown alone will not help.

While we suppress and manage the local threat, we must prepare for the next wave or several waves of the pandemic. Due to complex interdependencies of the global arena triggering systemic risks to our island nation, it is time we prepare for such risks. The transition of the political environment from pre-pandemic to post-pandemic will require the national leaders who were inward-looking with their ultra-nationalist and populist agenda to move toward a global and multilateral agenda and understand the complex systemic risks we face. Not only the top leadership, but the next lot of Parliamentarians who will be elected in a few months will need to understand that "we could harvest the benefits of globalization while building resilience and mitigating against the inevitable interdependency and vulnerability arising from increased connectivity and complexity."[15]

The world we live in has its complex interdependencies due to globalization. Managing these interdependencies is the key challenge which will get us ahead of the curve. Most leaders found a direction toward confining their focus and energy to local issues more than addressing global challenges to create a sustainable environment. It is time to rediscover ourselves while nature is reset. While industrialists mourn, wildlife will be left in peace. Was this a lesson to the fragmented human race?

COVID-19: International and Domestic Challenges Await Sri Lanka[16]

We're going to turn it around. And we have the cards, don't forget it. We are like a piggy bank that's being robbed. We have the cards. We have a lot of power with China.[17]

President Donald J. Trump
during the 2016 election campaign.

President Donald Trump was elected on a platform challenging long-standing American foreign policy premises with a particular criticism of US–China relations. Tensions in the US–China relationship were exacerbated due to Trump's continuous rhetoric and action during his Presidency, reminding the American polity that China's rise as a global power was not beneficial to the US in the economic and security domains. In the economic front, China's protectionist regulations, non-transparency, intellectual property theft, and economic cyberespionage has escalated toward a tense trade war and a national security threat.

China's economic dominance as the global manufacturing hub, providing financial assistance to many developing nations whilst expanding its tentacles toward the entire world through the Belt and Road Initiative to Asian Infrastructure Investment Bank (AIIB) has changed the geopolitical landscape in Asia. The tense US–China relationship is at direct risk of a military confrontation in four geographical locations in Asia — the Korean Peninsula, Taiwan, Senkaku/Diaoyu islands, and the South China Sea. Protecting vital US interests and regional allies and friends through its liberal order established since the Second World War is at the core of US foreign policy. President Richard Nixon's invitation to China in the 1970s of a diplomatic, economic, and security partnership to secure US military presence in Asia was a geostrategic maneuver to draw China away from the Soviet orbit. This helped to strengthen US interest in the region, protect its allies, and end the Cold War.

China's mask diplomacy to wolf warrior diplomacy

Today, thirty years after the end of the Cold War, a pandemic has triggered another cold war between the US and China, with former accusing the latter of a form of biological warfare. The US Secretary of State Mike Pompeo accused China stating that there was "enormous evidence" supporting the claim adding "there is a significant amount of evidence that this came from that laboratory in Wuhan…. I think the whole world can see now, remember, China has a history of infecting the world and running substandard laboratories."[18] Chinese media, responding to this direct accusation states, "If evil politicians like Pompeo continue to lie and bluff, then the Americans 'becoming great again' can only be seen as a joke."[19] Previously on social media, a Chinese diplomat, Zhao Lijian, strongly signaled China's anger on the assertion that the coronavirus was a bioweapon used by American soldiers. China is carrying out *wolf warrior* diplomacy,[20] retaliating aggressively and responding with firmness than never before while carrying out its soft power *mask diplomacy* — a term used to describe China's donation of millions of masks to countries affected by the pandemic along with medical equipment. The dual diplomatic postures have increased Chinese soft diplomacy and power projection.

China, as part of its *mask diplomacy,* provided medical equipment and a concessionary loan of US$500 million with a repayment term of 10 years, to assist Sri Lanka in its fight against COVID19. This will increase the island's existing debt profile with China and will certainly increase future borrowing from China due to unavoidable external shocks from the global recession. China was seen by Anil Jai Singh as "first off the block to capitalize on the vulnerabilities created by the spread of this pandemic. It has reached out to nations and offered support that obviously comes with strings attached. While there has been some pushback against coercive debt-trap diplomacy, the ability of the poorer or smaller nations to avoid succumbing to Chinese pressure will depend on the alternatives available."[21] According to the IMF, Sri Lanka's debt-to-GDP ratio is 82.7%, one of the highest ratios in South Asia. *The Economist*[22] in its "Which Emerging Markets are in Most Financial Peril?" statics recently ranked Sri Lanka at 61, a significantly reduced position compared to a few other South Asian nations.

Domestic challenges and strategic alignments

Months after President Gotabaya Rajapaksa's[f] appointment in November 2019, he was to prove his leadership to a significant external humanitarian crisis from a global pandemic. Similarly, his brother Mahinda Rajapaksa[g] faced a devastating humanitarian crisis after being appointed Prime Minister in 2004 — the Indian Ocean tsunami that took almost 35,000 lives in Sri Lanka. Rajapaksa proved his leadership skills managing the challenge, which eventually won him the Presidency in 2005. His brother Gotabaya demonstrated his leadership, contributing his military expertise, efficiently coordinating with armed forces, the police, intelligence, and healthcare officials. Sri Lanka is the second-best in the region for COVID-19 testing and perhaps the best in contact tracing with a low rate of death under 10. It appears as if "Rajapaksa decision-making" works well in a crisis.

Among powerful nations, China provided one of the most substantial donations back then for the tsunami-affected island of Sri Lanka. Similarly, China was the first to step in to assist in this emergency. Behind

---

[f]HE Gotabaya Rajapaksa is the 8th President in Sri Lanka, since his appointment in November 2019. He was the former Secretary of Defence from 2005 to 2015, when his brother Mahinda Rajapaksa was the President of Sri Lanka.

[g]H.E. Mahinda Rajapaksa is the Prime Minister of Sri Lanka since November 2019. He formerly served as the Prime Minister of Sri Lanka from 2004–2005 and the President of Sri Lanka since 2005 to 2015.

the crisis, a tense geopolitical storm is brewing between the US and China. Crises usually accelerate geopolitical fissures, drawing out underlying pre-existing geopolitical fault lines and building strategic partnerships and alignments among like-minded nations. This was how the Quad (India, Japan, US, and Australia) was created in 2004 after the Asian Tsunami. In the present day, as explained by Rajeswari Pillai Rajagopalan, "The United States has stepped up diplomatic consultations for cooperation with a geographically diverse group of countries, which has now been dubbed the Quad-Plus[23] as it includes South Korea, Vietnam and New Zealand in addition to the original Quad. China's actions are making this cooperation easier."[24]

The new grouping with like-minded countries will play a strategic role in the Indo-Pacific. Recently, the US National Security Advisor, Robert O'Brien, conveyed US support to Sri Lanka "to provide much-needed ventilators" and recognizing "Sri Lanka is an important part of a free and open Indo-Pacific region."[25] How will Sri Lanka face this new strategic alignment and manage its Chinese sphere of influence? Sri Lanka's erudite Foreign Minister Lakshman Kadirgamar noted in 2004 that: "China has never sought to influence the domestic politics of Sri Lanka," claiming that the country has never tried to dominate, undermine or destabilize Sri Lanka. "China has never tried to strike a quick bargain in a crisis. There have been no strings attached to Chinese aid".[26] Nearly two decades following this statement, China's interest and its role in the Indian Ocean has evolved with strength due to the tense geopolitical atmosphere.

Countering the Chinese infrastructure diplomacy in the Indian Ocean with alternative options is already afloat by the western allies. As explained by Hudson scholar Satoru Nagao, "Bangladesh has already chosen Japan's Martabali port project[h] instead of China's Sonadia port project.[i] If the Trincomalee Port[j] project — involving Japanese

---

[h]Martabali is a deep-sea port in Cox's Bazar, Bangladesh, which will be constructed as a multipurpose terminal by Japan.
[i]Sonadia port is located in Cox's Bazar, Bangladesh, and this was to be financed by China. However, in 2016, Bangladesh rejected the Chinese proposal of Sonadia Port deep-sea project. This was a strategic location in China's String of Pearls, similar to Gwadar Port in Pakistan and Hambantota Port in Sri Lanka.
[j]Trincomalee Port is situated in the heart of the Indian Ocean and this is the second largest natural harbor in the world. Currently, it has four multipurpose berths and

assistance — in Sri Lanka succeeds, then the importance of China's Hambantota port[k] will decline. Similarly, the Chabahar Port[l] project in Iran can mitigate the importance of the Chinese Gwadar Port in Pakistan."[m] Further, to strengthen the western grip in the Malacca Straits, India is modernizing infrastructure to deploy warships and planes in the Andaman and Nicobar Islands.[27]

The strategic relations established by President Mahinda Rajapaksa with the arrival of President Xi Jinping to Sri Lanka in 2014 will continue strongly under the current Presidency in a more complex setting. With Geopolitical Cold War 2.0 and domestic economic strain, President Gotabaya Rajapaksa has two daunting challenges ahead of him. He would have to navigate global shocks and balance the country's internal political challenges within a squeezed economy. As explained by Lee Kuan Yew Professor Razeen Sally, the present environment of unstable and contested geopolitics revolving around competition is going to squeeze global trade and globalization. Domestic malign mercantilism with more state intervention and restricted markets will see a different kind of capitalism coming out of this pandemic.[28] Sri Lanka should foresee this danger to avoid malign mercantilism drifting towards losing liberal values. The nation has to balance its foreign policy, protecting its liberal democratic values and its important relationship with China amid a geopolitical storm.

---

handles bulk cargoes. Sri Lanka wishes to develop it with the assistance from potential international investors.

[k] The port of Hambantota is also known as Ruhunu Magampura International Port, to be developed in Southern Sri Lanka. Hambantota Port is closely located to major international east–west shipping route and has direct roadway connection to the southern and eastern parts of Sri Lanka. China is engaging in construction and development of the Hambantota Port, one of the major projects in Sri Lanka.

[l] Chabahar is a seaport in Iran. Under the North–South Transport Corridor framework, India, Afghanistan, and Iran, signed the Chabahar Port Agreement in 2003 to utilize the Chabahar Port as a trade hub. India took over the operation in 2018 and in the process of refurbishing Chabahar Port.

[m] Gwadar is located in Pakistan and is the deepest seaport in the world. This port plays a prominent role in the China–Pakistan Economic Corridor (CPEC) and China's Belt and Road Initiative (BRI).

Collective Destinies in Pestilence[29]

No longer were there individual destinies; only a collective destiny.
Made for plague and emotions shared by all.

Albert Camus[30]

In 430 BC, an entire chapter of the Peloponnesian war documented by the Greek historian, Thucydides was about a deadly epidemic. According to him, while Athenians prepared for war with Sparta, its course changed dramatically due to a plague. First, Athenians believed it was the work of Spartans who have poisoned their waters, but eventually understood it was a plague. Over the course of history, epidemics have wiped out villages and populations and devastated and transformed empires. They wield much more power than any other security threat that could enter our society, and today we all directly confront this threat. While many nations and political leaders marched toward embracing ultra-nationalist sentiments, believing their national interest is important than the other nations, will eventually understand with the growth of the outbreak the importance of transnational cooperation and building trust among nations.

Wuhan is a city of 11 million people. It is described as a city geographically at the very heart of China. It is roughly equidistant from the cities of Beijing and Guangzhou (Canton) on a north–south axis and also is equidistant from Shanghai and Chongqing on an east–west line. Currently, its residents are not allowed to move out of the city. San Fiorano is also barricaded and closed off from the outside world with nine neighboring towns close to Milan that were the epicenter of the coronavirus outbreak. Italian Prime Minister[31] termed it as "Italy's darkest hour," as lockdown in the northern regions began and riots broke out in prisons as the country faced the biggest challenge since the Second World War.

The COVID-19 epidemic has spread to 114 countries, as of March 11, 2020, there are 118,000 confirmed cases with 4,291 deaths from around the world. The outbreak was declared a pandemic by the WHO. The daily developments of the outbreak are similar to the incidents illustrated in Albert Camus's 1947 novel *The Plague*.[32] Seen as a parable about the German occupation of France, the plot holds a far much deeper significance to everyday life through chronicling an outbreak in the North

African city of Oran. While people suffer from death and isolation, Camus wonders what it means to resist a challenging environment and outlines human courage through a profound optimism about human nature to rise from difficult moments through small kindnesses and solidarity. Just like the authorities blocking people of Oran, police have barricaded the entrance to the Italian town and anyone who attempting escape the blockade faces up to three months in prison or a fine of up to 206 euros ($223). It is as if I am going through the pages of Camus's chronicle when witnessing the human suffering documented from around the world. Given the current trajectory of the spread, it is poised to reach other cities which could follow the similar oppressive containment methods. It is worth preparing for the worse.

Distrust and cooperation

China is the *primus inter pares* among the developing countries. As an emerging power with significant economic strength, it is facing a security dilemma with the exiting global power, the US. Apart from the heightened trade war between the two nations and security concerns over Chinese products, another new dimension of conflict inhibiting the dire need for cooperation during epidemics is added to the agenda.

Some misleading reports were published, stating that the virus was a biological weapon from laboratories in Wuhan or that the US introduced the virus in Wuhan. Apart from nuclear weapons, China and the US engage in defensive biological warfare research for strategic deterrent or weapons of last resort. Distrust between the two nations at a time like this could aggravate this misleading information. What is required is to strengthen military-to-military bio-defense cooperation and trust and transparency between the two to minimize future hazards. Nations will need to work side by side to confront challenges from epidemics. Despite US–China trade wars, it is also an opportune time to strengthen collaboration for global health and epidemic preparedness.

Globalization in action

Was this a "black swan"[33] moment? A random and unpredictable event? Michele Wucker got it right by calling it a "gray rhino"[34] moment which is a *highly probable* but neglected threat that has an enormous impact.

No matter how powerful the nation, epidemics have no borders. The last time China had a similar outbreak was in in 2003 when the SARS epidemic which took many lives and weakened the economy even at its 10% growth rate. This time, the Chinese economy is at 6% growth, and the nation will face difficulty to introduce a stimulus with the current deficit. According to *Reuters*,[35] China's economic growth is expected to slow to 4.5% in the first quarter of 2020 — the slowest pace since the 2008 financial crisis and could cost the global economy US$1.1 trillion in lost income.[36] The disease will reshape economies around the world. It has already impacted oil prices, which witnessed the steepest decline since the 1991 US invasion of Kuwait.[37]

The estimates of the degree of infection are on the rise, and this would directly impact the Chinese economy and the entire global trade. It is commendable that the Chinese authorities have been transparent, sharing the DNA of the virus, unlike the previous SARS epidemic. In any government, the administrative capacity and competency could be weighed at a time of crisis, particularly at a time like this. So far, the Chinese authorities have proven their ability to follow the correct procedures and cooperate with the global community to overcome the challenges. However, at the beginning of the pandemic, there were lapses and delay in acknowledgment by the authorities. As clearly explained by Jennifer Bouey, Senior Policy Researcher at RAND Corporation, "the first common feature response of SARS and 2019-nCoV is the delay in acknowledging the initial case cluster to be a public health threat. If we recognize that stability is what the Chinese political system values most, and an acute public health threat, such as an epidemic, is precisely the "black swan" that can threaten such stability, then it is not too difficult to understand the Chinese government's reluctance toward acknowledging an epidemic. China's law prohibits anyone from talking about a public health threat before an official government announcement."[38]

Unlike in 2003, China is more globalized, with around 200,000 people a day travelling in and out of the mainland, resulting in a higher degree of risk for the outbreak. It is also a time of globalization in action, spreading the virus from one remote corner to another faraway city in a few hours. Unlike in the 1970s, where 310 million passengers travelled by air, presently, the number of annual air passengers is in billions.[39] Marc Lipsith,[40] a Harvard University epidemiologist working on coronavirus, says the virus "will ultimately not be containable" and, within a year, will infect somewhere between 40% to 70% of humanity. He adds, "But don't be too alarmed. Many of those people won't have severe illnesses or even show symptoms at all."

Sri Lankan economy: Navigating the global shocks

In Sri Lanka, one Chinese traveler was found COVID-19 positive, treated and sent back to China. Seen as a significant achievement by the authorities, the Health Minister took to the front page of the news, not realizing it was not the end but rather the beginning of many more cases to be diagnosed in the coming days. Along with the news cycle, the public focus will shift in a few days to upcoming Parliamentary election which will the cost taxpayers some several billion amidst the global outbreak and global economic slowdown, which has already hit the tourism industry.

The Sri Lankan economy, which is facing the lowest growth rate in South Asia, will experience further effects of the coronavirus. The tourism industry went through a hard recovery after the 2019 Easter Sunday terror attacks[n] and, while on the path to recovery, was hit by coronavirus. The number of Chinese tourists visiting the island nation will drop, and Chinese infrastructure projects will also face some impact due to the dearth of construction workers. Depending on the global impact on supply chains and how soon things will be back to normal, the Sri Lankan economy would have to navigate the shocks in the global arena. A note of caution on recent irrational government policies in the international arena (UNHRC)[o] and turning down the US MCC loan:[p] decisions taken for the sake of elections will have ripple effects post elections, especially with the prevailing global economic slowdown.

---

[n]Three churches and three luxury hotels in Sri Lanka were attacked on April 21, 2019, the Easter Sunday. The attacks were carried out by members of National Thowheed Jama'ath, a local militant Islamic group. There were more than 260 deaths and other casualties.

[o]Sri Lanka co-sponsored the 30/1 UNHRC Resolution on "Promoting reconciliation, accountability and human rights in Sri Lanka", which was adopted in 2015. This was never accepted by the Rajapaksa government as this had criticized both the government and the extremist group, Liberation of Tamil Tigers Eelam (LTTE) for violations committed during the civil war.

[p]The Millennium Challenge Corporation (MCC) is a bilateral US foreign aid agency and this approved a five-year grant as part of a Compact program for Sri Lanka, consisting of two projects: the land project and the transport project. This was criticized by many on issues pertaining to legal, environmental, and external interference, which led to the ending of the implementation of the project.

Coronavirus election and the National Security Policy for Sri Lanka

While the government in power is seeking two-thirds majority in the Sri Lankan Parliament in the 2020 Parliamentary Elections in April, the political environment will be different from the past elections. You could call it a "coronavirus election." Should there be elections with the global pandemic? Regardless of the global health hazard, does the government encourage public gatherings? Why cannot the government postpone elections? These are some useful questions to carefully think twice. Government efficiency and the President's unilateral decision-making on managing the epidemic will be a factor. President Gotabaya Rajapaksa, who came to power projecting a national security threat from the Easter Sunday bombings, will face another form of global security threat. Responding to disease outbreak requires a multifaceted effort by the whole government machinery. It involves provincial-, local-, and Mayor-level efforts as well.

Successfully managing the spread of the virus relies on the efficiency of the overall system of government, not one individual. Has Sri Lanka prioritized who receives the virus test? How fast can the results be delivered? Who is responsible to sanitize public transit places? How effective and efficient are the quarantine facilities managed? These are some vital questions that require answers. The Government's efficiency of managing the crisis will be a daunting challenge which will lead to building trust with the general public and the system in place, which will eventually secure the vote in the coming election. A slight lapse or mismanagement would have a drastic public reaction and outcome.

We must understand this new reality to reduce the risk of future epidemics. Having a security policy is an essential ingredient that can add value to the process of preparedness during a national security crisis. National Security Policy (NSP) will capture the holistic security threats (health, climate, economic, etc.) to the nation in the next several years. An NSP was compiled at the National Security Think Tank (INSSSL) during last three years with several military experts from tri-forces along with the researchers and handed over to the Secretary Ministry of Defence General Shantha Kottegoda in October 2019. The Sri Lankan NSP highlights that "a nation should develop the means and capacities to prevent and control epidemics that might cripple the country." The document is worth circulating to the public and line Ministries for further inputs and development. Unfortunately, these documents go classified and not shared with the public like the National Defence Policy (NDP), which was declassified and approved by the cabinet on November 11, 2019.[41] Not many Sri Lankans know that the nation has an NDP. These policies belong to the people and not to a particular regime or individual, therefore it should be carried forward with improvements and amendments, not to be hidden inside cupboards and shared with a restricted audience.

At a time of global crisis such as the COVID-19 pandemic, with mounting anxiety, uncertainty, and multiple socio-political and economic shocks which could create distrust among nations, what is required is cooperation, solidarity, and acts of human kindness to each other. While epidemics teach us, a collective destiny is what we possess; however, we still tend to be fragmented and glued to our destiny, securing our national interest while ignoring others.

Chapter 5

Domestic Political Stability, Leadership, and Economic Crime

Politicians are a lot like diapers. They should be changed frequently, and for the same reasons.

Mark Twain

Sri Lanka's Presidential Election 2019:
A New President and the Politics of Balances[1]

Introduction

"We have not lost in this election. In a way we have won the Southern vote; we just did not receive the votes from North-East and the upcountry ... I will ensure I will look after all of you." These were the departing words of Mahinda Rajapaksa after his loss in Presidential Election in 2015. The president who left office came back to power after four years, this time appointed as prime minister by his brother — Gotabaya Rajapaksa — a historical political incident where two brothers share the Executive and the premiership.

In 2015, votes from the ethnic Tamil-dominated former war zone in the north of the country and Muslim-dominated areas played a key role in President Maithripala Sirisena's victory. It took four years for a Rajapaksa to seize back the top seat by winning a significant percentage of the Sinhalese voter base. The new president, Gotabaya, secured 52.25% of the votes with a 1.3 million lead, a historic victory without many votes from the North-East. As articulated by the newly elected president, "I won from the Sinhalese votes; I expected more votes from the Tamil and Muslim community which I did not receive. I want them to join now." He has appealed to them to be a part of his grand vision to create a prosperous nation with a new political culture, with meritocracy and technocracy emblazed at the helm.

Reasons for Gotabaya's victory

There are three distinct reasons for Gotabaya's victory. First, the Sri Lankan economy has been badly managed and the direct effect of rising costs was felt by the entire country. Second, the flaws in the bipartisan model introduced in 2015 became unmanageable, gradually evolving into a complete loss of mutual trust between the Executive and prime minister. Finally, it was the national security threat that arose from the extremist terror attack on Easter Sunday in 2019. Following the attack, the people's trust in the government eroded significantly and reached its lowest ebb when a Parliamentary Select Committee[2] highlighted serious intelligence gaps and administration flaws in the government.

In the 2019 Presidential Election, Sri Lanka was at a crossroads, pitting the neo-liberals against the nationalists. As a symbolic gesture, the color of the new presidential flag depicts dark brown, signifying the rich soil of the nation. The values stem from the Deep South — the scarf was the symbol the Rajapaksas used to depict their closeness to the soil, and this had much more strength than any other political slogans used by their opponents. "I am from a southern Sinhalese Buddhist family and I was educated at a Buddhist school 'Ananda College'. I will ensure principles of Buddhist values will be at the forefront in my presidency," said the newly-elected president at his inauguration at the Ruwanwelisaya Buddhist shrine, the place where the ancient Southern Sinhalese Buddhist King Dutugamunu who united the nation left a magnificent edifice to the entire country.

Adopting global best practices

While embracing history is significant, it is also important to explore whether history has punished societies that have not evolved. Alexis de Tocqueville came from another nation to praise America's embodiment of progressive political ideals. Nations should adapt best practices and embrace the values of progressive development in other nations. Leaders should be quick to adapt best practices and values from them.[3] Many politicians in Sri Lanka's recent past spoke about bringing inspiration from the Singapore model, but their words ended up only as empty promises. The newly-elected president could enact this change. Perhaps, as a reflection of this change, Gotabaya, within his first week in office, reduced the number of cabinet portfolios and established a committee for future appointments at all government institutional levels.

Sri Lanka's economic geography matters as much as its political geography. Most past leaders failed to capitalize on the nation's economic and political geographical significance due to their narrow political principles and their belief in protectionist measures, thereby missing the opportunity to leap forward and be part of the global economy and its value chains. Even Singapore defines her geography by international connectivity. The balance between national and liberal values is clearly visible in the Singaporean context. Sri Lanka should develop its capacity to concentrate and harness the flows of goods, services, resources, money, technology, information, and talent, which will make it grow into a developed nation, just like Singapore. For this, Sri Lanka has to go beyond the ultra-nationalist spirit to embrace what is out there in the world.

The strategy of the new president comes during the significant time of the Fourth Industrial Revolution. The author was present in Davos when Professor Klaus Schwab, Chairman of the World Economic Forum, released his book, *The Fourth Industrial Revolution*,[4] in 2016, when Sri Lanka's gross domestic product growth rate was at 4.5%. The economy is expected to grow at its lowest rate of 2.7% in 2019. Political instability, followed by a weak security environment, was a significant factor that has pulled the entire country down. When compared to nations such as Bangladesh in the South Asian region, which has managed to stabilize its economy with an 8% annual growth rate, the Sri Lankan economy would need a quick recovery, with a particular increase in foreign direct investment inflows.

Value of democracy and technocracy

Will Gotabaya be able to manage the delicate balance between ultra-nationalist and liberal economic values? Seen as an efficient administrative technocrat with little experience in politics, will he embrace the values of the rich school of democracy in his government? How will he embrace his brother's pro-China foreign policy? And will he be able to create a balance between the triple spheres of influence — between India, China, and the US? These are some questions the new leadership will face, and Gotabaya will need to use all of his statecraft to answer them in the coming months. One significant internal value the new leader may wish to follow is technocracy. Sri Lankans are in search of a better government that could balance democracy and technocracy — an area in which the previous regime failed miserably. The gap was clearly identified by Gotabaya and he has promised a government with values of technocracy and meritocracy under his leadership. In both his election manifesto and at his inaugural speech, he re-emphasized these values.

Technocracy is the model and policy prescription that was put forward as a solution for modern democracies by Parag Khanna, a Professor at the Lee Kuan Yew School of Public Policy in Singapore — he published a book on the same subject.[5] He explained that there is a lack of technical experts to solve complex government problems in a democracy. Technocracy, as a form of leading governing practice to efficiently govern a polis (the ideal city), was introduced by the Greek philosopher Plato as the most preferred form of government, which should be led by a committee of public-spirited guardians." In such a system, the most qualified technical experts are chosen based on merit to govern the nation. This is a model adopted by progressive nations such as Singapore. According to Parag, "Technocratic government is built around expert analysis and long-term planning, rather than narrow-minded and short-term populist whims ... Real technocracy has the virtues of being both utilitarian (inclusively seeking the broadest societal benefit) and meritocratic (with the most qualified and non-corrupt leaders). Instead of ad hoc and reactive politics, technocracies are where political science starts to look like something worthy of the term: a rigorous approach to policy." What Sri Lanka clearly needs is to steer in this direction. Indeed, the island state's new leadership has already recognized the importance of this model. Accordingly, the "public-spirited guardians" will be chosen to address key complex issues not adequately addressed before.

Foreign policy management

Gotabaya is the second leader after Sirimavo Bandaranaike who managed to become the head of state without much political experience. While Sirimavo's domestic policies had limitations, leading to an erosion of the economy, her foreign policy imperatives were excellent.

On foreign policy, the newly-elected president Gotabaya Rajapaksa spelt out his policy in his election manifesto "to maintain friendly relations with other countries from a standpoint of equality," and to "adopt a non-aligned policy in all his foreign dealings and work with all friendly nations on equal terms."[6] His clear position was that "we will not be part of any big power rivalry, we will take a neutral position." Even before the President's maiden visit to India, Constantino Xavier, a Foreign Policy Fellow at Brookings India in New Delhi, explained that, "Gotabaya Rajapaksa will play the China card, but Beijing is now less inclined to repeat the large financial investments it did five or 10 years ago, due to growing domestic opposition and international scrutiny." Further looking at the Indo–Lanka foreign policy in the context of the greater global strategy at play in the Indo-Pacific, Xavier stated, "Prime Minister [Narendra] Modi's ambition to shape the Indo Pacific great game will fail unless he gets Gotabaya to play ball and keep China at bay."[7] It would be wise for

India not to use its closest neighbor in such a manner as described by Xavier, since a strong and deep Sino–Lanka relationship is also an essential element in Sri Lanka's foreign policy.

China's deep economic and infrastructure-driven diplomacy in the island state cannot be discounted. From South Asia, Sri Lanka was an initial partner of the Belt and Road Initiative (BRI) — a strategic step taken by Mahinda during his presidency. China's goals were explained by President Xi Jinping in his congratulatory letter to the newly-elected president: "To deepen our practical cooperation within the framework of the Belt and Road Initiative, to start a new chapter of China-Sri Lanka Strategic Cooperative Partnership and to bring more tangible benefits to our two peoples." During his visit to India from November 28–30, 2019, Gotabaya bluntly and rightly expressed the importance of the strategic asset of the Hambantota Port leased out to China during his interview: "The Sri Lankan government must have control of all strategically important projects." Viewing the lease of the Hambantota Port as an unfruitful exercise, he elaborated on its long-lasting strategic implications: "…these 99-year lease agreements [that Sirisena's government signed] will have an impact on our future." The Hambantota Port and Chinese infrastructure diplomacy have had many concerned that Beijing was indulging in "debt diplomacy." Gotabaya has, however, rejected the claim of a "debt trap" in his same interview: "It is also wrong to say there was a debt trap," and that the Hambantota Port was leased out due to the government's inability to finance the borrowings from the Chinese.

The total Chinese loan percentage is much less than the sovereign bonds and the debt issue is more of a "middle-income trap" rather than a "Chinese debt trap." The country has advanced from a low-income to middle-income status and no longer qualifies for concessional loans from international institutions. Andrew Small, Transatlantic Fellow at the German Marshall Fund's Asia Program and a renowned China expert, analyzed the Sri Lankan debt trap as a data point rather than a trend, stating that the perception that China plans to build military bases through debt-diplomacy is inaccurate.[8]

Having said that, the new president will have to astutely exercise his "neutral" foreign policy posture at a time of geopolitical significance in Sri Lanka's surrounding environment, especially the Indian Ocean, where neutrality has its own complexity. Sri Lanka should not accept binary choices when it comes to the Indo-Pacific or the BRI. It should be part of both strategies and it should reap maximum benefits for its people.

Conclusion

Gotabaya is seen by the general Sri Lankan public as a leader who is capable of delivering on his promises. During his term, Gotabaya will be faced with the challenge of balancing competing priorities. He needs to introduce technocracy and meritocracy into the country, but he needs to balance this by carefully making deep changes to the existing system. He will need to balance nationalist and liberal policies, adopt best practices that will connect Sri Lanka to the world, and make the small island nation gravitationally a large nation. For this, Gotabaya will need to balance his "neutral" policy stance with regional and global geopolitical dynamics.

Mahinda Rajapaksa's 50 years in politics? Triple Threats and Balancing Triple Spheres in Sri Lanka[9]

Chess teaches the Clausewitzian concepts of "centre of gravity" and the "decisive point" — the game usually beginning as a struggle for the centre of the board. Wei qi teaches the art of strategic encirclement.

Henry Kissinger[10]

In weiqi, the 2,500-year-old Chinese abstract strategy board game, the goal is to slowly and patiently build up assets to tip the balance of the game in one's favor. The emphasis is on long-term strategy, not short-term gains, argues Kishore Mahbubani in his latest book *Has China Won?* Is China playing weiqi in deferent geographical locations? Is China tilting the global power balance in its favor?

The world has managed to evade another human carnage of a World War since 1945 with an era of long peace, as written by historian John Lewis Gaddis in 1986,[11] extending further into the post-Cold-War era. We have lived 75 years of long peace, limited only to proxy wars. Has the balance of the game changed with the rise of China and escalated US–China geopolitical tension predominantly in Asia? China's rise was discussed by two intellectual heavyweights in international relations, John J. Mearsheimer and Kishore Mahbubani in a recent debate, with two divergent views. Mearsheimer sees a contested environment with a zero-sum game where China would eventually be compelled to take the US's global hegemonic position and its economic interest will transform into military interest. While Kishore sees a positive-sum peaceful rise of China in a civilizational context and other nations accepting China's rise rather than agitating against the rising power. Both scholars referred to George Kennan, the guru of containment in the Cold War, when discussing the need for strengthening strategic alliances to contain China. Professor Mahbubani states "America did not win the Cold War on its own. It formed solid alliances with its Western partners in NATO and cultivated key third world friends and allies, like China, Pakistan, Indonesia, and Egypt. To preserve these close alliances, America kept its economy open to its allies and generously extended its aid. The Trump administration has announced an America First policy and threatened to impose tariffs on key allies like the EU and Japan and third world friends like India."[12] Seeing the weak US alliances in the present context, Mearsheimer's view is that the next US administration would have to invest more and strengthen strategic alliances to contain China. In the present Cold War 2.0, with the US having a clear peer competitor, perhaps the geometry of power in international relations is certain to change from the unipolar world order, where alliances such as the Quad Plus and many more would emerge in the next decade.

The recent Indo–China border tension adds further strain on regional geopolitics. A senior Indian government official, after meeting with Prime Minister Narendra Modi to review the ongoing border tension observed, "From Australia to Hong Kong to Taiwan to the South China Sea to India and right up to the US, a bellicose China is staring at the world for domination at all costs."[13] With the heightening of tensions in the border, three senior diplomats, Ambassador Shyam Saran, Ambassador Gautam Bambawale, and Ambassador Ashok Kantha see the close India–US strategic engagement as a factor for Chinese behavior.[14] If the US–India strategic engagement is a factor, then there will be definite ripple effects in countries of South Asia, especially in Sri Lanka, due to its long-term relations with both countries. Many nations could end up with binary choices between China and US, unwillingly departing from their neutral stand due to geopolitical frictions.

Mahinda Chinthanaya, the foreign policy vision of Prime Minister Mahinda Rajapaksa, was spelt out in 2005 with a "non-aligned" posture. A similar "neutrality" is expressed by President Gotabaya Rajapaksa's foreign policy in the present day. Amid heightened geopolitical tensions, the challenge will remain in executing the neutral foreign policy. Many nations have secured their economic interest with China whilst balancing their security interest with the US. Australia is a clear example when it comes to securing export revenue with China and security alignment with the US. According to Australia's leading strategic thinker Hugh White, "Australia's future will be dominated by China, Treasury forecasts show that the Chinese economy will be about 80 per cent bigger than America's within a dozen years. In this environment, Canberra must prepare for the new strategic terrain in the wake of America's declining leadership, and we would be unwise to support Washington in a confrontation with China that America probably cannot win."[15]

Within South Asia, China's trade has grown in the last decade. China's trade with all South Asian countries is mainly export-driven and higher than that of India. India's trade volume with its neighbors has remained well below in value to that of China.[16] The growth of China's economic space is a clear indication of its growing influence and economic engagement in the region. With its closest neighbor India in a direct border dispute with China, Sri Lanka will have a greater challenge in dealing with these two powerful nations in its foreign policy realm. China's heavy financial assistance and economic interest in the island will be a vital factor in the foreign policy decision-making process of the Sri Lankan Government.

50 years of Rajapaksa politics

In the domestic arena, the difference between the eras of Mahinda Rajapaksa's Presidency (2005–2015) and Gotabaya Rajapaksa's Presidency is that the geopolitical context has changed significantly. In the backdrop of India–China border disputes and US–China geopolitical tensions, there will be a significant expansion of Chinese dominance in the island to contain the US–India influence. Among the many congratulatory messages for Prime Minister Mahinda Rajapaksa's 50th political anniversary on May 27, 2020, was from Indian Prime Minister Narendra Modi. This was the second telephone conversation the Indian Prime Minister had with the Rajapaksa family during the last few days. First was with President Gotabaya Rajapaksa on May 23, where the Sri Lankan President sought from the Government of India, a US$1.1 billion special SWAP facility to add to the US$400 million SAARC Fund, to deal with the foreign exchange issue the country is facing right now. The Indian Premier assured, "we are ready to help under terms that are favourable to Sri Lanka." This explains India is keen to sincerely assist to strengthen the Sri Lankan economy facing direct effects of the pandemic.

Mahinda Rajapaksa's illustrious political career, continuing his father's political legacy for half a century, is in itself a significant achievement. South Asia has many political dynasties but the Rajapaksa family stands out in the international sphere for two symbolic accomplishments. First, ending an almost 30-year war, which was seen as an impossible task by many back then and second, for the geostrategic Hambantota Port, a hot topic in the global arena, which signaled Rajapaksa's welcoming of the Chinese strategic relationship, which was further cemented by multiple bilateral agreements during the 2014 visit by President Xi Jinping to the island nation. Having lost the 2015 Presidential Election, he returned to power as Prime Minister in 2019. Mahinda Rajapaksa stands out as a symbolic leader surviving political office with internal and external pressure at various interludes.

Former President Sirisena, in a special video to celebrate the Prime Minister's 50 years in politics, states "I had to make him the Prime Minister to save our nation in 2018." This signifies that only Mahinda Rajapaksa stands out from the rest, trusted to protect the national values and interests of the nation. A political trust he has built over time with the Sri Lankan polity that is testament to authenticity of his leadership. In a tribute to Prime Minister Mahinda Rajapaksa, his son Namal Rajapaksa recalls the words uttered by his father on the night the war ended — "Our work has now only begun. Let us raise this country to its true potential now that the bombs are over. Let all my people live in peace."[17] A sincere vision to engage on a genuine path of reconciliation and peacebuilding was unfulfilled with much to be done to heal the wounds. The agitation and ideology of the LTTE remains as was seen on Victory Day with back-to-back cyberattacks on several official government websites, displaying the Tamil Eelam ideology.

While losing the Presidential race in 2015, Mahinda stood firm amidst an internal political storm against his family. Sri Lankan politics "can either transform you into a strong figure or it can break you in every way possible," says Namal. In an environment where the country needed the leadership to be a rock of stability following the 4/21 Easter Sunday attack, Mahinda Rajapaksa, seen as the most trusted leadership figure who could deliver stability and ensure national security, supported his younger brother Gotabaya to become the President of Sri Lanka. He is another proven leader who has been effective in the nation's complex security environment. Whilst balancing the triple spheres of influence (US, India, and China), the Rajapaksas will face triple threats, stemming from the rising geopolitical tension in the region to its foreign policy and the rise of the ideological warfare from the LTTE and the Islamic extremist ideology that led to the brutal Easter Sunday attacks.

Sri Lanka and the World: Whither Political Prudence?[18]

It isn't that there's no right and wrong here. There's no right.

V. S. Naipaul

There is piercing hopelessness for the future when listening to certain political rhetoric in Sri Lanka. The International Workers Day, a day to remember workers' rights, was initiated from the 1886 Haymarket Affair in Chicago. It grew from a general strike for the eight-hour workday and has, over time, developed into a showcase of political muscle at the May Day rally. The competition among the political parties is to attract the largest crowd, moving away from the initial idea behind the observance.

The line that divides the opposition and government in Sri Lankan politics has been blurred by a bipartisan mechanism introduced by the former government under President Sirisena. It is further blurred with 16 Sri Lanka Freedom Party[a] ministers having become part of the joint opposition or remaining ambiguous in their political affiliation. Political party loyalty and discipline has reached the lowest ebb in Sri Lankan politics.

The appointment of cabinet ministers in the beginning of May 2018, to what was perhaps the largest cabinet in the world, has been questioned by former members of the former President Mahinda Rajapaksa's government, who claim there is no scientific basis to the allocation of ministries to particular individuals. Yet such an accusation leaves the general public to wonder if the previous Rajapaksa government had a mechanism to select its cabinet ministers. Although there was a message to the public from certain politicians, including a senior cabinet Minister, who said:

---

[a]Sri Lanka Freedom Party is one of the major political parties, which was founded by S.W.R.D. Bandaranaike in 1951. This political party has a democratic and socialist agenda and remains more nationalist.

"Cabinet reshuffle will take place in a scientific manner" and that a "scientific formula" was introduced to allocate ministers, the substance of the formula was not revealed to the public. A government should allocate its cabinet ministers based on merit and achievements in their area(s) of expertise even though party leaders will be limited to selecting only 25 out of 225 members. Irrespective of the "scientific formula" used, it will not give results because most members of parliament were elected from a grave miscalculation, and not based on merit.

Sri Lankan political scientist Dr. Jayadeva Uyangoda rightly calls for academic scrutiny of this changing behavior of political party members toward their leadership, especially on the question of party discipline/indiscipline changing the dynamics of Sri Lanka's political party system. According to Dr. Uyangoda, "Sri Lanka's political parties have become new creatures with some unusually new characteristics. Monitoring these new changes requires not only scholarly vigilance, but also detachment from our old images of what democratic political institutions are." The new creature created by the system sows confusion for political society.

Moving from domestic political society to the international, China's President Xi Jinping spoke of Karl Marx's idea of the struggle of the proletariat, the ideal that underpins some international workers' movements. Xi said, "Writing Marxism onto the flag of the Chinese Communist party was totally correct."[19] Two centuries since Marx's death, while advancing a much more open economic system, the leader of the second largest economy of the world said Marx is "the greatest thinker of modern times." As a rising power, China liberalized its economy and ushered in globalization to move millions out of poverty.

Closer home in South Asia, India took up a somewhat similar trajectory. As China and India underwent these changes, their respective foreign policies were impacted. After 1990, with the end of the Cold War era, India underwent two important adjustments to its foreign policy: first was economic liberalization and deregulation, and the second was India's changing relationship with the US. In their book, *India at the Global High Table: The Quest for Regional Primacy and Strategic Autonomy*, Ambassadors Teresita and Howard Schaffer correctly identify this phenomenon. Over 50 years ago, the classical realist international relations theorist, Hans Morgenthau, had explained that: "The character of foreign policy can be ascertained only through the examination of the political acts performed and of the foreseeable consequences of these acts."[20] By assessing given actions, one could evaluate what statesmen have actually done for the foreign policies of their countries and the profound impact on the outlook toward the world outside. Sri Lanka, with its middle-path idealistic foreign policy, is stuck somewhat in the non-aligned past, which needs recalibration toward a more realistic approach in this century. The idealistic view adopted in the past could be due to the influence of Buddhist values on our leaders.

Today, China has expanded its trade with US. Nonetheless, Beijing has faced a serious trade war with Washington due to the US Department of Commerce ban on ZTE, one of the largest Chinese telecommunications companies in the US. In February 2018, US intelligence agencies warned Americans against buying products from ZTE and Huawei, another Chinese telecom company, claiming that the companies posed a security threat to American customers. The chairman of ZTE called this "unfair and unacceptable," decrying the US export ban as a massive disruption to its business since the company relies on US firms for key smartphone components.

This incident is a clear indication of how national security plays out in the present context despite an open trade policy. Meanwhile, Sri Lanka has opened its gates for the lowest price with a high percentage of tele-communication infrastructure based on ZTE and Huawei products. Such a predicament was anticipated and highlighted during a discussion of experts from national security think tanks in Sri Lanka in 2017. Its outcome was circulated among the highest policymakers.

Should such warnings from experts go unheeded?

Witnessing the 30/1 Debacle[21]

Despite all the difficulties, there needs to be a concerted effort to develop a negotiating framework that can command the widest possible support. Such a negotiating framework must include at least minimal acceptance, by both sides, of the norms and standards relating to inter-national human rights and a determination to restore peace, normalcy, civil society and democratic governance.

Dr. Neelan Tiruchelvam[22]

President Gotabaya Rajapaksa's government concluded its first 100 days on February 25, 2020. The previous Sirisena Administration maintained a website[i] to track the progress of the initial 100 days. It went defunct after most promises were not addressed. While unattainable promises are pledged during elections, Sri Lankan political history is filled with such false domestic and international promises and policy reforms. In the international arena, the country often loses its reputation and credibility due to unfulfilled pledges and duality of its own policy.

On October 1, 2015, Sri Lanka committed at UNHRC to probe allegations of human rights abuse during the protracted civil war by co-sponsoring the 30/1 resolution. Three foreign Ministers, Mangala Samaraweera, Thilak Marapana, and Dinesh Gunawardena, during the last five years have taken three dissimilar actions contrary to each other on the Geneva co-sponsored resolution by Sri Lanka. First, Minister Samaraweera co-sponsored the 30/1 resolution fully in 2015 along with 11 other nations. In 2019, Minister Marapana, in articulating his position on government reservation for having international judges "hybrid court," referred to a constitutional amendment with two-thirds of parliament and a referendum required to have foreign judges for its judicial process.[23] This year, the present Foreign Minister Dinesh Gunawardena explained his administration's position to withdraw from the co-sponsorship, an election pledge by President Gotabaya Rajapaksa.

The US "travel ban" on Army Chief, Lt-Gen Shavendra Silva[b] and his family came as a surprise.[24] Upon meeting Alice G. Wells, the US Deputy Assistant Secretary, in Oman at a conference in October 12, 2019, I advised the Sirisena–Wickremesinghe government that this could be in the works. The same travel ban was applied to the only Sri Lankan Field Marshal and the Cabinet Minister, Sarath Fonseka,[c] a few years ago despite former President's intervention. Lt-Gen Shavendra Silva's travel ban could be a revisit of the US policy carried out in the past toward the Rajapaksa regime.

The consequence of moving out of the 30/1 co-sponsored resolution will have a significant negative impact, heading toward a confrontational course in the global arena due to its weak internal policies. Long-term

---

[b]Lt. General Shavendra Silva is the Present commander of the Sri Lankan Military. During the Sri Lankan civil war, he gained fame as General Commanding Officer of the elite 58th Division.

[c]Field Marshal Sarath Fonseka is a retired military commander and a current politician in Sri Lanka. During the Sri Lankan Civil war, he was the Commander of the Sri Lankan Army.

implications of the withdrawal have not been considered. The government, while facing parliamentary elections, is pushing a short-sighted "irrational decision" in the global arena. The previous Sirisena government rushed to co-sponsor the resolution in 2015 without prior consultation of the parliament or any public discussion about the decision, which was also unacceptable in a democratic nation. I have analyzed the duality of policy within the government in my article titled "U-Turns are difficult,"[25] published in March 2019. Some of the advisers and policy experts have ill-advised the political leadership to move out from the co-sponsored resolution without calculating or understanding its long-term impact on Sri Lanka.

First, the country co-sponsored a resolution against itself in 2015, and now it wishes to symbolically withdraw from the co-sponsorship after five years. It is a blaring display of policy inconsistency. Withdrawing from the resolution will require 27 votes at UNHRC at the time of the vote and end of the moratorium period, a rather difficult exercise. Foreign Minister Dinesh Gunawardena explained closure is important at this stage because the resolution violates the country's constitution, a factor which should have been considered prior to the co-sponsorship; this was neither considered nor agreed upon as a violation of the constitution by his predecessors, a serious blurring in domestic policy, which shows how weak national policy decisions could be taken at the global arena. A U-turn from such statements is near impossible for the next several years, and the country will face significant consequences.

Such decisions should be taken not on the basis of the upcoming elections but by analyzing different scenarios and undertaking an in-depth foresight study, along with extensive discussions with foreign policy experts and think tanks, and weighing the impact. Unfortunately one such government think tank that could have sent some sensible recommendations was reset last month after appointing a former military officer. The nation has failed in this regard in many policy decisions in the recent past. I inquired on the withdrawal when meeting a distinguished Sri Lankan Foreign Service officer, to which the officer said: "we have not calculated the long term implications to the nation and what's the guarantee that China and Russia will support us in every occasion?"

The country will be seen by the international community as not possessing a clear policy strategy, changing according to the political circumstances. Political pledges and unfulfilled promises one after another prove a clear point for the diaspora and the nations supporting the

Resolution. Sri Lanka will be seen as subjected to selective targeting by the West and will invite new phase of risk factors. First, the nation will tilt toward its savior nations, China and Russia, at the Security Council; this will directly impact the so-called executing "balanced and equidistance" foreign policy of the President. Second, a clear indication that Sri Lanka will drift away from the international assistance for the reconciliation process, including inviting international judges and isolation from many friendly nations where our democratic values and economic interest are intertwined from the past. While we disengage from the international process, we will have a systemic barrier to improve the domestic mechanism to achieve reconciliation, accountability, and human rights targets in Sri Lanka. Third, working outside the UNHRC framework will limit regular visits by rapporteurs who played an important role in trust-building with the international community. How will a mechanism outside the UNHRC framework guarantee a genuinely inclusive process?

The UNHRC chief Michael Bachelet has taken a stronger position on Sri Lanka due to the unfulfilled targets toward the overall reconciliation process during the last decade, which continuously identified the diminishing hope. Bachelet said "that domestic processes have consistently failed to deliver accountability in the past and [I am] not convinced the appointment of yet another Commission of Inquiry will advance this agenda ... I am therefore troubled by the recent trend towards moving civilian functions under the Ministry of Defence or retired military officers, and renewed reports of surveillance and harassment of human rights defenders, journalists and victims. The increasing levels of hate speech, and security and policy measures appear to be discriminately and disproportionately directed against minorities, both Tamil and Muslim."[26]

Four years after co-sponsoring Resolution 30/1 and 40/1, the Sri Lankan government has fulfilled 6 out of 36 commitments on reconciliation, human rights, and accountability.[27]

Despite the slow progress post-2015, the Sri Lankan Government did invest heavily in transitional justice, human rights, and accountability along with international actors committing to international processes. The UNHRC has given a moratorium till March 2021 for the Government of Sri Lanka to implement the provisions of the resolution. Lapses in the progress and the present decision to symbolically withdraw from the co-sponsorship have sent the wrong message to the global arena. The past investments made by the previous government to fill in the foreign policy gap created by pre-2015 Rajapaksa regime with the international community will be lost, reversing the nation to a pre-2015 scenario. The government should have made amendments rather than completely reset the process, a loss for the country. Seen as a permanent solution, the entire exercise will only sweep the problem under the carpet, which will emerge at a later stage. The Government should have navigated with the international community, embracing global best practices, and addressed the domestic political concerns such as devolution of power to build a secular nation, which will lead to prosperity rather than bandwagon toward a more ultra-nationalist stance where dominated by irrational decision-makers.

The Resolution 30/1 debacle saw Sri Lanka's government reach a crossroads and take a step while many watched on helplessly. The choices are asserted and the path is set. Who speaks political rationale in Bedlam?

U-Turns are Difficult[28]

...members of the foreign policy elite are rarely held to account, they were able to make the same mistakes again and again.

Stephen M. Walt on US foreign policy

The US and Sri Lanka need to recalibrate their respective foreign policies. On both ends of global power scales, I suspect the world's superpower and the small southern Indian Ocean island both require a realist reframing of their foreign policy. This is also suggested by Stephen M. Walt in his 2018 publication titled *The Hell of Good Intentions*.

At home, Sri Lanka requires a foreign policy that reflects national interest. A senior foreign ministry official of State recently whispered to me that, "we have become a prostitute who is ready to sleep with anyone for any price." This erratic and impulsive style of governance will hold grave consequences to the nation. U-Turns are difficult, including the ones committed, such as 2015 30/1 Resolution at UNHRC. Neville Ladduwahetty[d] explains this clearly in his article "Government to Sponsor 2019 Geneva Resolution." He rightly explains the stand taken on 30/1 by the Foreign Ministry reflects the degree of disconnect that exist within the ranks of the government.[29]

---

[d]Neville Ladduwahetty is a Sri Lanka author and political analyst.

I was onboard a US military C2 flight heading toward the Eastern Indian Ocean waters to visit the USS John C. Stennis (CVN 74) aircraft carrier, a floating metal base of a 4.5-acre sovereign US territory. The nuclear-powered aircraft carrier was named after the only US senator carrying his personal philosophy to "Look Ahead" for the sake of the country. The aircraft can hold 5,000 personnel onboard and carry enough firepower. It is a gigantic piece of human innovation. In my opinion, it serves to project US power in the oceans.

Aircraft carriers which combine the Navy and Air force are an example of ensuring and insuring US's presence on the oceanfront. Gigantic maritime defense equipment such as USS John C. Stennis come at the costs of US$5 billion and another US$5 billion or more for research and development for technical upgrades of military hardware. The floating base can be seen as a global police officer in the 21st century. It aims to secure the rules of the ocean in a rules-based order.

The shift of emphasis from land power to sea power took place during the early 19th century with the Mahanian theory of winning the oceans as the key for global dominance. This theory was absorbed and acted upon in forming the US grand strategy for the following century. During the Cold War, it was the Atlantic, Pacific, and the Mediterranean seas that mattered more for the global geopolitics. Currently, the focus is on the Indian Ocean. With more than half of global trade traveling through the Indian Ocean, securing trade lines will be paramount for US and China in this century.

To engage in securing trade and projecting power from a distant place is a challenge. Carrier strike groups, with their aircraft carriers, provide a strategic advantage. US strength with its naval power could be seen as a capital-intensive navy with a slow return on investment. The US's peer competitor, China, is engaged in a stealth warfare strategy, with more investment in space and underwater, e.g. their submarines. The civil–military nexus in Chinese ship building today has given a clear advantage of a shorter manufacturing time to build naval crafts than any other military in the world. The US fleet has been reducing in size. In 1950, it held 634 ships; in the post-Cold War period, by 1997, it had scaled down to 365 ships; and today its naval fleet is reduced to 150 ships. This reduction is due to the high cost of unfruitful pointless wars. This high cost is the result of US's stubborn commitment to the strategy of "liberal hegemony" since the end of the Cold War. The US efforts to use power to spread democracy, open markets, and other liberal values into every nook and cranny of the planet was a strategy which was doomed to fail. A more realist strategy with a foreign policy of a more realistic view of American power is required, as clearly explained by Stephen M. Walt.[e]

The present US maritime strategy is derived from the British historian Julian S. Corbett, who wrote the 1911 book titled *Some Principles of Maritime Strategy*. The decrease in US fleet numbers pose the significant risk of limitations in fleet strength and size. The strategy to overcome this is to have more allied or likeminded nations that support American values to assist them. In Corbett's words, it would be a "fleet in being" — which is a collection of ships that can quickly coalesce into a unified fleet when necessary, and engage in limited defense.

Sri Lanka is at the center of the of sea lines of communications (SLOCs) in the Indian Ocean and is an important post for the US Navy. Stock Control Division Officer Lt. Bryan Ortiz from the John C. Stennis' has said: "The primary purpose of the operation is to provide mission-critical supplies and services to U.S. Navy ships transiting through and operating in the Indian Ocean, the secondary purpose is to demonstrate the U.S. Navy's ability to establish a temporary logistics hub ashore where no enduring US Navy logistics footprint exists."[30] If Sri Lanka allows full logistics hub clearance, then there is no guarantee another nation such as China would not demand for the same. In this future scenario, Sri Lanka could end up as a multi-logistics hub operations base for the US and Chinese navies. This may sometime transfer into a multi-base operation, depending on the domestic and foreign policy in the next 25 years.

The foreign policy of a nation should derive from its national interests and not succumb to another nation's interests. The Sri Lankan foreign policy is going in two directions, clearly shown by the Foreign Ministry, which is endorsing and negotiating time to implement the 30/1 resolution of 2015 while another delegation was sent by the President to Geneva to elucidate non-intervention, and that rather, the island nation could find a domestic mechanism to resolve its internal issue. The duality of this position shows the deep political polarization within the government and barriers to agreement between the foreign ministry and the President, being now displayed on the international stage.

---

[e]Stephen M. Walt is a Professor of International Affairs at the John F Kennedy School of Government at Harvard University where he authored the theory of defensive neorealism.

The democratic government did not take efforts to engage the public, or consult with them when co-sponsoring the resolution in 2015. If it had been done, the majority of Sinhalese Buddhists would have not supported this resolution. The nation's interest was not captured when formulating the path in Geneva. The President's U-turn from the government's 2015 position shows that he was excluded or was not allowed to voice his opinion from the earlier decisions of foreign policy in Sirisena–Wickremesinghe government.[f] Serious setbacks are clearly on the horizon to an already scarred nation owing to the mistrust and duality of views taken at the highest levels of State. Many nations have articulated a National Security Strategy, National Defense Policy, and Foreign Policy through a white paper or a policy document. This basic coherence in governance and leadership is absent in Sri Lanka.

From a non-aligned foreign policy, Sri Lanka has moved toward a multi-aligned foreign policy today, trying to align with the strongest triple sphere of influences i.e. the US, China, and India, and the rest. The danger of a multi-aligned policy is when alignment is tilted toward one power, the domestic politics will be in chaos. Shivshankar Menon, the former NSA of India, observes in his book *Choices* in 2016 that New Delhi had reason to want a change of government in Sri Lanka due to the then President Rajapaksa going back on his pledge in respect of Sri Lanka–China relations. The Chinese tilt of Rajapaksa was seen as a national security threat to India. Menon's assertion that Sri Lanka is an "aircraft carrier," parked 14 miles off the Indian coast, clearly underscored New Delhi's serious concerns regarding Sri Lanka being too close to China. If Sri Lankan geography is seen as an aircraft carrier by India, one could clearly understand why the extra-regional powers send their aircraft carriers and submarines to visit Sri Lanka or to use the nation as a logistics hub. A vertical axis of Sri Lankan geography with India and Russia plays one geopolitical note while the horizontal axis is with US and China. Balancing the two axes was a significant challenge with the dual foreign policy of Sirisena and Wickremesinghe. It is time the nation invests to institutionalize the foreign and defense policy of the nation. As Senator Stennis spelled out for the US, perhaps applicable to Sri Lanka, we need to "Look Ahead" for the sake of the country to institutionalize the nation's policies.

---

[f]The government that came into power from 2015–2019 lead by Sri Lanka President Maithripala Sirisena and Prime Minister Ranil Wickremamsinghe.

Comparing Crises: Presidency and Power in a Changing World Order[31]

We must make ourselves relevant so that other countries have an interest in our continued survival and prosperity as a sovereign and independent nation.

Lee Kuan Yew

Let us try to understand changing East–West political negotiations and geopolitical power dynamics through the Venezuelan crisis in South America and the 2018 "coup" in the South Asian island of Sri Lanka. Venezuela became an independent country in 1830 following Spanish colonization from the 16th century. Since the first discoveries of oil were made in the Maracaibo Basin, it has been the driving force behind Venezuela's political and economic affairs. Venezuela's primary geopolitical challenge is managing its relations with the US — the regional hegemon. The US is not only the largest military power in the region but also the largest consumer market and a key destination for Venezuelan crude oil exports. According to Amy Chua, in *Political Tribes*, she explains that white Venezuelans of European descent were an example of a market-dominant minority who were sidelined when Hugo Chavez, a representative of the country's darker-skinned majority, took power. The former Venezuelan President Hugo Chavez was seen as a misfit in the Western world order. Chavez built his domestic and foreign policies around the rejection of the hegemonic sphere of influence of the US while reaching out to the rising Asian global power China, and establishing closer links with Russia. The "Asianization" of Latin America is seen to sway to strong geopolitical influences from China. China was targeting US$500 billion in trade and US$250 billion in investment between 2015 and 2019. It threatens the once-subservient nation to US hegemony since the 19th century Monroe Doctrine. In a comparative analysis on the island of Sri Lanka, Sri Lanka's primary geographic challenge is managing geopolitical relations with India — the regional hegemon, who is well aligned with the US. Just like in Venezuela, the former Sri Lankan President Mahinda Rajapaksa is seen as a misfit in the Western world order. Rajapaksa aligned his foreign policy with China, opening the floodgates to Chinese strategic relations, letting China set its geopolitical footprint upon the nation. The Sri Lankan polity experienced a constitutional crisis in 2018. Sources connect the political fiasco to external geopolitical influences in the country. Venezuela was soon to follow in South America, facing a similar fate. This trend could follow in many other nations where the US is slowly losing grip as the sole global super power. Sri Lanka could also revisit this same situation in the coming months and perhaps in the next Presidential election. One cannot ignore the geopolitical influences from external powers. Such influence pushed to bring back Prime Minister Ranil Wickremesinghe and remove Rajapaksa out of office after a short stint, as he was seen as the illegitimate Prime Minister by the West. The nation had two Prime Ministers from October 26, 2018: one accepted by US and the Western allies and another accepted by China. In the same way, Venezuela presently faces the geopolitics of external powers. Venezuelan President Nicolás Maduro was declared illegitimate by the US and its Western allies after his second-term election in which he won 67.8% of the votes. This win is widely viewed as rigged, while an interim President Juan Guaidó declared himself as the legitimate leader. Mr. Guaidó argues that, as the president of the National Assembly, an opposition-controlled legislative body, he has the constitutional authority to assume power because Mr. Maduro had taken office illegally. According to Bloomberg columnist Noah Feldman, "the constitutional argument that Maduro isn't really President is nothing more than a fig leaf for regime change. Even as fig leaves go, it's particularly wispy and minimal. The U.S. policy is, in practice, to seek regime change in Venezuela. It would be better to say so directly."[32] In the same way, in the island nation of Sri Lanka, PM Wickremesinghe accused Rajapaksa of undemocratic conduct, calling his appointment unconstitutional and illegitimate. Not having the parliament majority support and the process of appointment by President Sirisena was seen as illegitimate. Back in Venezuela, President Maduro is supported and accepted by the Chinese and the Russian governments. While the tense situation unfolds, President Maduro is consciously escalating diplomatic tensions. He announced complete diplomatic shutdown with the US government, giving a 72-hour time period for the US diplomats to leave Venezuela. While one President calls for a diplomatic shutdown of the US within the nation, the interim president — President Guaidó — has invited the US to stay. The State Department has said it will not heed the order to leave the country. It accepts the interim President's request and rejects Maduro's order. At home, in a similar manner, Rajapaksa was rejected by the West with a strong voice from US. His cabinet was seen illegitimate while appealing to the judiciary to restore democracy. Sri Lanka was at a crossroads and deeply polarized. This divide further reared its head in the upcoming election. In Venezuela, the Trump Administration pressed its case, with the US Secretary of State Mike Pompeo calling on all countries in the Organization of American States (OAS)[g] to reject Maduro and "align themselves with democracy," calling the Maduro Administration "illegitimate and invalid." Pompeo, in his address to the 35-member OAS, said: "His (Maduro's) regime is morally bankrupt, it's economically incompetent and it is profoundly corrupt. It is undemocratic to the core."[33] A few days after this statement, three European Union nations, Germany, France, and Spain, were ready to recognize Juan Guaidó as Venezuela's interim president if elections were not called within eight days, in a threat to Venezuelan regime. The trade sanctions by the US will follow and isolation from the Western allies will be unfolding over the next several days. The trade sanctions echo the manner in which the EU was ready to withdraw its GSP plus and sanctions to follow in Sri Lanka. The Sri Lankan military was not involved in the constitutional crisis; the scenario in Venezuela was different as the military has already taken President Maduro's side and supports his Presidency. Just like Sri Lanka is playing a pivotal role in the Chinese Belt and Road Initiative and its close diplomatic and defense relations with Russia, the Venezuelan regime, from Hugo Chavez to Maduro, has invested heavily in China and Russian relations, which is a direct threat to the regional hegemon, the US. Venezuela has also been one of the largest markets for Russian arms exports in Latin America and has signed 30 contracts worth US$11 billion from 2005 to 2013, according to the Russian news agency TASS. In December, Russia dispatched a small group of aircraft to Venezuela in a show of solidarity with Mr. Maduro's Government. Two Tu-160 nuclear-capable bombers flew more than 6,000 miles in this exercise. Overall it has given Venezuela more than US$10 billion in financial assistance in recent years. In exchange, Rosneft, the Russian state oil company, has acquired stakes in Venezuela's energy sector. Venezuela's crisis has made it more vulnerable than ever not only due to Russian influence but more toward the Chinese influence, which has put US economic, security, and diplomatic interests at risk. From Maduro's last state visit to China requesting for more loans

---

[g] Organization of American States (OAS) is a continental organization of South American States founded on the purpose of solidarity and cooperation among its member states within the western hemisphere. It was created with the objective of countering the spread of communism during the Cold War.

from China, China's loans to Venezuela have grown to US$65 billion. However, the Venezuelan economy has stuttered, in perhaps the same way as the Sri Lankan economy, even as Sri Lankan leaders have obtained and are seeking more loans from China. These loans are seen by the West as predatory and debt-trap loans. Sri Lanka, in 2020, celebrated her 72nd year of independence from British colonial rule. Even after 72 years, policy-makers have failed to realize promises of economic prosperity. What we have today is a broken down nation. Three top ratings agencies, Fitch, Standard & Poor's, and Moody's Investor Services, have downgraded Sri Lanka's rating, raising the cost of international borrowing. Fitch has moved Sri Lanka from B+ to B, which leaves it just four notches above default status in 2019. The nation is turning to China and India for financial support as a balance of payment crisis looms over the debt-strapped island. According to Indrajit Coomaraswamy,[h] former Governor Central Bank of Sri Lanka, both India and the China are considering plans to scale up their respective offers to US$1 billion each. He says, "Sri Lanka's friends, the two regional giants, have stepped up to support us in this time when we were pushed into a rather difficult corner."[34] Power transitions from West to East only prove that it is imperative to calculate external geopolitical interference toward Sri Lanka. Lankan leadership needs to include this discussion in political discourse.

Importance of Meaningful Co-operation in Preventing and Interdicting Economically Motivated Crimes and Misconduct: The Sri Lankan Perspective[35]

The old world is dying, and the new world struggling to be born: now is the time of monsters.

Antonio Gramsci

It is fitting to quote Gramsci because the monsters we have created are real, especially the extremist threat that entered Sri Lanka on April 21, 2019.

---

[h]Indrajit Coomaraswamy is a Sri Lankan economist and the 14th Governor of the Central Bank of Sri Lanka.

Dr. Emma Sky has clearly explained the instability in the Middle East and its ripple effect on all nations in her new book titled *In a Time of Monsters: Travels through a Middle East in Revolt*. Instability in the Middle East is the direct geopolitical consequence we all are facing today. From the millions of refugees fleeing the horror, to the extremist terror that affected London, Paris, Brussels, and Colombo, all are products and results of geopolitics in the Middle East.

Sri Lanka, an Island nation strategically located between the busy East–West maritime trade routes in the Indian Ocean, celebrated its 72nd Independence in 2020. Owing to its location alone, Sri Lanka faces many issues involving geopolitical challenges, the nation's foreign relations, and its national interests, which scans several key challenges the nation is facing in the domestic arena and the international theatre. Many have authored papers and books, including mine titled *Sri Lanka at Crossroads*, published by World Scientific, Singapore.

The beautiful island nation of Sri Lanka is going through many challenges, such as bureaucratic inertia, mostly arising out of confusions in the human mind, directly affecting good governance. Though it appears that the politicians in power, who are elected representatives of the people, have control of the Government, in reality, the policy decisions of the political master based on inputs from an ill-advised, corrupt, and inept bureaucracy could lead a nation to disaster.

There is no need to delve on this area much as many have had the good fortune of viewing the comedy series "Yes Minister" and "Yes Prime Minister" aired by the BBC. The net result of this aforesaid confusion is many glaring incidents that received wide publicity. One is the question that arose concerning the authority of the President Sirisena in dissolving a Parliament and the appointment of the Prime Minister Mahinda Rajapaksa.[36] The second is the appointment of a non-citizen as the Governor of the Central Bank[37] and the value of his swearing allegiance to the constitution of the country in assuming duties as the Governor. Today, he is a fugitive of justice — involved in the Central Bank Bond Scam. Third was the inability to evaluate intelligence inputs, resulting in the inability to prevent the most brutal terrorist attack in Sri Lanka on the Easter Sunday in 2019, resulting in the loss of hundreds of lives. The targets of the terrorists were churches and hotels.[38] On a personal note, my family and I escaped death by the skin of the teeth from the terrorist bomb that exploded in the Shangri-La Hotel. The aforesaid confusion of the bureaucratic mind is such that even attending a gathering of this nature to exchange knowledge relating to the security of any realm is considered an unfruitful exercise.

Soon after this disgraceful terror attack, a Cabinet Minster[39] came on TV and said his father advised him not to attend church on Easter Sunday due to a prior terror warning, which raises a moral and philosophical question to our society. Allowing "few privileged individuals to live and many ordinary citizens to die" is a fundamental breach of the principal duties of the social contract between civilians and government in representation and securing the individual lives.

Corruption and economic crime are pillars that destroy good governance, leading to serious breaches of national security. Many texts have delved on this subject, and in my book,[40] an entire chapter is devoted to the importance of strengthening government institutions to fight corruption and economic crime.

Fighting corruption is a pet political theme in any country where it is rampant. Governments are voted out of the office on the promises made by those who seek office to fight it. But the successors can be no better and the predecessors have a distinct political advantage again. People's aspirations may be one thing but the views of the politician, ably assisted by the bureaucrat, are to "make hay while the sun shines." In the Sri Lankan parlance, the motto is "Earn for seven generations rightly or wrongly when you can." Corruption has become endemic in our societies, and it spreads like an uncontrollable ulcer. From the global CPI Index, Sri Lanka has failed to show progress as we were on the same score 38 in 2017 and 2018, and at the 89th place in 2018.[41]

In a recent online survey conducted by the INSSSL[42] Sri Lanka, we inquired how much so Sri Lankans worry about corruption: 93% clearly highlighted as a factor they worry a lot and 50% think amid the extremist security threat to the country, the 2019 presidential election theme should be on corruption. The next elected Executive and the Government would have to continue the anti-corruption campaign and strengthen legal and financial structures to minimize economic crimes in the country. While fighting domestic retail corruption and political corruption is important, it is also essential to improve Anti-Money Laundering/Countering the Financing of Terrorism (AML/CFT) mechanisms.

Economic crime as a phenomenon in criminology was identified by Edwin Sutherland in 1939.[43,44] This under-researched area in the past has dramatically changed and has become a recognized subject of scholarly study. Panama Papers,[45] bond scams, and Bitcoin[46] usage for terrorist funding posed challenges to Sri Lanka. Concepts such as occupational crime, corporate crime, organizational crime, environmental crime, business crime, and elite crime all come under the umbrella term of economic crime.

Strengthening interagency cooperation

One of the pivotal areas limiting the efficacy and efficiency in fighting economic crimes is the absence of meaningful cooperation between domestic agencies and between regional and international agencies in preventing and interdicting economically motivated crimes and misconduct. With cross-border fund transfer mechanisms and ease in technology in fund management, the task has become more challenging to detect financial crimes. Coordinating with other agencies, including Financial Intelligence Units (FIU) and sharing lessons regarding AML/CFT-related crimes is pivotal in this era.

Fighting transnational security threats — The 4/21 terror attack

Sri Lanka is facing a new kind of security threat from extremist terrorism that had links to ISIS/ISIL,[i] which carried out multiple suicide bombings on April 21, 2019.[47] To fight this new transnational security (TNS)[j] threat, Sri Lankan authorities require different skills and expertise, with greater assistance from multiple international agencies. A multi-pronged, multi-agency, multi-jurisdictional approach is required to eradicate the complex TNS threat.

Sri Lanka needs to establish meaningful cooperation to detect the funding sources flowing into the country. The FIU[k] of Sri Lanka was

---

[i]ISIS/ISIL also known as the Islamic State of Iraq and Syria or the "*daesh*" is a global terror organization and an unrecognized proto-state that follows the fundamental, salafi jihadist doctrine of Sunni Islam.

[j]Transnational security (TNS), according to Richard Schultz, Roy Godson, and George Quester, is a paradigm for understanding the ways in which governments and non-state actors functioning within and across state borders interact and affect the defense of states and their citizens.

[k]Financial Intelligence Unit (FIU) is the financial supervisory and monitoring institution of the Central Bank of Sri Lanka that directs anti-money laundering activities.

established in 2006 and played a pivotal role, especially during the final years of the three-decade war against the Tamil Tigers. The work of late Mrs. Joan Moonesinghe, who was the former Director of Bank Supervision at Central Bank of Sri Lanka, should be remembered as she played a pivotal role at that time. Sri Lankan FIU has faced twin threats, earlier from LTTE terrorist funding and now from extremist funding.

In the present day, especially after the 4/21 terrorist attack that devastated our nation and killed 250 innocent civilians, more than 40 accounts and illicit assets of millions were ceased by the authorities. There has been tremendous support from international agencies and intelligence agencies post the attack. While there were lapses in identifying the severity of the threat and lack of a coordinated mechanism among domestic agencies before the attack, an Integrated Threat Assessment Centre[l] (ITAC) was proposed by the Sri Lankan national security think tank INSSSL to improve coordination after identifying how weak coordination had been among agencies and policymakers.

According to former Deputy Governor H. A. Karunaratne, the FIU had flagged several suspicious transactions that occurred in the country's banking system before Easter Sunday attacks, and information on such were shared with law enforcement agencies.[48] Unfortunately, there was no forum for the FIU to highlight the importance of their findings. Had it been so, the FIU findings would have been prioritized and lives would have been saved, supplemented by the meaningful cooperation among FIU, Criminal Investigation Department (CID),[m] and Attorney General's Department. As the Governor of the Central Banks, Dr. Indrajit Coomaraswamy rightly stated after the terror attack, "We are setting up much stronger coordination between AG's Department, the CID and the FIU. Therefore, we will be able to move these cases much faster by having a better sharing of information among these institutes."[49]

State intelligence units have recently received information that extremist terror group members were receiving huge sums of money from

---

[l]Integrated Threat Assessment Centre (ITAC) is a proposed body to centralize security and intelligence activities of all law enforcement and security agencies of the country to determine threats facing Sri Lanka.

[m]Criminal Investigation Department (CID) is the primary investigative arm of the Sri Lanka police and carries out all activities related to investigations pertaining to national security.

informal channels such as the *undiyal*[n] system to carry out business activities in major towns. Several complaints were made by members of traders associations to the relevant authorities about these informal channels, but no visible action has been taken against these money launderers who were doing businesses with money sent to them through *undiyal* system by the international division of an extremist terror group.

The Sri Lankan FIU is mandated to ensure the transfer of financial intelligence to the domestic law enforcement agencies on the one hand and coordinate the exchange of information with foreign FIUs on the other. This is an essential mechanism for a nation like Sri Lanka to possess and function efficiently due to the significant threat by terrorism.

In this environment, AML/CFT mandate has to be taken seriously. FIUs should develop the capacity to fight AML/CFT threats. The Sri Lankan extremist group that attacked on Easter Sunday used bitcoin to make transfers to their accounts, which shows the sophistication and the complexity of terror funding.

War on drugs

Economic crime involves "massive amounts of money, time and geography."[50] This is clear when you explore the complexity of the illicit drug networks that use Sri Lanka as a strategic hub for trans-shipment and local distribution. Each month, large amounts of illicit drugs are nabbed by the authorities and the Sri Lankan President Maithripala Sirisena was strategically correct in declaring "war" on drugs. While bringing in notorious criminals using international assistance, President Sirisena was one of the first leaders to directly confront in this scale and destroy a considerable volume of illicit drugs in the presence of direct public observation.

Back in 2012, when I met President Felipe Calderon in Mexico, I remember his bold remarks to crush the drug mafia; a few months later, he lost his Presidential race due to massive social instability created by the drug cartels. In a different magnitude, President Sirisena also has got entangled after a successful attempt to crush the drug mafia in another massive security threat, which is extremist terrorism. The global illicit drug

---

[n]Undiyal is a Sri Lankan term for the Hawala system which describes the illegal transfer of money from one country to another without any physical movement of money from across borders.

networks possess more income than many developing nations. I also witnessed the control of these networks during a field visit to San Pancho, Mexico, where the drug mafia has burned down schools and conducted forceful recruitment for their criminal activity. A meaningful collaborative approach was impossible in this society due to the magnitude of the problem.

One of the biggest hurdles to fighting economic crime is that the perpetrators actively follow the concurrent interpretations of the authorities and change their actions accordingly. While the threat is constantly evolving and reshaping with technological advancements, the authorities struggle to find solutions for the evolving nature of the problem. For example, when offshore companies as a hiding place for illegal money becomes a popular concern, the perpetrators will migrate toward another complex mechanism.

Sri Lanka on the "Grey List"

In October 2017, the Financial Action Task Force (FATF) listed Sri Lanka as a jurisdiction with strategic AML/CFT deficiencies in the FATF's Compliance Document, which is more commonly identified as the "Grey List."[51] As explained by the Central Bank Governor, "Accordingly, the FIU-Sri Lanka is working towards strengthening its legal and regulatory framework, IT infrastructure including information systems, analytical skills and other capacities, to be in line with international standards, to perform its core functions efficiently. Sri Lanka has made a high-level political commitment to work with the FATF and APG to strengthen the effectiveness of its AML/CFT regime and address any related technical deficiencies."[52]

One of the real setbacks in many territories, including Sri Lanka, is that investigation is conducted after the crime has been committed, thus it is curative mechanism. The preventive measures are absent. The authorities should have mechanisms to trigger to prevent such economic crimes.

From action-centered to actor-centered

Sri Lanka usually has an action-centered approach, which is interrogation after the crime has occurred. The media reports the VIP, Minister, or Governor of the Central Bank was questioned by authorities for so many hours. This is seen by certain fractions of the society as a success story, but unfortunately, the action-centered approach has fewer results when compared with the actor-centered approach. An actor-centered approach is when authorities gather evidence collaboratively and engage in surprise house searches, seizures, and arrests to gather the relevant evidence. This approach is required in Sri Lanka, where media could highlight after the seizure and exposure rather than focus on people walking in and out of FCID.[o]

In this actor-centered approach, as rightly identified by Anne Puonti, there is "a closer collaboration between authorities, because the information needed is dispersed in various files at various agencies.[53] Combined with the efficient tracing of criminal proceeds, this approach has achieved good results in terms of convictions as well as forfeited money. The strategy has been promoted for years, but a recent project found that its application is not widespread."

Three legislations to fight economic crime

The Director of the Commission to Investigate Allegations of Bribery Corruption (CIABOC[p]) General Sarath Jayamanne said about the government: "I am not sure if they had done any research before this commitment,"[54] adding that absence of stringent laws made it difficult to take action against wrongdoers. "Furthermore, the lack of proof also made the prosecution harder, which was worsened by the resource limitation," he said. To bridge this limitation, in 2017, the CIABOC was given powers to amend three pieces of legislation, the Declaration of Assets and Liabilities Law, Bribery Act, and the Bribery Commission Act, which were last amended 1994.

Currently, the Declaration of Assets and Liabilities Law does not have requirements to declare income or expenditure during the year, and the new laws will assist to establish a separate directorate under CIABOC

---

[o]The Financial Crime Investigation Division (FCID) is the law enforcement agency of the government of Sri Lanka tasked with financial crime investigations and law enforcement, established by the 2015 November "Good Governance" government to investigate financial crimes as an agency of the Sri Lanka Police.

[p]Commission To Investigate Allegations Of Bribery Corruption (CIABOC) is a legislative body created under the 17th Amendment of the Constitution of the Democratic Socialist Republic of Sri Lanka to investigate allegations of bribery or corruption under the Bribery Act and the Declaration of Assets and Liabilities Law of 1975.

for asset declaration, which would be done online. The directorate will also have powers to carry out verification processes and forward any suspicious cases to CIABOC. The new laws proposed to the legislation are now with the Legal Draftsman and on final stage according to the Commissioner.

However, it was unfortunate that all these were lengthy processes and implemented at the end of the 2015 Government's term.

National Action Plan for combating Bribery and corruption in SL

CIABOC was entrusted with the task of formulating a National Action Plan for Combating Bribery and Corruption in Sri Lanka. The Action Plan is premised on four strategies namely, Prevention Measures, Value-based Education and Community Engagement, Institutional Strengthening of CIABOC and other Law Enforcement Agencies, and Law and Policy Reforms.[55] Four Handbooks was also released along with the Action Plan, exploring decisive factors which would shape the course of combating bribery and corruption. The four books include the Draft Proposal on Gift Rules; Draft Proposal on Conflict of Interest Rules; Integrity Handbook for State Officials; and Law Amendment Proposal for areas of bribery, asset declaration, Commission Act, election campaign finance, and whistle-blower provision.

Although the Bribery commission has compiled these important materials and strategies to fight economic crime in Sri Lanka, meaningful cooperation will be essential among government agencies and civil society to achieve some tangible results.

Conclusion

Many observers in and outside Sri Lanka wonder why, even after four years since President Sirisena's ascent to power, no high-level official is behind bars, although a lot of publicity was given to corrupt acts of the past. One could think, as explained by Alvesalo and Tombs,[56] that since the perpetrators are often of the same social class as the decision-makers, the level of interest may be impacted, thereby preventing arrests, or maybe the Government did not possess the required competency to carry out the investigations.

Meaningful cooperation is a top priority after learning from the hard way in Sri Lanka; the FIU, which had sufficient information on the accounts linked to the 4/21 terror attack, should have had much better cooperation with other agencies to interdict and prevent economically motivated crimes and save lives. Other nations could learn from the Sri Lankan experience.

Fighting TNS threats is a unique and challenging task faced by the nation today. Instead of merely looking at separate actions, we should analyze the interconnected nature of these actions.[57] To find patterns to connect these actions, the government should maximize their capabilities at FIUs and intelligence agencies to fight AML/CFT crimes, an imperative for nations like Sri Lanka engulfed with TNS threats. We could have prevented the 4/21 extremist attack if we had meaningful cooperation among inter-agencies within the jurisdiction and beyond.

While mechanisms to introduce legislation and implement the national action plan on combating bribery and corruption will add significant value to the entire system, Sri Lanka will need to improve cooperation among domestic and international agencies to overcome the challenges. For domestic cooperation, educating the bureaucracy is essential in this regard, who would take a central role in advising the policymakers.

Economic Crimes and the P118 of Sri Lanka[58]

If the top beam is askew, the bottom beams will be crooked.

Chinese proverb

There is a plague in the streets of Sri Lanka. If this plague has not entered your door steps, your family will still pay an indirect price. Most of us were aware of what ruffled the normal tenor of our lives but had no idea how to fight the plague. The plague is known as "corruption," and it might be inimical to the stability and integrity of the economy, which now threatens the entire nation.

Former President Sirisena explained that he is not in a position to open the newly built hospital in Hambantota, which he laid the foundation for several years ago when he was Minister of Health. "The building is completed but the hospital equipments has gone missing and all funding has been utilized, certain people who were after my term at the Ministry are directly responsible," said President Sirisena to the Director General of Bribery and the Key Note Speaker, Prof. Jayadeva Uyangoda, after a discussion on fighting corruption in Colombo.

Whoever is responsible for robbing public goods should be arrested, regardless of their political hierarchy or affiliation. If the powerful (top beam) in society could commit an economic crime of this nature, one may wonder how we create a society free of corruption and instill such values within the entire community. The President will need to take strict measures to arrest the culprits and strengthen weak government institutions, in order to fight corruption.

According to Auditor General Gamini Wijesinghe[q]: "More than half the state officials would be in jail by now if they were dealt with in the manner in which former presidential secretary Mr. Weeratunga was dealt with and sentenced to prison on charges of misusing State funds."[59] Due to large-scale corruption, the Auditor General suggested the new Audit Bill as a solution to ensure financial discipline in the state sector under the 19th Amendment to the Constitution. Such measures should be given utmost government support and top priority, especially considering the events which unfolded in the recent past. Passing the Audit Bill is not sufficient and the key focus should implementing it, explains the former Auditor General Sarath Chandrasiri Mayadunne.

Economic crimes, such as a powerful minister leasing the entire fishery harbor in Modara (Mutwal),[r] Colombo, a few years ago for a nominal fee was never investigated by the Bribery Commission. It is the duty of the commission to carry out investigation of all crimes, regardless of the culprit's social standing. According to Anura Kumara Dissanayaka,[s] leader of the JVP, "The Bribery Commission has summoned him on two occasions to appear before it to inquire into the harbour tender, but the Minister had not gone there. Instead he influenced the President to remove the Director General of the Bribery Commission."[60] The rule of law should apply equally to all citizens.

According to Prof. Jayadeva Uyangoda, a new "Perpetual Class" has emerged in the Sri Lankan society. This constitutes a new rich middle

---

[q]Gamini Wijesinghe was the 40th Auditor General of Sri Lanka until April 2019.

[r]Mutwal is a seafront municipal ward of Colombo that is located at the mouth of the Kelani river.

[s]Anura Kumara Dissanayaka is a Sri Lankan politician and the current leader of the Janatha Vimukthi Peramuna (JVP).

class, who are much more sophisticated when it comes to influencing politicians, political parties, and campaign funding. There are evident differences between this new rich middle class and past businessmen. This Perpetual Class (PC) exercises control and influence over ministers, high-ranking officials, and decision-making of the state using their financial power. Prof. Uyangoda further explains that there is a need and it is worth researching to understand the influence of such new middle class in our society.

The practice of political funding and lobbying has changed in many societies, including in the US. As Francis Fukuyama rightly identifies in his book, *Political Order and Political Decay*, there were only 175 lobbying firms in 1971, in 1981 number reached 2,500, and by 2013, a whopping 12,000 firms spent US$3.2 billion on lobbying. According to Fukuyama, "it's these firms that distort American public policy across many different areas."[61]

The 2015 Presidential Election followed by the August General Election was held under the central theme "Corruption of the family." Today, the theme has transformed from the Rajapaksa family to another direction, the "P118." The P118 is the list of 118 Members of Parliament (MP) who has accepted funds from Perpetual Treasuries, which has become the discussion among mainstream media in Sri Lanka. During the last few weeks, few MPs were questioned by the authorities; one MP, who authored a book of the infamous bond scam by Perpetual Treasuries, has also accepted Sri Lankan Rupees (LKR) 3 million, which he again justified as giving back to the poor of our society. According to some individuals, there is no such list. Since the government championed and introduced the Right to Information (RTI) Act,[†] the public has a right to know if such a list exists. The RTI Commission, showing its strength, recently ruled that two termination agreements entered into between Sri Lankan and AerCap, which caused great losses to Sri Lankan Airlines, will be released. The order by the commission explains: "where the public purse is concerned, and the alleged financial irregularities of a particular Public Authority are under scrutiny in an Appeal before us, this

---

[†]The Right to Information (RTI) Act introduced by the Government of Sri Lanka is an act of parliament that established that the people have the right to know information regarding which functions of the public are performed using state funds, thereby allowing access to information, responsibility to state institutions to publish information, and responsibility to release information.

Commission will be particularly watchful of the public interest." In the same manner, the commission could assist the public to reveal the P118 list; only this time, the "particular public authority" will be the Parliament of Sri Lanka. Since the RTI is in full motion, politicians also could assist the commission by revealing information to the public, including the former President Rajapaksa, who claimed he has files on the corrupt officials.

Economic crime is perhaps the largest national security threat the nation is facing right now and it directly relates to the financial accountability and transparency of the Public Authority and individuals representing in the Parliament who craft policy protecting the sovereignty of the people. If policymakers could be easily influenced by lobbying groups, foreign policy, national security, and people's sovereignty will be threatened.

In countries such as South Korea or Singapore, if found guilty of financial misappropriation, jail time is assured, regardless of political position. To set the nation in the right path, we should take a leaf from these nations and use drastic measures against corruption. In 1996, rumors spread that Lee Kwan Yew had received improper discounts on property purchases. Mr. Goh Chok Tong, former Prime Minister of Singapore, ordered a full investigation of such alleged improper activities, subsequently finding no evidence. He brought the issue to the Parliament, which held a full debate lasting three days. Lee Kwan Yew said, "I take pride and satisfaction that the question of my two purchases and those of the Deputy Prime Minister, my son, has been subjected to, and not exempted from, scrutiny... It is most important that Singapore remains a place where no one is above scrutiny, that any question of integrity of a minister, however senior, that he has gained benefits either through influence or corrupt practices, be investigated."[62]

Sharing the Singapore experience in an essay for an anthology compiled for the inaugural Anti-Corruption Summit held in London, Prime Minister Lee Hsien Loong identifies four factors key to the Republic's share of success on this score. First, the British steel frame bureaucracy left Singapore with a working system and sound institutions — "English laws, a working civil service, and an efficient and honest judiciary." Second, men who wore white shirts and white trousers symbolized their determination to keep the government clean and incorruptible under the strong and honest leadership of Lee Kwan Yew. Third, Singapore institutionalized a robust, comprehensive, anti-corruption framework that spans laws, enforcement, the public service, and public outreach.

The enactment of the Prevention of Corruption Act (PCA) puts the burden of proof on the accused to show that he acquired his wealth legally, and any unexplained wealth disproportionate to known sources of income is presumed to be from graft and can be confiscated. It also gives extra-territorial jurisdiction, so that the actions of Singaporean citizens overseas are treated the same as actions committed in Singapore, regardless of whether such corrupt acts have consequences for Singapore. "Our anti-corruption agency, the Corrupt Practices Investigation Bureau (CPIB), is well resourced and independent. It is empowered to investigate any person, even police officers and ministers, and conducts public outreach to raise public awareness and shape social norms. We pay public servants fair and realistic wages benchmarked to private sector earnings and, in return, demand the highest standards of integrity and performance." Fourth, over time, Singapore developed a society and culture that eschews corruption and expects and demands a clean system. "They do not condone giving or accepting 'social lubricants' to get things done. They readily report corrupt practices when they encounter them. Singaporeans trust that the law applies to all and that the Government will enforce the laws without fear or favour, even when it may be awkward or embarrassing. Businesses have confidence that, in Singapore, rules are transparent and fairly applied."

Sri Lanka has much to learn from the above four areas. Out of the 72-month Presidential timeframe, there are roughly 15 months or less before the next Presidential election. Can we expect some significant results in the next few months to take place by the Executive who was appointed by the people to hunt the corrupt?

Unexplained Wealth and For What Purpose? A Sri Lankan Perspective[63]

As the 19th century French economist Claude-Frédéric Bastiat explained: "When plunder becomes a way of life for a group of men in a society, over the course of time they create for themselves a legal system that authorises it and a moral code that glorifies it." Bastiat correctly identifies the way a group of people manage to plunder the wealth and use the state legal system to justify the unexplained wealth. Chasing behind unexplained wealth is proven to be complex, time- and resource-consuming, and highly controversial. The plunder of national wealth through corruption pushes poor countries into greater poverty. Sri Lanka is at the 91st place according to the latest CPI[u] Index, slipping further from previous year.

Corruption by public authorities

According to the former Sri Lankan Auditor General Gamini Wijesinghe, "Sri Lanka is the top-ranked country in the world in terms of public sector misappropriation and corruption."[64] His comment depicts the pervasiveness of corruption in the public sector of the country. He added, "the term Good Governance has been sullied at present," but continued to emphasize the need for it. He believes that Good Governance and the honesty of state sector workers are the most important factors for creating a fully functional and efficient state sector.

Panama Papers

In examining many disproportionate wealth cases, the Panama Papers is an example[65] where several prominent business persons in Sri Lanka were named. It is unfortunate that no legal action has been taken against the holders of unexplained wealth in offshore accounts.

In contrast, Pakistan took rigorous action against their Prime Minister for accumulating disproportionate wealth. From Panama Papers to London apartments, the Pakistan authorities have played a commendable role in bringing the corrupt, regardless of social hierarchy, to justice. Nations like Sri Lanka could learn from Pakistan, since no one in the Sri Lankan list from Panama Papers has been proven guilty. Panama Papers are likely to be just the tip of the iceberg, which has been made public, of a multi-national scale spanning international corruption and organized crime.

Unexplained Wealth Orders

It was the Greek philosopher Plato who said that "good people do not need laws to tell them to act responsibly while bad people will find a way around the law." Many affluent PE in the society manage to find a way around the law, and this is seen as two sets of laws applied to the same

---

[u] Corruption Perception Index issues by Transparency International (2017)

community. This will create an unjust system, and the public will lose trust in the state. In March 2017, Transparency International research identified London properties worth a total of £4.2 billion (US$5.4 billion) that were bought by individuals with suspicious wealth.

Unexplained Wealth Orders (UWOs) is a UK court order introduced in January under the 2017 Criminal Finances Act that requires the owner of an asset to explain how they were able to afford that asset, and is definitely a step in the right direction.[66] UWOs could be used against everyone, from a local drug trafficker to an international oligarch or overseas criminal. UWOs target two groups: first is a "politically exposed person" (PEP), such as a politician or well-connected civil servant, as well as people close to them, provided they are not citizens of the European Economic Area. The second is a serious crime suspect, whether in the UK or abroad. UWOs could be used when there is an obvious gap between the value of an asset (which must be worth at least £50,000) and the income of the person who appears to own it, such as a foreign leader who claims to subsist on a modest salary yet owns a range of overseas properties. Luxury apartments in London or large countryside mansions have long been attractive to those seeking to hide money because they are valuable assets and ownership is relatively easy to disguise. Transparency International UK cited UWOs as the most important piece of anti-corruption legislation, alongside the Bribery Act 2010, of the past 30 years. With the appropriate levels of resource and political commitment, UWOs could be an important and powerful tool in the effort to tackle serious crime and corruption in the UK and it could be introduced to many other nations. UWOs may relocate their assets and proceeds of crimes to other jurisdictions with weaker asset recovery regimes. In doing so, a global approach should be considered. Ireland has shown successful results; the main reason for the success of UWOs in Ireland was the creation of a highly effective multi-agency task force — the Criminal Assets Bureau (CAB).[67]

UWOs could also be introduced to nations like Sri Lanka, and governments that have come to power especially with a mandate to curb corruption should implement such measures. The Sri Lankan property industry is also booming, with many luxury apartments close to and above US$1 million, where most of their ownerships are probably from black money. UWOs will easily identify the corrupt in the society. While there is a significant economic inequality in Sri Lanka, with poverty rate above 20%, Aston Martins and Bentleys can be seen in the streets of Colombo. In such settings, UWOs will assist indirectly to minimize inequality in the society. It is pivotal to prevent the economic and social harms created by the laundering of illicit funds through the property market.

Conclusion

In conclusion, unexplained wealth should be taken as a pivotal measure to fight corruption in the society. Rule of law should be applied equally to everyone in the society. We cannot expect results if rules are applied only to a certain sector and not the entire society. Some of the key variables to focus are to develop the expertise and necessary allocation of skills, inter-agency cooperation, appropriate resource allocation, and finally political will.[68] The 2016 London Anti-corruption Summit proposed to establish an International Anti-Corruption Centre, which was commended by former President Sirisena. He stated that, "all of us as leaders need to act collectively to strengthen our own law enforcement agencies to track the corrupt and recover the proceeds of corruption." However, the prevailing political will in achieving said goals are questionable. The entire society has a role to play when fighting corruption, as the task is not only limited to the regulators, bribery commissions, and state sector. Private sector and individual voices in the society, including whistleblowers, could also play a leading role in combating cases of unexplained wealth.

Authentic Leadership of Martin Luther King Jr.[69]

Our lives begin to end the day we become silent about things that matter.

Martin Luther King, Jr.

We cannot imagine a bus today segregated according to skin color. That period of history is ugly. It took many lives and struggles to achieve the progress we enjoy in the present. A 39-year-old young Baptist minister was organizing a march on the final day of his life in Memphis in support of the city sanitation workers for economic equality. It was 50 years ago, on April 4, 1968, the youngest Nobel laureate at that time, the courageous iconic leader of the civil rights movement, Rev. Dr. Martin Luther King Jr. was assassinated outside his room at Lorraine Motel in Memphis, Tennessee. It was a single bullet that led to his fall.

On the balcony in front of his room 306, little did his killer understand the value of Martin Luther King's presence. The killer silenced an advocate against racial injustice and a voice for the voiceless African American at the time of segregation in American society. Dr. King strongly believed in using non-violence to win suppressed rights at that time, borrowing words and deeds of his mentor Mahatma Gandhi, who was also gunned down in another corner of the world.

Reading Dr. King in retrospect, Bill George, a Senior fellow at Harvard Business School and expert of leadership, explains: "King's legacy of staying true to his beliefs, pursuing his purpose, and exhibiting courage under pressure are profound lessons for leaders in all walks of life."[70] The most important lesson that all leaders can draw today from King's leadership, George explains, is to "recognize how you can make a difference in the world through your leadership, and then to step up to the challenge when opportunities present themselves. When you do so, undoubtedly you will encounter roadblocks and opposition. That's when it becomes imperative to have the courage and resilience to persevere in order to fulfill your mission. In a very real sense, the character you demonstrate in achieving your purpose is the legacy you leave to those leaders coming along behind you."

According to Peter G. Northouse, "Leadership is a process whereby an individual influences a group of individuals to achieve a common goal."[71] Dr. King's design of the process to influence a group and subsequently the entire nation toward one common goal was evident in his leadership. John P. Kotter's definition on leadership is fundamentally about change and what leaders do is create the system to elevate others to a whole new level to take advantage of new opportunities. Dr. King elevated the civil rights movement and all the followers to a different height through his non-violent marches across the nation, which eventually gained the attention of the Government at that time to address the issue.

Dr. King's inspiring oration and meaningful emotion swept the enormous crowd gathered at Washington on August 28, 1962. A strong and powerful message was articulated in his "I Have a Dream" speech to call for an end to racism and restore dignity to the society he was living in. The speech was a reminder that now is the time to take action and "is no time to engage in the luxury of cooling off or to take the tranquilizing drug of gradualism. Now is the time to make real the promise of democracy. Now is the time to rise from the dark desolate valley of segregation to the sunlit path of racial justice. Now is the time to lift our nation from the quicksands of racial injustice to the solid rock of brotherhood."[72] This was a strong appeal which still echoes in our society; to secure individual freedom and equality, regardless of race, religion, cast, class, or skin color was the central theme of Dr. King's dream, and to achieve his dream "that my four little children will one day live in a nation where they will not be judged by the color of their skin but by the content of their character,"[73] he had to transform the thinking pattern of the society at that time.

Dr. King's self-confidence and passion inspired others, especially his courage to be a fearless leader, putting himself in danger many times in his short life. Despite being imprisoned 30 times, he did not change his stance but navigated to achieve his goals despite the obstacles. Dr. King believed in mobilizing large crowds to overcome the obstacles: "fire hoses can't deal with a million people. Yes, the water will give out. Dogs can't bite a million people. The United States Army wouldn't know how to deal with a million people..."[74] he said.

One of his last writings was entitled "The World House," a brilliant piece worth revisiting today, especially to understand the importance of co-existence. Dr. King writes "A widely separated family inherits a house in which they have to live together. This is the great new problem of mankind. We have inherited a large house, a great "world house"[75] in which we have to live together — black and white, Easterner and Westerner, Gentile and Jew, Catholic and Protestant, Moslem and Hindu — a family unduly separated in ideas, culture and interest, who, because we can never again live apart, must learn somehow to live with each other in peace... We still have a choice today: nonviolent coexistence or violent co-annihilation. This may well be mankind's last chance to choose between chaos and community."

His strategic thinking as a leader is seen by the decisions he made to stage demonstrations at the right time for the television to make a significant impact to the entire nation. Dr. King voiced against the Vietnam War at that time, and this was called treasonous, consorting with a foreign power and against the national interest. At time of his death, he was under serious pressure from Government due to his anti-war stance. On his last visit to Memphis, Dr. King explained to his follower, Jesse Jackson: "You know, we got to go on to Memphis. We cannot leave those sanitation workers stranded. They have a right to watch their children graduate from high school and college. They have the same human rights that other people have. We're going on to Memphis. Then we're going to

Washington, if necessary, and tie up traffic and go to jail. We're going to force this Congress to shift from killing abroad to healing at home."[76]

Dr. King's assassination caused widespread emotional responses and subsequent political tensions. Around 76 riots broke out, with 2,000 people injured, 28,000 jailed, and 46 killed. Despite the ugly incidents on the same day in Indianapolis, Robert F. Kennedy (RFK) was addressing a gathering, which created a deferent tone, a hope of creating a different society. The ripple of hope created on this day by RFK was a cooler air that eased the strain at that moment, if not a flutter of hope. The plea was the same message of Dr. King for national transcendence of racial, ethnic, and generational mistrust to be healed, and it was the first time he spoke of losing his own brother. It was ironic and tragic that RFK was also killed two months later at another hotel, this time the Ambassador Hotel in California.

Looking back 50 years later, Dr. King's leadership and philosophy of non-violence shines for its authenticity. As his daughter Bernice A. King rightly said, "The leader of the movement [Dr. King] was able to define it very clearly, we lost his voice and no one has emerged since that time to articulate the way he did."

Endnotes

Chapter 1

1. The article was initially published by Hudson Institute, Washington DC, USA. http://www.southasiaathudson.org/blog/2019/5/7/easter-sunday-in-sri-lanka-crisis-correction-and-hope
2. https://www.nytimes.com/2019/02/28/world/middleeast/trump-isis-territory.htm
3. https://www.kbzk.com/cnn-europe-mideast-africa/2019/03/23/isis-has-lost-its-final-stronghold-in-syria-the-syrian-democratic-forces-says/
4. https://www.bbc.com/news/world-middle-east-45547595
5. https://www.rsis.edu.sg/rsis-publication/rsis/islamic-state-new-phase-of-global-expansion/#.Xuo-5C1h0_U
6. The article was initially published by Hudson Institute.
7. https://www.nytimes.com/2019/03/11/world/asia/modi-india-election.html
8. https://www.jstor.org/stable/10.1017/s0022381614000504?seq=1
9. IPCS, June 17, 2019.
10. This article was initially published by Hudson Institute, Washington DC, USA. http://www.southasiaathudson.org/blog/2019/11/20/implementation-of-a-national-defence-policy-for-sri-lanka
11. PSC Full Report: https://www.parliament.lk/uploads/comreports/sc-april-attacks-report-en.pdf
12. DCAF Security Sector Integrity: https://securitysectorintegrity.com/defence-management/defence-policy/
13. "Towards a Clear Defence Policy," in *P.V. Narasimha Rao Selected Speeches. Volume IV: July 1994–June 1995,* Government of India, 1995, p. 125.

14. https://idsa.in/policybrief/indias-defence-and-security-priorities-skalyanaraman-240518#footnote6_4dtemjx

15. SL landslide and rain: https://www.theguardian.com/world/2016/may/18/sri-lanka-hundreds-of-families-missing-after-landslide-buries-three-villages

16. SL Garbage dump collapse: https://www.nytimes.com/2017/04/15/world/asia/sri-lanka-garbage-dump-collapse.html

17. This article was initially published by Hudson Institute, Washington DC, USA. http://www.southasiaathudson.org/blog/2019/11/4/a-reappraisal-of-maritime-defence-for-sri-lanka?fbclid=IwAR058Q0nFV4dqTCohSQH-X0pKDUlFDc9gbXG9Hsd0qDQ61eGMyso8o5Rq5E

18. "Struggle to Build China Into a World Sci-Tech Power" — Speech at the National Sci-Tech Innovation Meeting, Meeting of the Two Academies, and the 9th Congress of the China Association of Science and Technology, May 30, 2016, 新华 *Xinhua*, May 31, 2016. Available at: www.xinhuanet.com/politics/2016-05/31/c_1118965169.htm

19. Godawaya: An ancient port city. See: https://www.archaeology.lk/668

20. *Financial Times*, "China signs 99-year lease on Sri Lanka's Hambantota Port." Available at: https://www.ft.com/content/e150ef0c-de37-11e7-a8a4-0a1e63a52f9c

21. Martello Tower Hambantota by Anuradha Piyadasa. See: https://www.archaeology.lk/5791

22. Statement of Admiral Harry B. Harris Jr., U.S. Navy Commander, U.S. Pacific Command Before the House Armed Services Committee on U.S. Pacific Command Posture, 14 February 2018, https://docs.house.gov/meetings/AS/AS00/20180214/106847/HHRG-115-AS00-Wstate-HarrisJrH-20180214.pdf

23. *The Economic Times* (2018). "Decoding Chinese submarine 'sightings' in South Asia, eroding New Delhi's strategic primacy." Available at: https://economictimes.indiatimes.com/news/defence/decoding-chinese-submarine-sightings-in-south-asia-eroding-new-delhis-strategic-primacy/articleshow/66631063.cms?from=mdr

24. R. D. Martinson and P. A. Dutton, "China's Distant-Ocean Survey Activities: Implications for U.S. National Security." CMSI China Maritime Reports 3, 2018.

25. "Xiang Yang Hong 01" research vessel starts its second section of 2019 northeast Indian Ocean Cruise." Available at: http://en.fio.org.cn/pages/newsshow/?3-5-1-735

26. UNCLOS Part XIII. See: https://www.un.org/depts/los/convention_agreements/texts/unclos/part13.htm

27. Fish Hook Sea bed SOSUS Network. See: https://defence.pk/pdf/threads/fish-hook-sea-bed-sosus-network.448398/

28. *The Times of India*, National Command Control Communication Intelligence (NC3I). Available at: http://timesofindia.indiatimes.com/articleshow/45237364.cms?utm_source=contentofinterest&utm_medium=text&utm_campaign=cppst

29. Parrikar, https://pib.gov.in/newsite/printrelease.aspx?relid=111697

30. *Daily News*, "Government to spend 900m for MRCC." Available at: http://www.dailynews.lk/2017/04/06/local/112650/govt-spend-rs-900-m-mrcc

31. *Sunday Times*, "Jaffna International Airport to be declared open." Available at: http://www.sundaytimes.lk/article/1106398/jaffna-international-airport-to-be-declared-open-today-flights-to-operate-from-november

32. The MCC Compact Grant program consists of two projects: the Transport Project and the Land Project. The latter includes creating an inventory and mapping state land parcels, creating a deeds registry improvement, land valuation system, and establishing a Land Policy Research Group (LPRG) to advise the government on land policy decisions. "Cabinet green lights MCC." http://www.ft.lk/top-story/Cabinet-greenlights-480-m-MCC-Compact-deal-with-US/26-688661

33. Y. Shlomi (2014). "Sri Lanka and the Tamil Tigers: Conflict and legitimacy," *Military and Strategic Affairs*, Vol. 6, No. 2, pp. 65–82.

34. *Ground Views* (2018). "War crimes in Sri Lanka: Stain or slander?" Available at: https://groundviews.org/2018/09/16/war-crimes-in-sri-lanka-stain-or-slander/

35. *The Guardian* (2018). "Sri Lanka declares state of emergency after communal violence." Available at: https://www.theguardian.com/world/2018/mar/06/sri-lanka-declares-state-of-emergency-after-communal-violence

36. Disaster Management Centre, United Nations Development Programme in Sri Lanka (2014). "National Report on Disaster Risk, Poverty and Human Development Relationship."

37. The Global Competitiveness Report 2018. See: https://www.weforum.org/reports/the-global-competitveness-report-2018

38. "Meethotamulla Garbage Dump — A man-made disaster creates history." Available at: https://apad.lk/index.php/meethotamulla-garbage-dump-a-man-made-disaster-creates-history/

39. F. G. Adams, J. R. Behrman and M. Boldin (1991). "Government expenditures, defence and economic growth in LDCs: A revised perspective," *Conflict Management and Peace Science*, Vol. 11, No. 2, pp. 19–35.

40. Commonwealth Observer Group (2015). "Sri Lanka Presidential Election." https://thecommonwealth.org/sites/default/files/news-items/documents/SL%20PE%202015%20COG%20Report%20FINAL.pdf

41. www.colombogazette.com (accessed February 2, 2015).

42. SPIEGEL Interview with Mangala Samaraweera, Foreign Minister. Available at: https://www.mfa.gov.lk/ta/6259-isaslecture-fm/

43. S. Bhatt, P. W. Gething, O. J. Brady, J. P. Messina, A. W. Farlow, C. L. Moyes *et al.* "The global distribution and burden of dengue," *Nature*, Vol. 496, pp. 504–507.

44. Department of Community Medicine, Faculty of Medicine, University of Colombo (2016). "Situational analysis on occupational health and safety in Sri Lanka," World Health Organization Collaborating Centre for Training and Research in Occupational Health.

45. S. H. Dahal (2003). *Internal Conflict and Regional Security in South Asia: Approaches, Perspectives and Policies.* United Nations Publications, UNIDIR.

46. National Archives, UK. "The human rights situation in Sri Lanka." Available at: https://webarchive.nationalarchives.gov.uk/20151002161647/http://arabic.fco.gov.uk//human-rights-in-countries-of-concern/sri-lanka/quarterly-updates-sri-lanka/

47. A. K. Jeewaka Saman Kumara (2015). "Non-traditional security disputes of Sri Lanka." Senior Lecturer, Department of Political Science, University of Peradeniya, Sri Lanka.

48. G. Vasudeva (2002). "Environmental security: A South Asian perspective," Tata Energy and Resources Institute, Arlington.

49. Mely Caballero-Anthony, Alistair D. B. Cook, Pau Khan Khup Hangzo, Lina Gong and Manpavan Kaur (2013). "Internal Conflict." In *Non-Traditional Security in Asia: Issues, Challenges and Framework for Action*, ISEAS, Singapore, p. 21.

50. Paper presented at the National IT Conference, October 3, 2018.

51. T. Kopan, K. Holmes and S. Collinson (2015). "U.S., China say they won't engage in cybertheft." [online] *CNN News.* Available at: https://edition.cnn.com/2015/09/25/politics/us-china-cyber-theft-hack/index.html (accessed October 1, 2018).

52. S. Shane and M. Mazzetti (2018). "The plot to subvert an election." [online] *The New York Times.* Available at: https://www.nytimes.com/interactive/2018/09/20/us/politics/russia-interference-election-trump-clinton.html (accessed October 1, 2018).

53. A. Gupta (2016). "Securing cyber space: A national security perspective," in C. Samuel and M. Sharma (eds.) *Securing Cyberspace: International and Asian Perspectives*, Pentagon Press, New Delhi, pp. 17–22.

54. B. Buzan (1991). *People, States and Fear: An Agenda for International Security Studies in the Post-Cold War Era.* Harvester Wheatsheaf, London.

55. F. Hare (2010). "The Cyber Threat to National Security: Why Can't We Agree?" *CCD COE* Publications, Estonia, p. 218.

56. Experts from the World Economic Forum's Expert Network, curated in partnership with Benjamin Fung, Canada Research Chair in Data Mining for

Cybersecurity, Associate Professor, School of Information Studies, McGill University.

57. RBR, https://www.rbrlondon.com/research/.

58. *The Indian Express* (2017). "'To counter China', India-Sri Lanka Joint Military Exercise in Pune from Oct 13." Available at: https://indianexpress.com/article/india/to-counter-china-india-sri-lanka-joint-military-exercise-in-pune-from-oct-13-4884495/

59. V. Kaura (2018). "Sri Lankan soldiers to visit Bodh Gaya: India employs military diplomacy, cultural outreach to offset Chinese offensive." Available at: https://www.firstpost.com/world/sri-lankan-soldiers-to-visit-bodh-gaya-india-employs-military-diplomacy-cultural-outreach-to-offset-chinese-offensive-4587471.html

60. H. Biyagama (2018). "National cyber security policy in the offing: Defence Secretary." *Daily FT.* Available at: http://www.ft.lk/front-page/National-cyber-security-policy-in-the-offing--Defence-Secretary/44-663274

61. This article was initially published by Hudson Institute, Washington DC, USA. http://www.southasiaathudson.org/blog/2019/10/17/aerial-fears

62. https://singularityhub.com/2018/09/07/the-4-waves-of-ai-and-why-china-has-an-edge/

63. https://www.bbc.com/news/world-middle-east-46822429

64. https://www.rand.org/blog/2018/06/toy-drones-and-twitter-the-ability-of-individuals-to.html

65. Initially published in http://www.icip-perlapau.cat/numero34/pdf-eng/Per-la-Pau-n34-ac-4.pdf

66. *National Reconciliation Reports (2011–2014)*, Lakshman Kadirgamar Institute of International Relations and Strategic Studies.

67. Sri Lanka shift on civil war anniversary (2015).

68. *Indian Express* (2017). "Tamil leaders in Sri Lanka celebrate LTTE chief Prabhakaran's 63rd birthday anniversary." Available at: https://www.newindianexpress.com/world/2017/nov/27/tamil-leaders-in-sri-lanka-celebrate-ltte-chief-prabhakarans-63rd-birthday-anniversary-1712398.html

69. https://www.newsfirst.lk/2016/01/09/pardoned-former-ltte-cadre-returns-home-praises-president-sirisena/124209/?shared=email&msg=fail&mode=list

70. Statement by Justin Trudeau, the Prime Minister of Canada, on the ninth anniversary of the end of the war in Sri Lanka (2018).

71. *National Reconciliation Reports* (2011–2014), Lakshman Kadirgamar Institute of International Relations and Strategic Studies.

72. The discussion was held at the Lakshman Kadirgamar Institute, Sri Lanka. 7. Interpeace organization.

73. World Economic Forum GCI Report (2017).

74. A. Abeyagoonasekera (2018). "Racism, riots, and the Sri Lankan state," IPCS.

75. Weerasinghe (2018). "Education: Towards sustainable peace and shared economic prosperity. Education empowerment and transformation."
76. Published in *The Diplomatist*, February 2018.
77. A version of this paper was published by International Peace Research Initiative (IPRI), NIAS, India, on April 21, 2020.
78. *RAND.*   https://www.rand.org/blog/2019/05/sri-lankas-easter-attacks-dismantling-myths-to-prevent.html
79. https://www.vaticannews.va/en/church/news/2020-04/sri-lanka-easter-2019-church-bombing-ranjith-forgiveness.html
80. BBC, "Easter Sunday Attack 21/04/2019 documentary." https://youtube.com/RQCp50EDrD
81. https://www.parliament.lk/uploads/comreports/sc-april-attacks-report-en.pdf
82. http://www.colombopage.com/archive_19B/Dec02_1575307825CH.php l

Chapter 2

1. https://www.colombotelegraph.com/index.php/geopolitical-scales-of-one-belt-one-road/
2. https://nationalinterest.org/feature/traveling-china's-new-silk-road-13635
3. P. Khanna (2019). *The Future is Asian.*
4. https://foreignpolicy.com/2018/12/10/the-death-of-global-order-was-caused-by-clinton-bush-and-obama/
5. The article was initially published by the IPCS, New Delhi.
6. "Strategies for the Indo-Pacific: Perceptions of the U.S. and Like-Minded Countries," Hudson Institute, December 2019,
7. http://embassy.nettech.it/content/sri-lanka-italy-relations
8. S. R. Nagy (2019). "Coming in from the cold? Canada's Indo-Pacific possibilities & conundrum," in *Strategies in the Indo-Pacific: Perception of the US and its Like-minded Countries*. Hudson Institute, Washington D.C.
9. R. D. Kaplan (2010). *Monsoon: The Indian Ocean and the Future of American Power*, Random House, New York.
10. https://lk.usembassy.gov/remarks-adm-harry-harris/
11. https://thediplomat.com/2015/01/china-india-and-sri-lankas-change-of-guard/
12. Published by Heidelberg University, May 5, 2019.
13. C. Xueyuan, BRI Seminar, Colombo. Available at: http://lk.china-embassy.org/eng/xwdt/t1614328.htm
14. R. Chaudhury (2019). "How India views the Indo-Pacific".
15. D. Sevastopulo (2017). "Trump gives glimpse of 'Indo-Pacific' strategy to counter China," *Financial Times*, November 10, 2017. Available at: https://www.ft.com/content/e6d17fd6-c623-11e7-a1d2-6786f39ef675.

16. N. Satoru (2019). "Competing visions: BRI vs FOIP?"
17. K. Ranasighe, South Asian BRI.
18. H. Pant (2019). "India, BRI, and Delhi's Indo-Pacific Strategy."
19. *The Hindustan Times* (2017). "India has its reasons to boycott China's Belt Road Initiative," May 17. Available at: https:// www.hindustantimes.com/editorials/india-has-its-reasons-to-boycott-china-s-belt-road-initiative/story-kbLQ7Km9b9fNJTpL5hlMSO.html (accessed October 11, 2018).
20. J. Mearsheimer (2001). *The Tragedy of Great Power Politics*, W. W. Norton & Company, New York, pp. 157–158.
21. R. Chaudhury (2019). "How India Views The Indo-Pacific."
22. Brewster, *India as a Pacific Power, op cit.*, pp. 40–41.
23. Grare (2017). *India turns East*, Penguin.
24. "Vice President Mike Pence's remarks on the Administration's policy towards China," Hudson Institute, October 4, 2018. Available at: https:// www.hudson.org/events/1610-vice-president-mike-pence-s-remarks-on-the-administration-s-policy-towards-china102018 (accessed March 7, 2019).
25. *Ibid.*
26. H. Davidson (2018). "Warning sounded over China's 'debtbook diplomacy,'" *The Guardian*, May 15. Available at: https://www. theguardian.com/world/2018/may/15/warning-sounded-over-chinas-debtbook-diplomacy (accessed October 10, 2018).
27. M. Fernandez (2019). "Is China's investment in Sri Lankan project a debt trap?" *Al Jazeera*, January 16. Available at: https://www.aljazeera.com/news/2019/01/chinas-investment-sri-lankan-project-debt-trap-190116190240067.html (accessed January 19, 2019).
28. "Sri Lanka probes Chinese firm over claims it bribed former president Rajapaksa," *Reuters/SCMP*, July 24, 2015. Available at: https://www.scmp.com/news/asia/south-asia/article/1843557/sri-lanka-probes-chinese-firm-over-claims- it-bribed-former (accessed January 11, 2019).
29. A. Aneez and R. Sirilal (2014). "Chinese submarine docks in Sri Lanka despite Indian concerns," *Reuters*, November 2. Available at: https://www.reuters.com/article/sri-lanka-china-submarine/chinese-submarine-docks-in-sri-lanka-despite-indian-concerns-idINKBN0IM0LU20141102 (accessed October 10, 2018).
30. R. Singh (2018). "Pakistan, China scaling up military at lightning speed; fund crunch crippling India, warns army," *Hindustan Times*, March 13. Available at: https://www.hindustantimes.com/india-news/army-says-it-lacks-funds-to-buy- ammunition-counter-china-pakistan/story-4bfbXOgIr-eRlRvrmDN0SxL.html (accessed October 12, 2018).
31. CNN (2019). "Jimmy Carter, Trump discuss administration's China trade talks." https://edition.cnn.com/2019/04/15/politics/jimmy-carter-trump-china/index.html
32. J. Mearsheimer (2019). *The Great Delusion*, Yale University Press.

33. L. Seligman (2019). "U.S. military wary of China's foothold in Venezuela," *Foreign Policy*, April 8. Available at: https://foreignpolicy.com/2019/04/08/us-military-wary-of-chinas-foothold-in-venezuela-maduro-faller-guaido-trump-pentagon/

34. S. Walt (2018). *The Hell of Good Intentions: America's Foreign Policy Elite and the Decline of U.S.*

35. P. Khanna (2019). *Future is Asian.*

36. A. Abeyagoonasekera (2019). *Sri Lanka at Crossroads*, World Scientific, Singapore.

37. A. Abeyagoonasekera (2019). "Geopolitical scales of One Belt One Road," Hudson Institute.

38. Kadirgamar Institute (LKIIRSS), Seminar on the 21st century MSR, November 7, 2014.

39. R. Wickramasinghe (2019). Interview with China Central Television (CCTV), April 15. Available at: http://www.adaderana.lk/news.php?mode=beauti&nid=54397

40. The article was initially published by Hudson Institute, Washington DC. Available at: http://www.southasiaathudson.org/blog/2018/11/25/disruptions-and-democracy-the-sri-lankan-political-crisis-through-a-geopolitical-lens

41. http://southasiajournal.net/trumpism-and-the-diplomatic-dragon-balancing-interests-in-the-new-year/

42. Bay of Bengal Initiative for Multi-Sectoral Technical and Economic Cooperation (BIMSTEC) workshop at the National University Singapore (ISAS) on 24th September 2018. The workshop themed "BIMSTEC at 20: Priorities and Prospects" was organized by Institute of South Asian Studies (ISAS), Consortium of South Asian Think Tanks (COSATT) and Konrad Adenauer Stiftung (KAS).

43. C. Xavier (2018). "Bridging the Bay of Bengal: Towards a stronger BIMSTEC," Carnegie. Available at: https://carnegieendowment.org/files/CP_325_Xavier_Bay_of_Bengal_INLINE.pdf (accessed October 11, 2018).

44. D. R. Chaudhury (2018). "India planning to set up SEZ in Myanmar's Sittwe," *Economic Times*, August 2. Available at: http://economictimes.indiatimes.com/news/politics-and-nation/india-planning-to-set-up-sez-in-myanmars-sittwe/articleshow/53496839.cms (accessed October 11, 2018).

45. https://www.news.lk/news/politics/item/22108-take-collective-steps-against-drug-menace

46. https://www.outlookindia.com/newsscroll/india-stresses-on-connectivity-within-bimstec-region/1373183/?next

47. https://www.ips.lk/wp-content/uploads/2017/03/Nation_10June_Regional-economic-integration.pdf

48. https://lki.lk/publication/bimstec-and-sri-lanka-a-potential-agenda-for-2018-2020/

49. *Ibid.*
50. https://bimstec.org/?page_id=266
51. S. Kelegama (2016). "Regional economic integration in the Bay of Bengal," *Daily Star*, February 25. Available at: http://www.thedailystar.net/op-ed/economics/regional-economic-integration-the-bay-bengal-660181 (accessed October 11, 2018).
52. R. Bhatia (2017). "Brighter prospects ahead for BIMSTEC." Available at: https://www.gatewayhouse.in/brighter-prospects-bimstec/ (accessed October 23, 2018).
53. https://www.kas.de/c/document_library/get_file?uuid=f3daf8b4-8354-3f53-7a56-8da3f660e28a&groupId=252038
54. World Bank, "Poverty and Equity Data Portal Pakistan." Available at: http://povertydata.worldbank.org/poverty/ country/PAK.
55. "The Global Competitiveness Report 2017–2018." Available at: http://www3.weforum.org/docs/GCR2017-2018/05FullReport/TheGlobalCompetitivenessReport2017%E2%80%932018.pdf.
56. World Bank, "South Asia: Growth and Regional Integration," Washington DC. Available at: http://documents1.worldbank.org/curated/en/843381468334773128/pdf/378580SAS.pdf (accessed August 3, 2020).
57. *Ibid.*
58. U. Sinha (2016). *Riverine Neighbourhood: Hydropolitics in South Asia*, Pentagon Press, New Delhi.
59. P. Kher (2013). "Political economy of regional integration in South Asia," UNCTAD. Available at: http://unctad.org/en/PublicationsLibrary/ecidc-2013misc1_bp5.pdf.
60. M. Arndt (2013). *Regional Multilateralism in South Asia*.
61. K. Ohmae (1995). *The End of the Nation State: The Rise of Regional Economies*, p. 80.
62. *Ibid.*
63. P. Kher, "Political economy of regional integration in South Asia," UNCTAD. Available at: http://unctad.org/en/PublicationsLibrary/ecidc-2013misc1_bp5.pdf.
64. Conferences on Interaction and Confidence Building Measures in Asia (CICA). Secretariat Seminar on "Military-Political Dimension" among CICA member countries, Asthana, Kazakhstan, October 16, 2018.

Chapter 3

1. This article was published by ORF. "Raisina Debates," January 14, 2020. Available at: https://www.orfonline.org/expert-speak/strategic-stability-in-the-new-decade-ports-of-asia-in-a-period-of-escalation-60183/

2. http://www.ft.lk/front-page/President-Rajapaksa-says-leasing-H-tota-Port-was-a-mistake-calls-for-renegotiation-with-China/44-690388
3. https://www.theatlantic.com/politics/archive/2020/01/what-iranian-way-war-looks-like/604438/
4. US IPSR 2019 Indo-Pacific Strategy Report refers to China as a Revisionist Power.
5. https://menafn.com/1099389015/On-Hambantota-port-Prez-Gotabaya-Rajapaksa-was-quoted-out-of-context-says-PM-Mahinda-Rajapaksa
6. https://www.timesofisrael.com/shin-bet-chief-said-to-warn-chinese-investment-in-israel-poses-security-threat/
7. https://www.congress.gov/congressional-report/116th-congress/senate-report/48/1?overview=closed
8. https://www.businessinsider.com/sri-lanka-port-city-dubai-2018-9?r=US&IR=T
9. https://www.iiss.org/blogs/analysis/2019/12/sri-lanka-and-india-address-shared-ct-challenge
10. http://www.xinhuanet.com/english/asiapacific/2020-01/02/c_138674497.htm
11. https://www.orfonline.org/expert-speak/strategic-stability-in-the-new-decade-ports-of-asia-in-a-period-of-escalation-60183/#_edn9
12. The article was initially published by *The Diplomat.* Available at: https://thediplomat.com/2018/10/sri-lanka-the-indian-ocean-and-the-new-era-of-great-power-competition/
13. The article was initially published by Hudson Institute
14. Published by ORF India on February 20, 2020.
15. Leo Kelion, "Huawei set for limited role in UK 5G networks," *BBC*, January 20, 2020. Available at: https://www.bbc.com/news/technology-51283059 (accessed August 5, 2020).
16. https://www.orfonline.org/raisina-dialogue/
17. BBC, "US charges three researchers with lying about links to China," January 28, 2020. Available at: https://www.bbc.com/news/world-us-canada-51288854 (accessed August 5, 2020).
18. https://www.state.gov/blue-dot-network/
19. H. Kissinger, *World Order*, Penguin Books, 2014. "Talented strategist Klement von Metternich was guided by the motto that to maintain stable international relations you needed to acknowledge the true interests of all actors and not just those of your own."
20. G. Wignaraja (2019). "Grappling with great power rivalries: Reflections on Sri Lanka's engagement with the United States and China," SWP Working Paper, November. Available at: https://lki.lk/wp-content/uploads/2019/12/BCAS_2019_Dr_Ganeshan_Wignaraja_Sri_Lanka.pdf (accessed August 5, 2020).

21. Initially published in http://southasiajournal.net/patterns-to-politics-entering-2019/
22. http://penelope.uchicago.edu/Thayer/e/roman/texts/plutarch/lives/alexander*/3.html
23. https://frenndw.files.wordpress.com/2011/03/geopol-the-geopolitics-reader.pdf
24. Initially published in https://www.orfonline.org/expert-speak/rajapaksas-leadership-in-sri-lankas-68634/
25. http://www.dailymirror.lk/print/front_page/Interview-with-BBC-Maithri-continues-to-deny-knowledge-of-Easter-attack-beforehand/238-190223
26. https://www.bbc.com/news/world-europe-19401598
27. http://www.sundaytimes.lk/200614/news/jica-suspends-funding-for-cable-project-406001.html
28. https://www.presidentsoffice.gov.lk/index.php/2020/06/18/president-xi-applauds-sri-lankas-successful-fight-against-covid-19/?lang=en
29. https://m.thewire.in/article/external/shivshankar-menon-interview-china/amp?__twitter_impression=true
30. https://www.deccanherald.com/opinion/beijing-s-season-of-all-round-assertion-849286.html?fbclid=IwAR1dVUluJ-3Iz07Z60KolDA5fD5_Mrcu8mnzIfapoQkaiEe9hPqCz9CwceY
31. https://timesofindia.indiatimes.com/india/g-haan-trump-wants-to-expand-g7-to-g10/11-to-include-india/articleshow/76116297.cms
32. http://www.southasiaanalysis.org/node/2234
33. https://www.9dashline.com/article/covid-19-chinas-adventurism-with-taiwan-and-the-south-china-sea
34. https://asia.nikkei.com/Politics/International-relations/India-and-Australia-sign-military-pact-as-China-tensions-rise
35. https://twitter.com/detresfa_/status/1259711974792810498
36. https://www.orfonline.org/research/india-has-a-bigger-worry-than-lac-china-now-expanding-military-footprint-in-indian-ocean-67732/

Chapter 4

1. http://www.dailymirror.lk/features/Leviathan-in-an-island-democracy/185-153274
2. Published in http://southasiajournal.net/sri-lanka-sustaining-democracy-%EF%BB%BF/
3. http://southasiajournal.net/disruptions-and-democracy-the-sri-lankan-political-crisis-through-a-geopolitical-lens/
4. https://www.goodreads.com/work/quotes/57250303-on-grand-strategy

5. Published by US Department of Defence (NESA Center), April 21, 2020. Available at: https://nesa-center.org/managing-systemic-risks-during-the-pandemic/
6. J. Lynn (2010). "WHO to review its handling of the H1N1 flu pandemic." *Reuters*, January 12. Available at: https://www.reuters.com/article/us-flu-who/who-to-review-its-handling-of-h1n1-flu-pandemic-idUSTRE5BL2ZT20100112
7. E. Rutnam (2020). "Sri Lanka must ensure China is held accountable: US Lawyer." Available at: http://www.dailymirror.lk/hard-talk/Sri-Lanka-must-ensure-China-is-held-accountableUS- Lawyer/334-185719
8. R. Keohane and J. Nye (1977). *Power and Interdependence: World Politics in Transition*. Little Brown, Boston.
9. E. Lorenz (1963). "Deterministic nonperiodic flow," *Journal of the Atmospheric Sciences*, Vol. 20(2), pp. 130–141.
10. I. Goldin and M. Mariathasan (2015). *The Butterfly Defect*. Princeton University Press, Boston, MA, USA.
11. J. Dempsey (2020). "The coronavirus pandemic should end Europe's comfort zone," March 24, Carnegie Europe. Available at: https://carnegieeurope.eu/strategiceurope/81352
12. R. Bhatia, Gateway House. See: https://www.gatewayhouse.in
13. S. R. Hoole, "Democracy in crisis: Avoiding dictatorship." Available at: https://www.colombotelegraph.com/index.php/democracy-in-crisis-avoiding-dictatorship/?fbclid=IwAR2K2nKiIA-BHblxYwIKLpDT7_HdEaRFfaqs-VGYrMATbBjXB4e3I5C7mr8
14. R. P. Rannan-Eliya, "Sri Lanka needs rapid expansion of testing," *Daily Mirror*, http://www.dailymirror.lk/news-features/Sri-Lanka-needs-rapid-expansion-of-testing/131- 185909
15. I. Goldin and M. Mariathasan (2015). *The Butterfly Defect*. Princeton University Press, Boston, MA, USA.
16. Observer Research Foundation (ORF) New Delhi. Available at: https://www.orfonline.org/expert-speak/sri-lanka-facing-geopolitics-of-covid-19-to-cold-war-2-0-66169/
17. https://www.csmonitor.com/USA/Politics/2016/0502/Should-Trump-be-using-rape-to-describe-US-China-relations
18. https://foreignpolicy.com/2020/05/04/pompeo-continues-china-blame-game/
19. https://www.scmp.com/news/world/united-states-canada/article/3082665/china-has-history-infecting-world-us-secretary
20. Wolf Worrier Diplomacy, https://www.timesofisrael.com/chinas-wolf-warrior-diplomats-show-teeth-in-defending-virus-response/
21. A. J. Singh (2020). "The Quad and the pandemic: A lost opportunity," *The Diplomat*. Available at: https://thediplomat.com/2020/05/the-quad-and-the-pandemic-a-lost-opportunity/

22. *The Economist* (2020). "Which emerging markets are in most peril." Available at: https://www.economist.com/briefing/2020/05/02/which-emerging-markets-are-in-most-financial-peril

23. https://nationalinterest.org/feature/how-america-leading-quad-plus-group-seven-countries-fighting-coronavirus-138937

24. https://www.cfr.org/blog/pandemic-and-china-are-strengthening-us-india-relations-now

25. O'Brien 'National Security Council', @WHNSC Twitter message, https://www.newsfirst.lk/2020/05/09/us-national-security-advisor-calls-on-president-gotabaya-rajapaksa/

26. J. Dhanapala and J. Goonaratne (2012). "Sri Lanka: China as a growth of modernization," in *A Resurgent China: South Asia Perspectives*, eds. S. D. Muni and T. T. Young, Routledge, London, pp. 245–246.

27. S. Nagao, "Countering China in the Indo-Pacific," Hudson Institute. Available at: https://www.hudson.org/research/14402-countering-china-in-the-indo-pacific

28. R. Sally LKY School Online Discussion, *Asia Thinker Series*, May 6, 2020.

29. http://southasiajournal.net/collective-destinies-in-pestilence-by-asanga-abeyagoonasekera/

30. https://www.japantimes.co.jp/opinion/2020/04/24/reader-mail/collective-action-meet-individual-needs/#.Xtudky9h0_U

31. https://www.ft.com/content/7e5ee68e-6200-11ea-b3f3-fe4680ea68b5

32. https://www.foreignaffairs.com/articles/united-states/2020-03-05/us-chinese-distrust-inviting-dangerous-coronavirus-conspiracy

33. Black Swan moment describes an event that comes as a surprise. The theory was developed by Nassim Nicholas Taleb.

34. "Gray Rhino" was coined by Michele Wucker, a fellow YGL and policy analyst who came up with the term after the 2012 Greek financial crisis.

35. https://www.weforum.org/agenda/2020/02/how-coronavirus-disrupts-global-value-chains/

36. https://www.theguardian.com/world/2020/feb/19/coronavirus-could-cost-global-economy-1tn-in-lost-output

37. https://edition.cnn.com/2020/03/09/business/oil-price-crash-explainer/index.html?utm_campaign=wp_todays_worldview&utm_medium=email&utm_source=newsletter&wpisrc=nl_todayworld

38. Jennifer Bouey, Testimony presented before the House Foreign Affairs Subcommittee on Asia, the Pacific, and Nonproliferation on February 5, 2020. Available at: https://www.rand.org/content/dam/rand/pubs/testimonies/CT500/CT523/RAND_CT523.pdf

39. 2018 saw 4.2 billion air passengers for the year. Available at: https://data.worldbank.org/indicator/IS.AIR.PSGR

40. https://www.businessinsider.com/coronavirus-outbreak-could-hit-3-billion-adults-harvard-expert-2020-3

41. Approved by Government of Sri Lanka (Cabinet Paper No 19/3132/103/173) on November 11, 2019.

Chapter 5

1. http://southasiajournal.net/sri-lankas-presidential-election-2019-a-new-president-and-the-politics-of-balances/
2. PSC Full Report. Available at: https://www.parliament.lk/uploads/comreports/sc-april-attacks-report-en.pdf
3. M. Linsky (2009). *Practice of Adaptive Leadership*, First edition, Harvard Business Press, Harvard, MA, USA.
4. K. Schwab, "The Fourth Industrial Revolution." Available at: https://www.weforum.org/about/the-fourth-industrial-revolution-by-klaus-schwab
5. P. Khanna (2017). *Technocracy in America: Rise of the Info-State.*
6. Gotabaya's election manifesto. Available at: https://gota.lk/sri-lanka-podu-jana-peramuna-manifesto-english.pdf
7. C. Xavier (2019). "How India should deal with Gotabaya's Sri Lanka," *Hindustan Times*, November 19. Available at: https://www.hindustantimes.com/analysis/how-india-should-deal-with-gotabaya-s-sri-lanka/story-GkOygslgsitytFjvF3QKaJ.html
8. https://fp.brecorder.com/2018/06/20180611380847/
9. Initially published in https://www.orfonline.org/expert-speak/mahinda-rajapaksas-50-years-in-politics-67407/
10. H. Kissinger (2011). *On China.* Penguin Books Ltd.
11. J. L. Gaddis (1986). *The Long Peace.*
12. K. Mahbubani (2020). "Has China won? The Chinese challenge to American primacy." *PublicAffairs* [Kindle Edition].
13. https://www.hindustantimes.com/india-news/pm-modi-s-doklam-team-back-in-action-to-stand-up-to-china-in-ladakh/story-F1E9vWFXP9qGghwExg90ZM.html?fbclid=IwAR0ZH9bER_Kw1sJ7uL4iYu6owQmAevIx0LnyAaWP1XsmZuDgay2wCwmlKCk
14. https://www.thehindu.com/news/national/pla-actions-at-lac-in-ladakh-denote-shift-from-past-experts/article31665294.ece?homepage=true
15. CIS Australia, "China debate: John Mearsheimer vs Hugh White." Available at: https://www.youtube.com/watch?v=oRlt1vbnXhQ
16. https://www.brookings.edu/research/indias-limited-trade-connectivity-with-south-asia/
17. N. Rajapaksa (2020). "50 years of political legacy: A legend who I am fortunate enough to call my father," *Newswire*, May 27. Available at: http://www.newswire.lk/2020/05/27/50-years-of-political-legacy-a-legend-whom-i-am-fortunate-enough-to-call-my-father-namal-rajapaksa/

18. This article appeared in IPCS, New Delhi, for Dateline Colombo.
19. https://www.reuters.com/article/us-germany-marx-china/no-regrets-xi-says-marxism-still-totally-correct-for-china-idUSKBN1I50ET
20. https://www.mtholyoke.edu/acad/intrel/morg6.htm
21. The article was initially published by Hudson Institute, Washington DC, on May 3, 2020.
22. http://www.dailymirror.lk/dbs-jeyaraj-column/Neelan-Tiruchelvam-s-Absence-Felt-In-The-Making-Of-a-New-Constitution/192-161598
23. Foreign Minister Referring to para 68 (C) of the OHCHR Report (A/HRC/40/23). Full statement available at https://www.mfa.gov.lk/statement-by-hon-tilak-marapana-p-c-minister-of-foreign-affairs-of-sri-lanka-and-leader-of-the-sri-lanka-delegation-to-the-40th-session-of-the-human-rights-council-on-agenda/
24. https://www.theguardian.com/world/2020/feb/14/us-sanctions-sri-lanka-army-chief-shavendra-silva
25. https://www.colombotelegraph.com/index.php/u-turns-are-difficult/
26. https://colombogazette.com/2020/02/27/un-rights-chief-rejects-sri-lankas-new-commission-of-inquiry/
27. Verite Research, SL resolution 30/1. Available at: https://www.veriteresearch.org/wp-content/uploads/2019/03/Verite-Research_UNHRC-Monitor-No4-March-2019.pdf
28. The article was initially published by Hudson Institute Washington DC. Available at: http://www.southasiaathudson.org/blog/2019/3/19/u-turns-are-difficult.
29. http://www.island.lk/index.php?page_cat=article-details&page=article-details&code_title=200824
30. https://www.wsws.org/en/articles/2019/01/17/slus-j17.html
31. This article was initially published in http://southasiajournal.net/comparing-crises-presidency-and-power-in-a-changing-world-order/
32. https://www.bloombergquint.com/markets/u-s-recognition-of-venezuela-s-guaido-is-disguised-regime-change
33. https://www.nytimes.com/2019/01/24/world/americas/donald-trump-venezuela.html
34. Sri Lanka's friends, the two regional giants, have stepped up to support us in this time when we were pushed into a rather difficult corner.
35. https://www.emerald.com/insight/content/doi/10.1108/JFC-01-2020-0009/full/html
36. https://www.euronews.com/2018/11/09/sri-lanka-president-signs-papers-to-dissolve-parliament-sources
37. http://www.island.lk/index.php?page_cat=article-details&page=article-details&code_title=174552

38. https://www.newsfirst.lk/2019/04/23/easter-bombings-who-knew-but-turned-a-blind-eye/
39. https://www.newsfirst.lk/2019/04/23/easter-bombings-who-knew-but-turned-a-blind-eye/
40. A. Abeyagoonasekera, *Sri Lanka at Crossroads*, World Scientific. Singapore.
41. https://www.transparency.org/en/cpi
42. INSSSL Survey on National Challenges Sri Lanka is Facing, 2019.
43. Geis, Meier and Salinger (1995).
44. Friedrichs (1995), pp. 2–5.
45. *The Times of India* (2018). "From Panama Papers to upcoming prison term: How Nawaz Sharif was finally nailed." Available at: https://timesofindia.indiatimes.com/world/pakistan/from-panama-papers-to-upcoming-prison-term-how-nawaz-sharif-was-finally-nailed/articleshow/64974498.cms
46. http://www.dailymirror.lk/breaking_news/ISIS-'funded-SL-Easter-bombings-with-Bitcoin-donations'/108-166328
47. https://www.nytimes.com/2019/04/23/world/asia/sri-lanka-bombing.html
48. http://www.dailymirror.lk/business-news/SL-to-crack-down-on-terrorist-financing-with-new-vigour/273-168481
49. http://www.ft.lk/top-story/Time-to-get-down-to-business--CB-Chief/26-679330
50. Geis *et al.* (1995), p. 15.
51. https://www.cbsl.gov.lk/en/news/the-financial-action-task-force-endorsed-the-progress-made-by-sri-lanka
52. http://fiusrilanka.gov.lk/docs/AR/FIU_AR_2017.pdf
53. https://core.ac.uk/download/pdf/14915359.pdf
54. http://www.ft.lk/front-page/New-legislation-to-fight-corruption-in-Parliament-soon/44-683036
55. https://www.ciaboc.gov.lk/media-centre/latest-news/741-press-statement-launch-of-the-national-action-plan-for-combating-bribery-and-corruption-in-sri-lanka
56. Alvesalo and Tombs (2001c) cyberespionage.
57. Salminen (1998), p. 15.
58. https://www.colombotelegraph.com/index.php/economic-crime-the-p118-of-sri-lanka/
59. http://www.dailymirror.lk/breaking_news/Half-of-state-officials-should-be-in-jail-by-now-AG/108-151469
60. A. Siriwardena and Y. Perera (2017). "Rajitha received Rs. 10 M from President's Fund: Anura Kumara." *Daily Mirror.* Available at: http://www.dailymirror.lk/article/Rajitha-received-Rs-M-from-President-s-Fund-Anura-Kumara-135293.html?fromNewsdog=1&utm_source=NewsDog&utm_medium=referral

61. F. Fukuyama (2014). *Political Order and Political Decay: From the Industrial Revolution to the Globalization of Democracy.* Farrar, Straus and Giroux, US.

62. https://www.mlaw.gov.sg/files/news/press-releases/2016/05/AntiCorruption 2016PressReleaseAnnexB.pdf

63. Paper presented at the *36th International Economic Crime Symposium* held at Jesus College Cambridge University, September 2–9, 2018.

64. https://www.newsfirst.lk/2018/08/17/sri-lankas-public-sector-is-the-most-corrupt-in-the-world-auditor-general/

65. L. Harding (2016). "What are the Panama Papers? A guide to history's biggest data leak," *The Guardian,* April 5.

66. F. Keen (2017). "Unexplained Wealth Orders: Global lessons for the UK ahead of implementation." Royal United Services Institute. London. Available at: https://rusi.org/sites/default/files/201709_rusi_unexplained_wealth_orders_keen_web.pdf

67. *Withersworldwide,* "UWO: Are Russians in the UK at risk of investigation?".

68. F. Keen, "UWO: Global lessons for the UK ahead of implementation," RUSI Occasional Paper.

69. This article was initially published in http://southasiajournal.net/authentic-leadership-of-martin-luther-king-jr/

70. https://discoveryourtruenorth.org/leadership-lessons-from-martin-luther-king-jr/

71. https://www.sagepub.com/sites/default/files/upm-binaries/33554_Chapter1.pdf

72. https://www.vox.com/2016/1/18/10785618/martin-luther-king-dream-speech

73. https://www.vox.com/2016/1/18/10785618/martin-luther-king-dream-speech

74. https://www.theatlantic.com/magazine/archive/2018/02/martin-luther-king-jr-poor-peoples-campaign/552539/

75. https://www.beaconbroadside.com/broadside/2010/01/martin-luther-king-jr-the-world-house-excerpt.html

76. https://www.history.com/news/mlk-assassination-jesse-jackson-interview

Index

About the Author

Professor Asanga Abeyagoonasekera is the Founding Director General of the Institute of National Security Studies Sri Lanka (INSSSL), the National Security Think Tank under Ministry of Defence, Sri Lanka. During his nearly two-decade experience in government, he has served in policy advocacy, advisory positions, and expert panels, including the panel which compiled the National Defence Policy of Sri Lanka in 2019. He has testified at the Presidential Commission of Investigation (PCoI) into the Easter Sunday terror attacks in 2020.

He is a Visiting Professor of Geopolitics and Global Leadership at Northern Kentucky University (USA), International Security (University of Colombo), International Political Economy (RIC, University of London), and a Senior Advisor and member of Academic Advisory Committee of Zheijiang University (China).

Asanga writes regular columns for Hudson Institute (Washington DC, USA), ORF (India), and *South Asia Journal*. He contributes articles on geopolitics and regional security. He has authored many academic journal articles and presented in defense, foreign policy think tanks, universities and government ministries, including Quai d' Orsay in Paris, LKY School of Public Policy in Singapore, and Jesus College (University of Cambridge). His major field of interest is geopolitics of South Asia, Indian Ocean Region, and regional security in South Asia.

He has served as the former Executive Director of the Sri Lankan government think tank on foreign policy, the Lakshman Kadirgamar Institute of International Relations and Security Studies (LKIIRSS) and as Advisor to Minister of External Affairs, Sri Lanka, from 2012 to 2015. He was educated at Harvard Kennedy School, Jackson Institute for Global Affairs at Yale University, Lee Kuan Yew School of Public Policy (Singapore), University of Oxford (England), Indian School of Business (India), and Edith Cowan University (Perth, Australia).

Asanga was recognized as a Young Global Leader for the World Economic Forum. He is the author of *Sri Lanka at Crossroads* (2019) and *Towards a Better World Order* (2015). Asanga is an Alumnus of US State Department International Visitor Leadership Program, Asia-Pacific Center for Security Studies (Hawaii), and the National Defense University (Washington, DC, USA).